PHILOSOPHY BEHIND BARS

C000103458

Growth and Development in Prison

Kirstine Szifris

BRISTOL
UNIVERSITY
PRESS

First published in Great Britain in 2021 by

Bristol University Press
University of Bristol
1-9 Old Park Hill
Bristol
BS2 8BB
UK
t: +44 (0)117 954 5940
e: bup-info@bristol.ac.uk

Details of international sales and distribution partners are available at bristoluniversitypress.co.uk

British Library Cataloguing in Publication Data
A catalogue record for this book is available from the British Library

ISBN 978-1-5292-0554-1 hardcover
ISBN 978-1-5292-0555-8 paperback
ISBN 978-1-5292-0558-9 ePub
ISBN 978-1-5292-0556-5 ePdf

Cover design: riverdesignbooks.com
Front cover image: Alamy.com KR062T

Bristol University Press uses environmentally responsible print partners.

Printed in Great Britain by CMP, Poole

For Eugene

Contents

List of Boxes

Chapter 8

Chapter 9

Acknowledgements

This book is the culmination of 10 years of work. Starting as an MPhil student, moving through a PhD and into a university position, there have been many stages to this project, and many people to thank along the way.

First, I must acknowledge the role of my supervisor, Professor Alison Liebling. Although she stopped officially being my supervisor three years ago, she still acts as a mentor and a guide, regularly giving me time to discuss my thoughts and ideas, for which I am extremely grateful. She has read several drafts, offered encouragement and provided clarity throughout. She set me on this path when I was an MPhil student, as I nervously moved into a new discipline and was attempting to find my feet. Sitting in her office, I recall mentioning in passing the philosophy class I had run as a teacher. It was some years later that I realized why she had suggested I run these classes in prisons. With her vast knowledge of prisons and years of experience immersing herself in prison environments, she saw the potential in the idea and, I guess, in me. And now, here we are.

The other person who has given me endless support is my stepdad, Mike Scott. He has read everything I have ever written, given me encouragement, and patiently corrected all my commas, which I apparently have no understanding of how to use. Without his help, this book would not have been possible.

Others have read drafts of the book and chapters along the way – most notably Dr Pete Traynor, whose early feedback gave me encouragement regarding the importance of the book, and whose comments helped clarify my content. I am also grateful to my non-criminology draft readers, Duncan Parsons and Ritchie McCabe, whose comments on the first couple of chapters helped me get my 'voice' right. I must also thank my Examiners, Professor Antony Bottoms and Professor Fergus McNeill, both of whom thoroughly engaged with my work, challenging my thoughts, while offering support and feedback, and ultimately improved my thinking and my conclusions.

Many others deserve a mention and I will list them in brief. Vi, Yaz, Joni, Alice, Lauren and Sarah kept me sane. Hannah and Rhiain kept me grounded. My mum, my brother and his family gave me comfort and my own 'safe space' when I struggled. My colleagues at the Policy Evaluation and Research Unit kept my thinking fresh and I am grateful, in particular, to Professors Chris Fox and Steve Morris for managing my workload and for giving me space to write, as far as they were able. Morwenna, my prison education friend, kept me connected. Finally Dan, who kept me fed and picked up my spirits as I struggled over the finishing line – I could not have done it without you.

My final acknowledgement, however, goes to the research participants. Not many people can say that they have spent time in prisons engaging in philosophical conversation, and I am privileged to have had the opportunity. The men with whom I worked proved to be earnest, insightful and deeply intelligent. Their philosophical insights broadened my horizons, challenged my skills and forever changed my worldview. I am grateful that they took the time to provide a space where, for a short time, my status as 'teacher' and 'academic' could fall away and I could be a philosopher, for a time.

Foreword

Nigel Warburton

Philosophy is, above all, conversation. Not just any conversation, but conversation that engages with some of the most profound questions we can ask ourselves, moving easily from the abstract to the particular and back again. That conversation can be face-to-face, virtual, through the written word, or we can engage with thinkers of the past, whose best ideas have come to us in books and essays, and more recently in audio and video recordings. Philosophy values reasons, arguments, refutations and evidence above rhetoric and power games. At its best, studying it can be transformative. We see the world differently after thinking from different perspectives, examining the best arguments in favour of a position, or responding to a counterargument.

Some well-known philosophers have themselves spent time in prison – these include Boethius, Niccolò Machiavelli, Antonio Gramsci and Bertrand Russell; Ludwig Wittgenstein wrote much of the *Tractatus* while a prisoner of war, and Jean-Paul Sartre was briefly imprisoned in occupied France. But, despite the fantasy of a prison cell as providing quiet time to reflect and study, the reality is rarely like this. Prisons can be noisy, frightening and disorienting places, and some people survive only by keeping their heads down and their opinions private. Yet many people within them still do find ways to reflect philosophically and to discuss ideas with fellow prisoners and staff.

What happens when a sensitive teacher facilitates this kind of conversation in prisons? Here, Kirstine Szifris describes her experience as a philosophy teacher working with groups in two very different institutions – Grendon and Full Sutton. In the first, her students are long-term prisoners who have opted to take part in this therapeutic community, and who have already had extensive experience of talking in groups, respecting others' opinions and building up trust to reveal psychological vulnerabilities. In Full Sutton, in contrast, an aura of distrust and suspicion prevails, and for many prisoners the primary motivation is survival rather than growth, a motivation that can make them wary of revealing too much, and distrustful, too, of the motives of the teacher.

Szifris is a participant observer in these two very different environments – a teacher facilitating discussion, but also an ethnographer noting the complexities of the assumptions, roles and masks that prisoners adopt towards one another, and towards her. This makes for fascinating reading, not least because she has captured the prisoners' voices and ways of thinking, as well as their more philosophical takes on the materials she presents them with. Throughout, too, we learn how Szifris has herself been affected by her interactions.

Philosophy Behind Bars builds a powerful case for bringing philosophy teaching into prison. It provides deep insights into the ways in which well-led philosophical discussions not only provide enjoyment, intellectual stimulation, and a chance for constructive social interaction, but also contribute to participants' understanding of their own identity and values.

Philosophy, Identity and the 'Ship of Theseus'

'With philosophy you can bring out your own ideas and then, through the group you can rework it, remodel it, change it, look at it, to get to somewhere. So it's your part in building that and, I suppose, it's more empowering in that sense because you are doing it yourself.' (Michael, HMP Grendon)

In the 1st century AD, Plutarch wrote of the 'ship of Theseus', a well-known philosophical paradox, revived by Thomas Hobbes and rearticulated over time by philosophers and teachers. The story provides a basis to discuss identity.

In Plutarch's story, Theseus was a hero who had sailed the oceans with great success. The people of Athens kept his ship in a harbour, as a museum piece, to honour his triumphs and to preserve it for future generations. To maintain the ship, they replaced old, broken pieces with fresh, new pieces. Eventually all the pieces of the ship were replaced, and the question became, 'Is this still Theseus' ship?' According to Plutarch, half the philosophers of the day said it was, and the other half said it wasn't.

> The ship wherein Theseus and the youth of Athens returned from Crete had thirty oars, and was preserved by the Athenians down even to the time of Demetrius Phalereus, for they took away the old planks as they decayed, putting in new and stronger timber in their places, insomuch that this ship became a standing example among the philosophers, for the logical question of things that grow; one side holding that the ship remained the same, and the other contending

that it was not the same. (Plutarch, 'Theseus', taken from *The Rise and Fall of Athens: Nine Greek Lives*, translated by Ian Scott-Kilvert, 1960)[1]

In the 17th century, Thomas Hobbes resurrected the paradox of Theseus' ship. He imagined a young sailor, too poor to buy his own ship, who took the old pieces and stowed them away. Eventually the young sailor had enough pieces to make his own ship out of the old pieces of Theseus' ship. So now there were two ships. And the question became, 'Which ship is Theseus' ship?'

The story of Theseus' ship, and the questions it raises, provided the basis of the opening philosophical discussion for an 'Introduction to Philosophy' class I delivered in two prisons in England during 2014 and 2015. It is a poignant and meaningful stimulus for those who live a life inside prison. For the participants, serving long sentences for serious crimes, questions of identity become acutely relevant.

In the first session, the participants enthusiastically engaged with the paradox of Theseus' ship. The topic raised further questions: what identifies a particular ship as *Theseus'* ship? If it is no longer Theseus' ship, at what point did it change? Was it when the first piece was replaced? Or the last? Or somewhere in between? Is it the physical body of the ship that matters to its identity or something less tangible – the spirit, the essence of the ship? Or, perhaps, is it the way in which people identify the ship that matters? Is it the external identity, the identity assigned by others, that gives the ship its identity? It became clear that these last three questions, relating to identity, were very pertinent to the circumstances in which the participants found themselves.

At the start, the participants focused on the facts: who owned the ship? Why did they want to preserve it? Who was Theseus? As they moved through the conversation, they began to think more broadly about identity, what it means to change, and what makes us who we are. One of the sessions concluded with a discussion about the difference between how others see us (our external self) and how we see ourselves (our internal self). Through this, we discussed the difference between the body and the mind, the relevance of our histories, pasts and social identities, and morality. Where do our morals come from? How do they relate to our identities?

Overall, conversation flowed. Some offered nuanced views, listening carefully to the arguments presented. Others listened

---

[1] See www.philosophy-foundation.org/enquiries/view/the-ship-of-theseus

quietly, sitting back and taking stock of what was being said, never butting in but ready with a response when asked. A few let forth a stream of consciousness, relating ideas with half-understood concepts learned through voraciously reading whatever they could find in the prison library. These individuals would take the conversation to unusual places, seemingly taking the opportunity to articulate their perspective on the world – a perspective developed from behind the door of a prison cell, usually alone, and without anyone to challenge their thinking.

Philosophy as a discipline encompasses the range of human achievement, driving forward civilizations, providing insight and guidance to the individual in times of crisis and celebration, and producing fundamental shifts in the way we understand the physical world. Through my lessons I brought the ideas of some of the great Western philosophers to the prison classroom as part of an in-depth study into the relevance of philosophical conversation to the lives of people in prison. The work involved inviting people to engage in the research and participate in philosophical discussion in an attempt to cultivate a community of philosophical inquiry.

Initially, the aim of my research was to explore the relevance of philosophy education in prisons. As the research progressed, however, it developed into an exploration of identity. With similar populations, but contrasting characters, HMP Grendon and HMP Full Sutton provided the backdrop to what was an 'ethnographically led' piece of research that placed the experience of the prisoner-participants at the heart of the process. Questions around the possibility of growth and the meaning of personal development emerged. In the context of a prison, so often understood to be a place of boredom, stagnation and survival, understanding the relevance of philosophy became a study into how people find spaces to 'be'. As the research unfolded, I discovered it was necessary to consider issues of trust, relationships, openness, community and wellbeing to articulate the importance of self-expression, self-reflection and meaningful interactions.

At the heart of this book, then, lies a question of *identity*. How does the prison environment impact a person's sense of self? How can the individual maintain a sense of self? Can they grow and develop, or does imprisonment just mean boredom and stagnation? Prisons are places where some people spend significant portions of their lives. Self-reflection, a reappraisal of life choices and the need for opportunities to engage in different activities are all present in the literature that considers pathways out of crime. My research findings, systematically collected and analysed through interviews, feedback forms and extensive fieldwork notes, clearly point towards the need for spaces for prisoners to engage in activities that do not relate to their offences.

This is not about redemption, correction or rehabilitation, however, but about growth and personal development. Drawing both on prison sociology and my own research, we shall see that the prison environment fundamentally works against this. The lack of trust, the underlying tensions within the prisoner community and the language of risk that surrounds prisoners all cultivate a difficult environment for the individual to navigate. As a result, prisoners put up 'fronts' and develop identities as a way to cope.

First, however, we must understand what is meant by the word 'philosophy'.

What is philosophy?

The word 'philosophy' comes from the Greek *philo*, to love, and *sophia*, wisdom (Butler-Bowdon, 2013). It has been described as an 'activity' (Thompson, 2003), a method of finding 'truth' (Butler-Bowdon, 2013), an 'inquiry' (Grayling, 1995) and as 'thinking about thinking' (Honderich, 1995). The teachings of Socrates, Plato, Hume, Descartes, Bentham, Mill and Arendt have shaped our understanding of nature, the development of science and mathematics, the notions of justice and fairness, of moral reasoning, and the development of critical reflections on normative values and received dogmas (Grayling, 1995). Philosophy, arguably, lies at the heart of progress and civilization, of politics and science, of moral thinking and action. Despite its relevance to the development of our societies, philosophy as a discipline can sometimes remain obscure and out of reach.

So what does it mean to study philosophy? To philosophize? To be a philosopher? What does it mean to 'do' philosophy? The answers to these questions vary depending on who you ask, which can differ according to your profession, politics and personal perspective. Some see philosophy as the province of (often) old, (usually) white men, sitting in armchairs musing about the world. The conversations of philosophers can be complex, abstract and somewhat exclusive, with texts that can be technical and difficult to read. To study philosophy is to study the great thinkers, to engage with the tomes they wrote and to gain an in-depth understanding of the history of ideas. Further, to be a philosopher, some would say, you must be writing it down, articulating your own thoughts and ideas, contributing to and extending philosophical discourse, and allowing others to analyse and critique the logic of your stance.

However, another important school of thought sees philosophy as a *conversation*, an interactive dialogue of discovery and exploration. This perspective considers philosophy as something that belongs to everyone, an activity in which everyone can engage. Tim Sprod, a teacher involved in the Philosophy for Children movement,[2] explains:

> Philosophers, at least in the English-speaking world, tend to assume that philosophy, being a difficult and technical discipline, is not for ordinary people.... For the ordinary member of the public, however, philosophy is often quite different: an approach to things, an underlying way of looking at the world, a collection of important guides to life. It can be talked about in ordinary language on ordinary occasions – around a coffee table, or over a beer – whenever we slow down a little and think a bit more reflectively. We pass on our philosophy of life to others whenever we muse a little and talk about what is important to us in the big picture. (Sprod, 2001, p 101)

For this school of thought, studying philosophy does not mean studying philosophers, and nor is it to present a refined logical argument with complex clauses and conclusions. Instead, it is to actively *philosophize* – to think, with others, about the big questions of who we are, how we ought to behave and how we want to live. As an activity of the mind, this type of philosophy involves thinking through a problem in a structured, open and inquiring manner. Engaging in *active* philosophizing means examining our own perspectives, considering the lens through which we see the world (Butler-Bowdon, 2013). In other words, philosophy asks us to consider not simply *what* we think, but *why* and *how*.

This perspective sits within the 'Socratic' tradition. Socrates is significant as he is credited with changing both the focus and the method of philosophical inquiry. Unlike previous philosophers, Socrates was interested in how we *ought* to live (he is often referred to as

---

[2] Philosophy for Children (commonly referred to as P4C) was originally developed by Matthew Lipman and Margaret Sharp in the 1970s. They drew on a pedagogy based on Vygotskian learning theory and set out a method of engaging children in philosophical conversation. I was trained in this particular method (one among many) by the SAPERE charity (www.sapere.org.uk).

the 'father of ethics'), and practised philosophy through conversation. He was known for wandering around marketplaces, engaging people in conversation and asking questions. His quest to clarify moral terms such as 'justice' and 'courage', for example, involved interrogating people of all classes and character, often revealing contradictions in other people's ways of thinking and challenging received knowledge (Janaway, 1995).

In other words, Socrates embodied the role of philosophical dialogue as a means of interrogating and understanding philosophical ideas. These ideas have been translated into a method of teaching philosophy in schools and the community. In the following section, we look at philosophy education in general. As we do so, we will recognize that the same potential applies to philosophical activity in a prison context.

Philosophy education

Beyond defining philosophy as a subject, discipline, methodology or way of thinking, philosophy takes a significant place in the spectrum of subjects taught in educational institutions. If a person takes a 'philosophy class', the assumption might be that they will study the different philosophers or philosophies. They will learn about Mill's utilitarianism, Rawls' social contract, Descartes' dualism and so forth. Activities might involve people sitting in libraries reading original texts, listening to lectures while taking copious amounts of notes, and then summarizing and reflecting on their learning by writing an essay. If they are fortunate enough to be engaging in a philosophy course in person, on a campus or in a college, then they may have the odd weekly seminar where they have the opportunity to engage in philosophical discussion with their peers.

Since the late 1970s, there has been a growing movement towards an educational pedagogy that aims to engage learners in *active* philosophizing. The most well-known and far-reaching initiative is the Philosophy for Children movement. Organizations such as The Philosophy Foundation and methods including Community of Philosophical Inquiry (or CoPI), developed by Catherine McCall, have extended and developed dialogic methods of teaching philosophy. This is what I (and others) refer to as *active* philosophizing. Not reading and learning who said what and when, but *being* philosophers – turning over ideas, testing out hypotheses, exploring your own and other people's ways of thinking.

There has also been a growing interest in taking philosophical conversation into the prison environment. I am aware of initiatives across the UK, the Netherlands, Spain, Norway and the US. The initiatives vary in how they are funded, who runs them, how they are structured and the types of prisons involved, but they all have one thing in common: a desire to give people in prison the same opportunities to share their own thinking and to discuss the thinking of others.

A key aspect of dialogic philosophy relates to the sense of community it can cultivate. The term 'community' in this context refers to the acts of listening and participating in dialogue in an intellectually safe environment (Lien, 2007). Organizations and proponents of this approach often use the term 'community' to emphasize the importance of learners having this opportunity. Most importantly, however, the concept of community refers to the ability to engage in such dialogue in an *intellectually safe* environment (Lien, 2007) – in other words, in a space where learners can put their point across, test out ideas, change their mind and disagree without risking their membership or status within the group. As will become apparent, achieving a community and an intellectually safe space can present complex challenges in any environment, and even more so in the context of a prison community.

Referred to variously as 'community philosophy', 'conversational philosopher' and 'dialogic philosophy' among others, there has been increased interest in philosophical discussion in schools. Further, community philosophy groups such as Socrates Café and Philosophy in Pubs provide space for philosophical inquiry for people in their everyday environments. Programmes and gatherings that draw on these methods aim to create individual communities of philosophical inquiry. In practice, such spaces operate in an exploratory, non-adversarial manner.

In a philosophical inquiry class, in any of these contexts, a facilitator guides participants through the discussion as a co-inquirer, seeking knowledge and understanding along with the participants. With dialogue as its primary means of encouraging learning, the classroom is characterized by conversation. Based on the Socratic tradition (Barrow, 2010), the facilitator assists people in finding their *own* knowledge through collaborative conversation, and encouraging logical thought processes (Kennedy, 1999; Lien, 2007). The original Philosophy for Children pedagogy draws on Vygotskian learning theory, which asserts that children learn to think for themselves by engaging in the social practice of thinking together (Murris, 2008). It also draws on the work of John Dewey (Millett and Tapper, 2011), who argued that education should be interactive and social practice, that it ought to provide the opportunity to explore the facts of a curriculum with reference to the learner's own experiences, thus allowing the teaching of a subject matter to become an experience in its own right (Dewey, 1990 [1992]).

Community or conversational philosophy groups aim to encourage clear articulation of ideas and provide an opportunity for self-expression. The pedagogy of such programmes aims to develop open, collaborative and inquisitive conversation among participants to pique curiosity, and to encourage a systematic and rational method of approaching a problem. This means individuals can engage in philosophical conversation without having read or pursued study in the writings of the historical figures of philosophy. They can consider questions such as, what is our identity? On what principles do I base my actions? How should we, as people and members of a society, behave? What does it mean to live 'the good life'?

The practice of philosophical conversation provides the opportunity to explore these questions with others. In a discursive environment, strengths, weaknesses and discrepancies in a speaker's views are brought to the fore. Being exposed, but in a safe, non-adversarial and inquiring atmosphere, allows participants to explore their own and each other's ways of thinking. Through such discussions, it is possible to develop a deeper and more insightful understanding of how we, and others, think.

Fundamental to this practice is the philosophical question – engaging in philosophical inquiry involves asking questions that are general and abstract, that seek to understand the principles that lie *behind* an opinion (Thompson, 2003). To then *answer* questions philosophically means seeking to be accurate and precise in language in order to clarify our thoughts and refine our ideas (Pecorino, 2016). Philosophers' ideas are well thought out, carefully considered and based on strong, logical argument forms. As a result of the depth of philosophical investigation and the accuracy required within the language, philosophical writings can become technical, convoluted and confusing. Scholars can dedicate their lives to interpreting the writings of a particular philosopher who often offers long, almost indecipherable, explanations for their conclusions and their reasoning (Thompson, 2003).

From this perspective, the medium of philosophical exploration is language. It is through language that we 'express our beliefs and assumptions' (Grayling, 1995, p 5) and through dialogue with others that our assumptions can be questioned and interrogated. Through these activities, our opinions, ideas and thoughts can be brought to the fore and tested. If done well, it is possible to cultivate a positive environment that allows expression without judgement. Grayling (1995) claims that philosophical dialogue is characterized by critical inquiry and rational thought. By this he means the ability to develop understanding of an issue by questioning our own (and others') assumptions and reflecting on the veracity of any conclusions drawn. However, this also means that to engage in philosophical dialogue, participants must be willing to honestly and openly reflect on their own opinions. This activity comes with an important caveat; as Pecorino (2016) points out, philosophy is not a way of life, and nor is it a theory, belief or wish. Rather, it is a pursuit or activity of thought whereby we look for answers through a process of investigation and argument (Law, 2007).

To translate this vast body of philosophical thinking into a prison community, my philosophy classes broadly followed the principles of Philosophy for Children, but with some important alterations to suit the population with whom I was now working.[3] In general, such sessions need not cover specific philosophers or philosophies, and can, instead, encourage philosophical conversation with a focus on the everyday (see McCall, 2009). The teaching method is about learning ways of approaching different issues and relating them to people's lives. This makes it accessible to people in prison in their very particular circumstances.

However, the majority of my sessions outlined complex philosophical ideas. In focusing on different philosophers and schools of thought, but also using the pedagogy of philosophical dialogue, the participants were able to develop an understanding of the history of ideas alongside their own thinking. I covered Socrates, Plato, Hume, Descartes, Bentham, Mill, Kant, Russell and Arendt, among others. Some sessions discussed schools of philosophy, such as the Stoics or utilitarianism, while others focused on a particular philosopher. I delivered each session in stages designed to draw participants through an idea (see Chapter 3 for examples of teaching materials). I developed stimuli in line with the Philosophy for Children ethos, in that the content aimed to provoke dialogue that involved '… common central and contestable concepts like truth, justice, friendship, economy, person, education, gender' (Kennedy and Kennedy, 2011, p 266).

The project sought to develop spaces that would allow for this critical self-reflection and collaborative inquiry. More specifically, I sought to do this with prisoners in the context of a prison education department. There are numerous reasons why the prison is a complex place to attempt to establish such a space. Beyond the practicalities

---

[3] In Chapter 2, I provide an overview of the piloting work undertaken as part of this process that allowed time to develop appropriate materials and techniques prior to the main project.

of accessing a prison, recruiting participants, navigating the prison bureaucracy and dealing with multiple disruptions and lockdowns, the prevailing atmosphere of a prison environment has its own challenges.

In particular, issues of trust, power, identity, self-reflection, relationships and wellbeing take on particular meaning in the prison environment. Inter-personal conflicts, projected egos and hidden identities, religious tensions and complex vulnerabilities all shape the prison philosophy experience. Further, the role of education in the prison environment can get entangled with correctional ideas that it ought to be about helping the 'offender' to stop 'offending'.

This affects the way education is viewed by different people in the prison environment as well as the types of educational activities available to people in prison. Therefore, we need to place education in the prison context, and have a clear understanding of its purpose in the lives of people in prison.

Education in prison

Every prison in England and Wales delivers some form of educational activity. While basic literacy and numeracy is a priority in all adult prisons, educational opportunities vary between them. Although most offer a reasonably full timetable, many of the courses are short-term, with the exception of distance learning courses, including degrees offered by the Open University which involve a significant amount of self-directed learning.

In Grendon and Full Sutton, external providers delivered educational courses such as literacy, numeracy, employability skills, horticulture, cooking and art. There were also chess clubs and reading groups. Overall, however, education was geared towards vocational skills. The scope and nature of the education delivered in these prisons reflected the policy climate around prison education in the UK at the time, which maintained that education in prison should relate directly to employability. This focus was a result of a gradual change in policy over the previous decade, and had led to a narrowing of the curriculum available to prisoners.

Such narrowing of the prison education curriculum is not unique to the UK. Despite a body of evidence from Europe and North America in favour of a broad curriculum (see Duguid, 2000; Behan, 2014), education in prison places a heavy emphasis on vocational skills, with rates of employment sitting alongside reconviction rates as a means of measuring the success of in-prison programmes. In reality, there is little research into the link between employment-related education

education should be about growth + development

in prison and post-release outcomes (see Szifris et al, 2018). While employment skills may be a key part of the rehabilitation process for some, as this book will demonstrate, education can play a much greater role in the lives of prisoners.

My intention in this book, therefore, is to set out the argument that ✳ education should be about growth and development. In doing so, I do not provide an exhaustive or in-depth account of the theoretical underpinnings of pedagogy, the purpose and aims of education more generally, or the history of prison education. Rather, I provide some context to the research, and thereby offer some rationale for taking philosophy into prisons in the first place.

In addition to what is available from the education department in a prison, a range of groups offers programmes and activities to people living and working in prison. Organizations such as Prison Dialogue have been offering opportunities for staff–prisoner dialogues since the early 1990s, the Prison Reading Groups have been working in prisons since 1999, and User Voice, a charity that sets up prison councils, has been active since 2009. Various prison–university partnerships are now flourishing in the UK, which offer the prisoner-students the opportunity to learn alongside students from the outside, although there are still problems with providing long-term opportunities for people in prison interested in engaging in higher education. Prisons also often have writers-in-residence, mentoring and listening opportunities, with activities such as Shakespeare Behind Bars offering alternative activities for the prisoners. However, while innovative educational practices in prisons have a long history, they can be a little ad hoc due to challenges in accessing prisons and finding the means to fund them. As a rule, these activities are an exception as opposed to the norm.

Despite education being widely delivered in prisons around the world, research into prison education remains sparse. In particular, education in the context of prison remains under-theorized, with the underlying principles and purpose of education in prison remaining vague. When asked, policy-makers, practitioners, prison governors, prisoners and other interested organizations offer different justifications for providing education in the prison environment: the role and purpose of education changes according to who you ask. There seems to be a basic agreement that education is, in some way, 'good' for prisoners.[4] We do not fully

---

[4] Although few studies focus on what education can do for the individual, some important recent exceptions include the work of Helen Nichols (2021), Anne Pike and Susan Hopkins (2019) and Morwenna Bennallick (2019), all of whom place the prison experience at the heart of their research.

understand what it means to the person serving a sentence to engage in an educational programme, nor how education can benefit the individual in prison. This study focuses on one type of educational programme, that of philosophy, to begin to answer these questions.

As a consequence of conducting this research, however, I conclude that it is important to recognize the wider conversations around the prison system. For many, prison is synonymous with punishment – it is not meant to be easy. However, when working with and among prisoners, it becomes apparent that this over-simplistic perspective misses an important point. People in prison are human beings who, despite the walls that separate them, remain part of our society. Our laws and, I hope, morals, require us to treat prisoners with humanity and dignity.

For me, the corollary to this is that people in prison ought to have the opportunity for growth and personal development. This means going beyond programmes focused on 'offending' and convictions, and moving towards programmes for self-development. Today, the majority of activities in the prison environment relate either to addressing individual 'offending' needs or to provide 'purposeful' occupation while in prison; that is, so prisoners do not spend their time idle. I, and many others alongside me, argue that we should recognize that prisoners are people with lives that are still being lived.

As such, we must aim to meet prisoners as human beings, to treat them with respect, and provide opportunities that allow the whole person to flourish. For those who believe in 'corrections', this approach, in theory at least, ought to provide more desirable outcomes. Following programmes that encourage self-reflection, identity development and personal development should allow individuals in prison the opportunity to change and to move towards forging a crime-free path. For those who believe in a humanistic approach, we provide an environment of humanity, care and respect, regardless of convictions.

Calls for such an approach are not new (Gehring, 1997). Within the prison education literature, a variety of scholars, most notably Stephen Duguid (2000), have argued for the use of a broad curriculum within prison that will address the whole person. In particular, Cormac Behan and Kevin Warner (among other Irish academics) have published widely on the need to ensure that prison education remains true to the pedagogical principles of the adult education tradition. This includes providing room for self-directed study, focusing on developing the whole person, and seeking to instil enthusiasm for a subject within the learner. They warn against the narrowing of education to fit the current penal policy agenda, that prison education is most effective when it is based on the principles of adult education (see, for example, Behan, 2007). In particular, Aislinn O'Donnell (2013), a fellow teacher of philosophy in prisons, argues that the transformative nature of education occurs when the individual develops a love and appreciation for a subject. She goes on to argue that the educator's job is to provide a space in which learners can explore their own interests, such that it is flexible enough for the teacher to respond to, and to encourage learners in their personal pursuit of knowledge. She argues that personal development is emergent, and that education, rather than attempting to transform people, should focus on developing personal interests and enthusiasm for a subject, which will allow personal transformation to take place.

To complicate matters, even outside the context of a prison education department, the purpose of education more generally is the subject of much debate. For vocationalists, education should be about training individuals for the workforce. Liberal education focuses on the 'whole' person while humanist educational theories have similar aims but focus more on the emotions of the learner (Nichols, 2021). In the field of adult education, some theorists take a humanist approach, arguing that education enables learners to become active participants in the wider world (see Paulo Freire, 1996 [1970], *Pedagogy of the Oppressed*). Psychological perspectives focus on problem-solving skills (see Gagné, 1977, *Conditions of Learning*), while others focus on the role of education in developing self-actualizing people and altering self-concept (see Rogers, 1969, or Knowles, 1975). In common, adult educational theorists tend to recognize the self-directed nature of learning as an adult, and the role of experience and personal philosophy in shaping the educational activity (Jarvis, 1995).

Much of this work draws on the work of adult education theorist Jack Mezirow and his theories of transformative learning. Mezirow argues that education alters our 'frames of reference', thereby changing the way we see the world and challenging our assumptions and beliefs. A developed 'frame of reference' is inclusive, integrative and open in that the learner is able to integrate new knowledge into their worldview, be open to new ideas, and able to include other people's perspectives in their own (Mezirow, 1990). Mezirow placed critical reflection at the heart of the learning process, defining it as follows:

> To make meaning means to make sense of an experience; we make an interpretation of it. When we subsequently use this interpretation to guide decision making or action, then

making meaning becomes learning. We learn differently when we are learning to perform than when we are learning to understand what is being communicated to us. Reflection enables us to correct distortions in our beliefs and errors in problem solving. Critical reflection involves a critique of the presuppositions on which our beliefs have been built. (Mezirow, 1990, p 1)

Mezirow goes on to explore ideas around critical reflection, meaning-making, frames of reference and habitual patterns of expectation. He frames learning as a process of problem-solving, 'from the infant's problem of how to get fed to the adult's problem of how to understand the meaning of life' (1990, p 5). He claims this involves a process of reflection on prior learning experiences to determine whether these experiences are still relevant in the light of new knowledge. Mezirow also argues that *critical* reflection is fundamental to this, defining it as a process of questioning the '... values that have been very close to the centre of one's self-concept' (1990, p 12).

The premise of a philosophical conversation class (and my own view on education) aligns most closely with the teachings of liberal education. For example, Durkheim (1973), who is often referred to by liberal educationalists, suggested that education ought to develop learners' understanding of themselves as members of a community and a society. Liberal education cultivates the '... whole human being for the functions of citizenship and life generally...' (Nussbaum, 1998, p 9). As such, it aims to develop the whole person by encouraging critical self-examination and developing empathy (Nussbaum, 1998).

Although I agree with some of the tenets of a liberal education (I am, for example, wary of the notion of education as a means for instilling 'citizenship' in a learner), I am neither an expert nor a proponent. As a practitioner (I studied for a PGCE in 2008–09 with a range of philosophical perspectives of education being discussed as we trained), these high-level theoretical conceptualizations of education are not always at the centre of day-to-day work. In the classrooms, the corridors and the playing field, in my experience teachers rarely explicitly state their philosophical perspective. Instead, we engage in educational delivery as human beings, seeing our learners as fellow human beings whom we wish to see flourish and develop in the classroom. It is only now, as a researcher, I come to realize that my teaching philosophy loosely fits within the liberal paradigm. For me, the progress of my students, their self-realizations, personal growth and the skills gained remain the focus of my classroom, both in prison and outside.

In considering what prison education *ought* to do, it is important to understand what it *does* do. What do we know about the outcomes of providing education to prisoners? While few studies have been conducted into the role of education in prisons, there have been several important insights into the impact of education from the research that has been carried out. One broadly accepted finding is that participating in educational activities *in general* reduces the likelihood of reoffending and increases the likelihood of finding work. Such conclusions tend to come from post hoc studies that take a set of prison leavers, categorize them as 'did education' and 'did not do education', and compare their post-release outcomes. Those who 'did education' tend to fare better. However, there are issues of selection bias in these studies (see Ellison et al, 2017). More importantly for this study, however, these studies fail to get to the heart of the matter – what does education actually do? What does it mean to people who are in prison? And how does it relate to their lives inside?

Beyond stark measures of employment and recidivism, there are some studies that suggest education plays a particular role in the context of a prison. The experience and meaning of engaging in education while in prison relates directly to the prison and the prison experience. As Anne Reuss has argued, education can act as a refuge within the prison. Others have described education as having a different 'emotional climate' for prisoners (Crewe et al, 2013), where prisoners can engage in mutual support (Casey et al, 2013). Yet others have demonstrated that education relieves the boredom of prison life (Hughes, 2009), which can help prisoners cope with the challenges of the environment (Maruna, 2010).

Furthermore, research has shown that education can lead to better self-understanding, encourage self-reflection, build confidence and develop a sense of self-worth by providing the opportunity to discover talents (Waller, 2000; Hughes, 2009; Maruna, 2010). In this sense, prison education departments stand apart from the rest of the prison environment. Rather than focusing on the negative – for example, assuming a prisoner is 'broken' and requires 'fixing' – prison education focuses on the prisoner as a person and as a learner (Costelloe and Warner, 2008). Teachers are seen as being separate to the prison regime and education is provided, and engaged with, for reasons outside the penal framework of corrections and criminogenic risk factors.

What, then, is the purpose of prison education? When taking education into the prison setting, the broader issues of justice become more relevant. Should education be a means of developing the morality of prisoners or be used for behaviour change? Should we be actively trying to make prisoners 'better' citizens or 'better' people? Or should our primary concern be to develop skills so they can engage in work both in prison and on release? These questions are tied up with others that relate to the purpose of prisons that go beyond the discussion here.

I do not wish to 'sit on the fence' on the problem of prisons. Having spent 10 years working in this field, what I am left with is an unshakable sense of *in*justice – an interesting observation when we consider prisons are part of our *justice* system. I recognize the need, for a range of reasons, to sometimes remove people from their day-to-day lives. However, when you work with and among those who have been removed, the decision to do this is no longer abstract. Their stories, individual circumstances, their lives, hopes and dreams all become a reality, and the truth of what it means to send someone to prison becomes more apparent. As such, my own view of education differs from the notion that education ought to be 'correctional' to encourage 'better' behaviour (whatever that means). Instead, as a teacher, my role should always be to deliver the material of the course in an interesting and accessible manner, to develop learners' interest in a subject and, in the spirit of transformative learning, open their minds to different ways of thinking about the world. The purpose of engaging people in prison in philosophical conversation is simply to give them the opportunity to engage in such conversation and have the opportunity to do that kind of reflection.

This research presented here includes an in-depth exploration of the relevance of education to lives more generally. These ideas of the larger role education can play in the lives of people (and particularly people in prison) point towards education for education's sake. I take the view that the aim of education ought to be for growth and personal development. Although I recognize the role of education in providing greater access to employment, it goes beyond this by recognizing that education is also about understanding ourselves, the world and our place in it; it is about developing new interests and ways of thinking that can lead to personal transformation. In the following and final section of this opening chapter, I come to the exploration of the definition of 'identity'. What does it mean to be who we are? And how does our context shape us?

Populations of interest and different environments

As Mezirow said, 'No need is more fundamentally human than our need to understand the meaning of our experience' (Mezirow, 1990, p 11). The prison context shapes the experience of the prisoner. Understanding these different environments provides an insight into the meaning of these experiences.

In 2021, according to the World Prison Brief, there are around 11 million people in prisons across the world, and approximately 80,000 in the UK. With walls and bars separating the people inside from the wider community, the rhetoric around prisons swings between discussions of 'protection of the public' and 'rehabilitation'. In reality, prisons constitute a fundamental part of our criminal justice system and are, at their heart, a form of punishment. While in the UK we maintain that people are sent to prison *as* a punishment as opposed to *for* punishment, few take an interest in what actually happens behind prison walls. For those of us who do, the realities of prison, and the stories of the people sent there, become central to our way of thinking about the criminal justice system.

My work took place in two prisons – a therapeutic community prison (Grendon) and a maximum security prison (Full Sutton). I delivered two classes in each prison, with 24 prisoners in total attending the course. These participants took part in in-depth interviews, provided written and verbal feedback and attended 12 philosophy classes, each of which were between 2½ and 4 hours long. In addition, the research involved engaging with the wider prison education department, spending extensive time in the prisons to understand the wider prison community, and informally interviewing members of staff, non-participant prisoners and volunteers.

Traditionally characterized by a macho culture and power plays based on old gang ties, the informal economy and muscle, prison life today also incorporates hierarchies based on religion and piety, and stigmatization based on offence type and definitions of the 'other'. While the research, and the discussion that follows, focuses on this small number of participants, they represented the wider populations of the prisons in a range of ways. Three particular and distinct groups of prisoner emerged: vulnerable prisoners, Muslim prisoners, and the other, more 'typical', prisoners.

Vulnerable prisoners (VPs) are those deemed 'at risk' if they were to be held within the wider prison population, and are subject to greater protections. They suffer an extra level of stigmatization in entering prison as they are segregated from the mainstream population and held on separate wings (known as vulnerable prisoner units, or VPUs) and rejected by the prisoner society. They tended to keep themselves to themselves, were outwardly compliant, and cautious in their participation in the philosophical discussions.

Muslim prisoners are subject to particularly acute levels of distrust from the establishment's staff. The participants in both prisons included those who had been raised as Muslim and those who had converted while in prison. In Grendon, their religious identities, while important, were not overly relevant in the classroom. However, religious identity was at the forefront of interactions in Full Sutton, and my classroom included several Muslims who had been convicted of terrorist-related offences. As I will discuss later on, issues of power, piety and religion create specific tensions in the high security environment.

The third, important group can be loosely characterized as the more 'typical' prisoner. The 'typical' prisoner is either a young(ish) male who has committed some form of property offence or violence against a person, or an older prisoner who has 'been around the block' a few times and understands the 'game'. These men had, on the whole, been convicted of 'higher-status' crimes (murder, robbery, drug trafficking, for example), and carried themselves with an air of independence and stoicism. Some were white, some were not; some were religious, some were not. They engaged in the course openly, often offering me advice and guidance; they took a knowing protective attitude towards this young woman who was somewhat inexperienced in the complexities of prisoner politics and attempting to get them to engage in philosophical dialogue.

The lens of the prison sociologist often focuses on this 'typical' prisoner. Even those studies that attempt to incorporate a picture of the different types of prisoner often neglect to develop a comprehensive understanding of some types of prisoner. In particular, the literature often overlooks women, people convicted of sexual offences and the ageing population. Although other research refers, in some way, to vulnerable prisoners, these populations often sit on the periphery of the descriptions of prison life. In particular, those convicted of sexual offences are referred to as 'private sinners' (Cohen and Taylor, 1972), 'retreatists' (Crewe, 2009) and 'nonces' (prisoner terminology employed in Sparks et al, 1996). They keep themselves to themselves, comply with the regime, and are precluded from engaging with the mainstream population due to their crimes.

As in wider society, Muslim prisoners are often incorrectly subject to particularly acute levels of distrust from the establishment's staff and, as in wider society, are often incorrectly grouped together as though they are one homogenous group. More recently, research has begun to focus more fully on Muslim prisoners, the role of faith and conversion and issues of trust (see Beckford, 2005; Liebling and Williams, 2017).

Both Grendon and Full Sutton held all three types of prisoner, but with an important distinction. In Grendon, the men were differentiated by their status as members of a therapeutic environment, and were integrated within the prison and within their communities. In Full Sutton, the men were not integrated; VPs were held separately from the mainstream population in a VPU that, in reality, made up around half of the prisoner population.[5] The division between Muslims and non-Muslims, while not formal or physical, was just as real. This sense of community in Grendon, and sense of division in Full Sutton, played out in the philosophy classroom. However, as we shall go on to see, philosophical dialogue served as a means to overcome division.

While I provide a more in-depth account of these environments in the chapters that follow, in brief, the mainstream population in Full Sutton had a particular atmosphere with a particular set of tensions along religious and racial lines. The philosophy classroom was characterized by machismo and argument. The population of the VPU tended to be older, more compliant and, as referred to previously, were formally segregated from the wider population. Here, in Full Sutton, the philosophy classroom took a more careful tone, with prisoners wary of offering opinions.

The therapeutic community of Grendon was unique. The prisoners were integrated and, despite the intensity of the therapeutic work, lived in a comparatively cooperative and open atmosphere. Philosophical conversation flowed from the outset, with prisoners willing and able to engage in the subject matter.

I worked in the 'deep' end of the system. All prisoners were in prison for a long time. The shortest sentence was 8 years, and the longest serving prisoner had been in prison for 39 years when I met him. Some were old, some were young, but all were living a significant proportion of their life in prison. When I met them, they were living their life in a very specific kind of environment. As we shall see, these environments shaped the nature and content of the philosophical conversations. Further, they shaped the meaning of the conversations for the individuals, and provided an interesting insight into what it means to be human, and also what it means to grow and develop when living a life inside prison.

---

[5] As a result, in Full Sutton one class was delivered on the mainstream side of the prison and the other on the VPU. In reality, I was in the education department, in the same classroom, for both sides of the prison. The prison regime moved the relevant populations around in such a way that they never met.

What does it mean to 'be' when in prison? What does it mean to grow and develop when you live a life consigned to the prison system? How can the individual maintain a sense of identity in the prison environment?

Identity: a person in context

Philosophy offers the space to engage in both a personal and a social project, to explore the self and the views of others. Taking philosophy into the prison classroom meant giving prisoners the space and time to self-reflect and engage in dialogue in the company of others.

Identity sits at the heart of this discussion. My understanding of identity has been shaped by the philosophical discussions I undertook with the participants in prison, supplemented by reading in philosophy, sociology, mathematics and psychology. The issue of 'identity work' is of particular relevance to the lives of people in prison, a place where the individual is removed suddenly from their day-to-day lives and thrust into the life of a prison, often woefully unprepared. The participants had much to say on this topic, as will become apparent.

The prison context led to two distinct conceptualizations of identity coming to the fore: the 'survival' identity and the 'growth' identity. A survival identity refers to the 'front' many prisoners develop to survive the prison experience. Studies in prison sociology offer important insights into the prison context and how this can encourage 'survival'. A 'growth' identity refers to being future-oriented with the capacity to develop and flourish. Desistance literature (the study of how people *desist* from crime) engages with issues of identity, change and self-reflection, providing much needed insight into how people who have been convicted of crimes engage in 'identity work'.

Philosophical understanding of identity is often concerned with questions of *being* (Noonan, 2011). What characteristics or attributes can be assigned to a specific individual? What is human nature? What does it mean to be who we are? The social sciences also address questions of identity, but, instead of focusing on what identity is, consider the question of the *nature* of a person's identity. Scholars often distinguish between personal identity and social identity. The former refers to a person's continuous sense of self – their self-understanding and perception of what makes them who they are. The latter is determined by how they are identified by others, their place within a social structure and with whom they identify (Jenkins, 1996; Jewkes and Bennett, 2008).

The term 'identity' can take on different meanings. In the context of this work, in discussing identity I am referring to the identity that relates to how we understand ourselves and how others 'see' us. I focus on the idea that we construct a narrative or 'story' that explains who we are to ourselves. McAdams' (1993) theory of the internal narrative provides the framework for this understanding of identity and is used widely in desistance theories (see, in particular, Maruna, 2001). As such, I focus on issues of self-reflection, self-understanding and self-articulation.

However, our understanding of ourselves is shaped by those around us. As Hannah Arendt points out, any internally constructed concept of the self must be performed in public (Arendt, 1998 [1958]). Through articulation of the self in a public setting, and through reactions of others that consolidate or undermine our sense of self, identities are shaped and moulded according to culture, society and the environment in which we find ourselves (Arendt, 1998 [1958]). In this sense, our identity is understood to be in a constant state of development; our self-understanding is shaped and acted on by the people with whom we interact. We are, always, a 'person in context'.

We are always a person in context

The dichotomy of 'survival' versus 'growth' helps us understand the prison experience. Prisoners in Full Sutton were, in general, preoccupied with survival, while those in Grendon focused more on progress and growth. These ideas are given much greater attention later on (particularly in Chapters 3 and 4) and, as I present the findings of the research, we will develop a much greater understanding of what they mean in the context of being a person in prison.

Through prison sociology and desistance literatures, and my own experiences of working with and among prisoners, I articulate an initial theory of development and growth that describes the role of philosophy education in both prisons. Importantly, I provide an insight into the perspectives of the prisoners themselves, offering a unique discussion of prison, the prisoner and what it means to be human. I aimed to ensure my research worked with, as opposed to against, that which a prison already offers, focusing on developing the strengths of prisoners and looking to provide a space where, for a short time, their status as prisoner can fall away and they can be philosophers for a time.

2

Towards Theory: People, Places and Voices

'Subjectivity guides everything from the choice of topic that one studies, to formulating hypotheses, to selecting methodologies, and interpreting data' (Ratner, 2002, p 1). This book is not simply a subjective memoir, but an account of a piece of research. This involved systematic pre-, during and post-participation data collection, and took place dynamically alongside delivery of the course. As an ongoing process, analysis included reflection and refinement of data collection tools, ensuring that data provided relevant and focused insights as the research progressed (Foster, 2006). The methodological framework draws on Derek Layder's adaptive theory (1998). Following this framework, as the book progresses, I move between my data and literature to illuminate and illustrate the findings. This chapter provides a brief overview of this process, both with respect to delivery of the philosophy course and with respect to data collection and analysis. A full, more technical account of the research, can be found in the Appendix.

I delivered the course alongside conducting the research. Although such a dual role raises issues around objectivity, taking on both tasks has provided a clear advantage in that I was not simply an objective observer, but also a subjective participant in the research process (LeCompte, 1987). This has enabled me to provide an in-depth account of the course, placing the prisoner-student experience, which I shared, at the heart of the process. The central aim of this research has been to explore *what* role philosophy *might* play in the prison environment, and to do this through a consideration of identity. In doing so, the aim is not to demonstrate philosophy's superiority over other programmes or courses, but to highlight how it can be complementary, and also, in what ways it might 'work'. I focus on mechanisms, developing theories around the 'how' and 'why' of philosophy education as well as outlining 'what it does'. I prioritize the role of philosophy for the individual as I am interested in the role of education in developing the whole person.

At the outset, no literature was available regarding the use of philosophy education in prisons.[1] This research has therefore been aimed at theory-building, and draws on a range of data collection techniques to build a picture of the meaning and practice of philosophy in prison. Subsequent chapters present the findings of this research project in their refined form, culminating in a discussion of the wider implications for this type of education in prisons. I provide an account of how I reached these conclusions, demonstrating that they are fundamentally grounded in the experiences of the prisoner-participants while at the same time taking account of broader academic writings of educational theory, philosophy, prison sociology and criminological literature.

Throughout, I allowed the themes emerging from the data, and my own personal insights, to guide me through the process, drawing on existing literature as and when it became relevant. I used multiple streams of data collection, including extensive fieldwork notes, interviews and feedback forms. I spent significant periods of time in the two prisons, getting to know the environment and speaking with prison officers, educators and non-participant prisoners. I worked closely with the research participants, slowly developing relationships and noting their insights as the course progressed. All were formally interviewed before and after participating in the course and some part way through, as I developed theories and areas of focus. I took an iterative approach to the research and so, after each stage, amended and developed interview questions to reflect the changing focus of the research. Observational notes became more specific and refined. This allowed for the continuous development of theories, concepts and ideas that could be tested and developed on return to the field.

I now provide an overview of the process of delivering the philosophy course and a brief account of the research process. Further, I outline the preparation I engaged with prior to entering HMP Grendon and HMP Full Sutton, which included two pilot projects in two other prisons. Finally, as you will note from the opening chapter, the book offers accounts of philosophical discussions that serve to illustrate

---

[1] In the years since, a few papers have begun to emerge. See, in particular, Bovill and Anderson (2020).

the findings of the research. I therefore conclude this chapter with a discussion of how I placed the voices of the participants at the heart of the research.

First, however, I provide a brief account of the people and prisons involved in the research that provided the context.

Prisons and people

Both Grendon and Full Sutton are located in England. With one a therapeutic community (TC) (Grendon) and the other a high security, dispersal prison (Full Sutton), the two locations provided distinct settings for the research. The prison populations were similar (in terms of sentence length and offence category) but also distinct (both with respect to the demographic make-up of the population and the integration of different populations in the prison).

At the time of my research, Grendon was a Category 'B' prison with a capacity of 238 prisoners (Inside Time, 2014).[2] Unique in the prison estate, Grendon's regime ran on the principles of a democratic TC. It was, and remains, the only prison entirely run on this basis, other such places in the UK being single wings or small parts of wider prisons.

In contrast, Full Sutton was a Category 'A' dispersal prison,[3] and held over 600 prisoners. As a high security prison, Full Sutton tended to take those who had committed very serious crimes or posed particular

---

[2] In the wake of the abolition of the death penalty, the justice system in England and Wales had to consider the question of what to do with those individuals who had committed the most serious offences. Following the Mountbatten Report (Home Office, 1966) into prison security, the prison system introduced a system of categorization of prisoners related to their 'risk' of escape and the danger they present to the public, with Category 'A' being the highest level of security and 'D' being the lowest (Price, 2000). This system allows the prison service to organize the prison estate according to the 'level of security deemed necessary to safely hold them in custody' (Price, 2000, p 3). The current system of categorization remains unchanged from Mountbatten's original recommendations in 1966.

[3] The term 'dispersal' refers to the decision to 'disperse' Category 'A' prisoners among a Category 'B' population while maintaining the highest security. The other possibility was to hold the prisoners considered to be the highest risk in specially designated wings or prisons. This led to examples such as Durham's E wing, the focus of Cohen and Taylor's (1972) seminal study of prisons in *Psychological Survival*, who describe a 'prison within a prison' where small numbers of the most notorious prisoners were held in severe isolation from the wider prison community. Their account of E wing indicates that such limited ability to socialize led to particular problems for the individuals, and fell out of use in favour of the dispersal approach.

security risks. The prison ran a more traditional regime, with prisoners offered opportunities to engage in work or education during the core working day.

The different statuses of the prisons meant very different regimes. In Grendon, prisoners engaged in extensive group therapy, had responsibility for running wings, and were expected to engage in the life of the community. They were afforded significant amounts of time out of their cells, with mornings involving general therapy and afternoons offering specialized programmes such as art therapy and psychodrama. Prisoners engaged in the prison regime and were expected to work cooperatively with the community to develop insight into their behaviours and their pasts in order to move forward. Those who did not would run the risk of being voted out of the community by their peers.[4]

In Full Sutton, prisoners were escorted around the prison more closely than those in Grendon, were subject to more frequent searches, and followed a stricter regime. Although there were psychologically based offender behaviour courses delivered in Full Sutton, the focus of the prison was on security and purposeful activity. As a consequence, prisoners in Full Sutton tended to spend their days in workshops or in education.

Prisoners in Grendon had, in general, progressed further in their sentences than those in Full Sutton. Although they held similar populations, Full Sutton housed men either at the start of their sentences or those who struggled to comply with the expectations of prison life (and who had therefore not 'progressed' in the system). Both prisons held men with a range of offence types and, with a focus on those with 'long' sentences (defined as four or more years, but often substantially longer), they tended to include people convicted of more serious crimes. In particular, both prisons held prisoners convicted of sexual offences who were usually categorized as 'vulnerable'. Of particular note for this research was that Grendon integrated 'vulnerable' prisoners into the rest of the population. In Full Sutton, and in most other prisons in the UK, VPs were held on separate wings with distinct regimes to protect them from the wider population.

---

[4] During my time in Grendon two of my philosophy students were removed before the end of the course, one to move to a secure psychiatric unit and another because he contravened the rules of the community (they are not included in this research) with at least a further two leaving Grendon without completing therapy in the year following my research (these two have been included).

The integration of VPs in Grendon was due, in part, to its ethos as a TC. Grendon's inhabitants comprised those who had been deemed 'suitable' for such an environment by staff at another prison and who had demonstrated a willingness to engage with the therapeutic work. As such, they were expected to comply with the tenets of the community, or risk de-selection.

The men who volunteered to engage with the philosophy course included a range of individuals. They had various educational backgrounds, criminal histories and motivations for engaging. Their ages ranged from 25 to 64, with the majority being under the age of 40. All had significant sentences, although they varied in type and length. Around a third were serving life sentences, with a further three serving indeterminate sentences for the protection of the public (these sentences are no longer in use, but were previously used to give minimum terms but with no maximum). The remaining participants (13) had fixed-term sentences, with only one of those with a fixed-term sentence having a sentence length of less than 10 years. Some prisoners had entered prison for the first time on their current sentence, while others had had spells in prison since they were young men. However, the variation in both prisons was large, with some prisoners having served cumulatively a much larger number of years in prison (one participant had served over 30 years in prison across two life sentences, while another had only been in prison for 18 months).

These heavy sentences reflected the crimes for which the participants had been convicted. In total, seven had committed sexually motivated crimes, eight were serving time for murder, three for property offences, two for kidnap, one for drug trafficking and one for grievous bodily harm. A further two participants had been convicted under the Terrorism Act (known as TACT prisoners). Several participants' criminal careers revolved around, and were a result of, drug addictions, and many had childhood stories characterized by abuse and neglect. Others were more 'traditional' prisoners, seen as being part of the 'old guard' hierarchy relating to criminal gangs more common in the latter half of the 20th century. They often had criminal careers involving large-scale drug trafficking and racketeering. Finally, some of the prisoners came from more ordinary backgrounds, having completed school with varying degrees of success to go on to careers in industries such as catering, healthcare and management prior to their conviction.

Educationally, too, each of the groups represented a range of backgrounds. In Grendon, one of the participants had not completed any schooling prior to prison and had only engaged very minimally with education while in prison, despite having been there for over a decade. Another had come to prison as a teenager and started at Literacy and Numeracy Level 1, but by the time he participated in this research, was in the process of completing a challenging Open University degree in the Natural Sciences. Another was studying for a Master's in Mathematics, another had a degree prior to coming to prison, several had completed some university-level education in prison, while a couple had rarely engaged in formal learning. A similar story can be told in Full Sutton – some of the prisoners held, or had studied towards, degree-level qualifications while others came to the philosophy course having never engaged in formal education.

In general, the participants in my philosophy classes were highly intelligent, articulate and, even if they had not gained qualifications, were engaged in some form of self-improvement while in prison. For some, their mission for self-improvement had been ongoing for some time. They came to discussions with an established breadth of knowledge and a range of discursive skills. For others, engaging in the philosophy course represented a first foray into the realms of learning for the sake of learning.

The participants had a variety of reasons for signing up to the course. For some, it was an opportunity to engage in something intellectually stimulating as an addition to their current studies, while for others it was simply something to do. Others were intrigued by the word 'philosophy'. Some had very specific reasons for joining the course. For example, one of the participants in Grendon discussed struggling to 'find his voice' in group therapy sessions, and thought the discursive nature of the philosophy class might improve his confidence (which he later reported it did). Another in Grendon had developed a relationship with a girl he had known at school. She was now well educated and he wanted to be able to engage in conversation with her on a more intellectual level. He reported that he had won some arguments with her since being in the philosophy class (for which I refused to take the blame or credit). In Full Sutton, reasons for engaging in the course were rarely this specific. For these participants, such a class seemed to represent a rare opportunity for intellectual stimulation.

Previous experience of philosophy varied among the participants. Many had never studied philosophy or engaged in the subject before, while others had read some philosophy in their own time. For instance, one had read Bertrand Russell's *History of Western Philosophy* (2005 [1946]) and Plato's *Republic* (1992 [380 BC]). Others had studied philosophy formally, with one participant studying Philosophy, Politics and Economics through the Open University.

The different backgrounds, experience, knowledge and levels of articulacy in the class meant that each participant came to the discussion with their own unique skills. Further, as would be expected in philosophical discussions in the wider community, all had strengths and weaknesses, and all had specific preferences with respect to the different topics covered.

Taking philosophy into the prison classroom

This research project has been driven by my belief in and passion for education. I moved from being a professional teacher to being a researcher in 2010 with a specific aim to involve myself in prison education. The route has been somewhat convoluted, as I started my undergraduate studying for a dual honours in Maths and Philosophy but ultimately graduated with a Maths degree, before going on to study for a Postgraduate Certificate in Education (PGCE). I taught for a few years in the UK and abroad, during which time I trained in Philosophy for Children and ran lunchtime and after-school sessions for teenagers in a local comprehensive.

The first school I worked in was based in a relatively deprived area in the former mining areas between Sheffield and Chesterfield. The school had the highest number of 'looked-after' children (meaning they were cared for by someone other than their parents) in the county, and many of the young people with whom I worked had complex issues. My interest in prison education came from teaching two particularly difficult young men. They were in the bottom set for maths and often caused problems in the classroom, from answering back, to fighting, to turning up late and refusing to do the work. I was a newly qualified teacher and it took time to find my feet. Eventually, I started to gain some ground with them, and, after several months of effort, I felt they had started to learn something. Just as this happened, though, they were both permanently excluded, for separate reasons but in quick succession. While I understood the reasons, I just felt despondent. What would happen to their maths education now?

My approach to this research project has been shaped by these experiences. I moved into criminology with an express desire to understand what happened to an individual's educational trajectories if mainstream schooling failed. One of these two young men went to a pupil referral unit, a school specifically for those whose behaviour is not compatible with mainstream education. I developed an interest in 'hidden' educational institutions that sit outside of the 'normal' school system. Eventually, I started thinking about education in prison and my training and background in the teaching profession proved invaluable in understanding the prison classroom. It meant I could smoothly engage with the staff and culture of a prison education department, I understood the language of the environment and have usually been accepted without question in staff rooms. Perhaps more importantly, though, it has shaped my perspective of what teaching ought to do, what it means to learn, and what it means to have a positive learning environment.

My ultimate concern, with respect to students under my care, is to provide an environment that facilitates learning. By learning, I refer to the acquisition of knowledge, development of skills or pursuit of new or existing interests. I also specifically use the word 'facilitate' to illustrate my understanding of the role of a teacher not as an instructor, but as someone who develops a space in which learners can pursue learning in their own way and in their own time. Such a perspective encourages an individualized, personal and holistic approach to education whereby the teacher looks to meet the student where they are in their learning journey. I take a self-conscious approach to teaching, which draws close to the humanistic perspective articulated in Chapter 1 (see also Liebling, 2015).

Following this perspective, my role as a philosophy teacher, first and foremost, was to develop the participants' skills in active philosophizing and encourage their acquisition of knowledge in the subject of philosophy. It was therefore important to create a positive learning environment for all participants. Inherent in this is a recognition that all learners, participants, pupils or students must feel safe and able to engage in the learning process. A teacher's role involves some pastoral care whereby the wellbeing of their learners underpins practice. In the prison environment, this meant striving for an environment where the participants felt able to engage in conversation without fear of being undermined, with an understanding that their contribution had equal value, and where they were, first and foremost, learners in a classroom.

In both prisons, the 'Introduction to Philosophy' course I delivered lasted for 12 weeks, and was held in the education department alongside other educational programmes. Each session had the same structure. Participants would arrange themselves at desks, seated in a circle so all participants faced each other. I would place myself, seated, as part of the circle, so that I could facilitate the discussion as a co-inquirer.

The start of the first session involved a brief discussion around the purpose and expectations of the dialogue. In subsequent weeks, I began each session by asking for feedback from the previous session and for a brief recap to get the dialogue going. The participants would occasionally have written some reflective thoughts for me to read and respond to, or would bring along questions and new ideas.

Once introductions and feedback had ended, I would introduce the day's topic. I introduced topics and ideas in stages, drawing the participants through philosophical ideas. I took care to introduce each stage naturally, allowing conversation and dialogue to flow, but using each new stage as a means of redirecting and reinvigorating the conversation. At the end of each session, I gave the participants a handout with optional further reading to take away. The readings always related to the topic discussed, but often focused on a different philosopher, or different ways of thinking about the topic covered in the class.

I based each session on a different topic. Some of the sessions focused on a particular philosopher, such as Kant or Descartes. These sessions introduced the philosopher's ideas in stages, drawing the participants through their arguments, demonstrating how a philosopher builds from first principles. Sessions based on a school of philosophy, such as the Stoics or utilitarianism, introduced the participants to the ideas of several philosophers, which provided the opportunity to discuss arguments for and against a philosophical school of thought. The final 'type' of session focused on classic philosophical problems, such as 'Theseus' ship' introduced in Chapter 1.

To develop materials, I drew on a range of resources for inspiration and guidance. As an amateur philosopher with an interest in community philosophy (as opposed to a scholar who has studied philosophical works in-depth) I drew on popular philosophy books and secondary sources that provided summaries of philosophers' works. In particular, the work of Nigel Warburton and that of Peter and Emma Worley at The Philosophy Foundation provided excellent starting points, along with Stanford's *Encyclopaedia of Philosophy*, offering a more in-depth description of different perspectives. However, I built the stimuli myself, drawing on sources and thinking through how they might fit together. Initially, the topics reflected my own interests, focusing on identity, morality and society. As the course progressed, I incorporated the participants' views and consequently the topics came to reflect their interests.

My experience as a teacher in the prison classroom provided a specific and unique perspective in the data. From the topics I chose to discuss, to the direction of the philosophical dialogue and the nature of the social interactions, my own background, personality and interests have driven much of this project. The findings were shaped by my approach to philosophy, the topics I chose to cover, the way in which I conducted myself in the classroom and the relationships I developed with the participants. These, in turn, were derived from my understanding of what a 'good' learning environment looks like – one that builds learners' confidence, that encourages a thirst for knowledge, that looks to work with learners' strengths and interests, and, most importantly, one that encourages them to think critically about what is presented to them, allowing space and time for them to challenge both what is being taught and the way in which the teaching is being delivered.

For me, a positive learning environment is one that is 'buzzing' with energy and enthusiasm, where learners have not only learned something but have also enjoyed themselves in the process. To achieve this, in my experience, it is imperative for learners to understand that I, as their teacher, care about their progress in my classroom, about their educational journey and consequently, about them as people who live in the world.

However, in discussing an ideal learning environment, it is also necessary to question whether it is possible to truly achieve such an environment in a prison. Or, perhaps more importantly, to ask whether the context of a prison changes the meaning of a learning environment. In prison, motivations for entering education, the ability to progress within the classroom and the capacity to apply the learning beyond the classroom are all constrained by the prison environment. Although I delivered the course in two prisons, in reality, I delivered the course in three distinct environments – a therapeutic community, a maximum security mainstream prison and a maximum security vulnerable prisoners unit. The nature of the three populations with whom I worked presented distinct challenges. Furthermore, the different environments in which the course took place became relevant to the role of philosophy to the participants.

Preparation

Before entering the field, I engaged in two 'pilot' research projects. These served as opportunities to develop teaching materials and data collection techniques. This meant, in starting my research proper, I could avoid the inherent pitfalls that can occur when conducting large research projects. The first involved piloting the materials and model – a sort of 'proof of concept' piece of work – and the second, piloting the research methods. The latter involved developing a theoretical framework that helped direct the research project.

The first pilot entailed delivering four philosophy sessions in HMP High Down (London). This constituted my first experience of engaging prisoners in philosophy education and formed the basis of my MPhil dissertation. While my teaching practices drew on Philosophy for Children pedagogy, my teaching style developed significantly. I adapted the methods to suit the population with whom I worked, and developed my own methods of delivery. Fundamentally, having come from teaching maths in secondary schools and setting up philosophy classes on the side, this work constituted an opportunity to develop techniques and materials suitable for adult, male prisoners.

The second pilot took place in HMP Low Moss (Glasgow). This constituted an initial phase of data collection to develop an understanding of the relevance of philosophy to the lives of prisoners. As such, this pilot formed the first stage in 'theory-building', providing an initial framework for analysis (Bendasolli, 2013). At the time of the pilot, Nikki Cameron, a teacher in Low Moss, had been delivering philosophy classes for two years. Cameron's philosophy classes broadly followed the same principles as my own, basing her stimuli around an information leaflet. In that way, participants had all of the material for the basis of their discussion in front of them from the outset. The uptake of philosophy by the men in Low Moss had gradually developed to allow the growth of delivery from one class per week to around seven per week. I took the opportunity to observe established philosophy sessions, and to interview philosophy students.[5]

I collected data for the pilot across two waves, each consisting of four full days in the education department in Low Moss. Both waves involved observing philosophy sessions and interviewing participants. In total, I interviewed 20 participants, which included a mixture of long- and short-term prisoners who had a range of index offences. Some of the interviewees had been attending the course for nearly a year while others had only attended for a few weeks.

This research allowed me to develop a 'primitive conceptual framework' (Layder, 1998, p 117). The prisoners discussed how philosophy had helped them gain an understanding of themselves, their past, their present and their future. They discussed their enthusiasm for the intellectual fulfilment of philosophical dialogue, relating how

---

[5] I recount the findings of this research in detail in a paper entitled 'Socrates and Aristotle: The role of ancient philosophers in the self-understanding of desisting prisoners' (2017). Credit for the title of this paper must go to my supervisor Professor Alison Liebling, who has the habit of developing snappy ways of summarizing the core of a piece of research.

they would take it back to their wings and recreate the discussions with their 'pals'. Philosophy provided them with a better understanding of the world, providing access to wider societal conversations that had previously seemed obscure and irrelevant. They found the conversations helpful in developing their understanding of their fellow inmates, creating a sense of community and camaraderie among them. They argued that it was relevant to the prison atmosphere as a whole, both helping them cope with their situations and teaching them to have self-control – to think before they spoke, and to recognize that they did not necessarily know all the answers.

Analysis of findings concluded that philosophy is relevant to the self-understanding of participating prisoners (Szifris, 2017). The dialogic nature of the classes encouraged development of language for alternative self-definition – as a method to expose participants to new and different ways of thinking, and as a means to develop social skills in a community of peers.

The pilot work in Low Moss provided a clear foundation for the next stage of the research. Many of these themes are present in the findings from my own philosophy course. They were developed and refined so that they relate to the particular environments in which I was working. Grendon and Full Sutton had very particular environments that framed the outcomes and context of this research project. However, there are some key overarching themes that extend from my pilot research into the work in Grendon and Full Sutton – those of community, self-understanding and broadened perspectives.

Developing theory

I have already stated that this research focuses on *theory-building* as opposed to theory-testing (Bendasolli, 2013). In other words, without existing research to guide the work, I began with an open question asking what relevance philosophy has to the lives of people in prison. Using a technique developed by Derek Laydor known as 'adaptive theory', I moved between extant, relevant literature and emergent themes in the data as the research progressed. I gradually built and refined my thinking, making use of orienting concepts and theoretical memos to track and develop ideas.

I have focused on mechanisms, developing theories around the 'how' and 'why' of philosophy education, as well as outlining 'what it does' (Pawson and Tilley, 1997). I have prioritized the role of philosophy for the individual (as opposed to its role in crime reduction, for example, although I do touch on this through desistance literature) as I am interested in the role of education in developing the whole person (Dewey, 1990 [1902]). In this way, we can make the link from personal development to desistance, crime reduction and increased employability through recognition of the individual's own agency, interests and strengths, without having to compromise on the aims of an education course.

The research design reflects the exploratory and theory-building nature of the research. Derek Layder's (1998) adaptive theory has provided a methodological framework, while the theoretical framework draws on desistance literature, prison sociology and philosophical pedagogy to enhance and develop understanding of the emergent themes. However, as a *criminological* piece of research (as opposed to educational), I sit within the criminological, and more specifically, prison sociological paradigm. The focus in this research has been on the personal experience of engaging in philosophical dialogue from the perspective of *being a prisoner in the prison environment*. As such, although educational theory is touched on to provide context and develop understanding of pedagogy, data have been analysed from the perspective of a criminologist and prison sociologist.

Data collection included interviewing the participants before and after course delivery, using semi-structured interview schedules that were refined and developed during the piloting phase and throughout the research process. At the same time, this research was specifically designed to ensure that the voice of the prisoner-participant lies at the heart of the theory. Therefore, I drew on qualitative arguments that the individual at the centre of the research ought to be heard most clearly in the emerging theory (Rubin and Rubin, 2012). As a subjective participant, I realized that, in delivering the philosophy course, my own experience and insight hold relevance as well, and so I kept systematic and extensive fieldwork notes throughout. However, I have endeavoured to begin with the participants' own words, starting analysis with the post-participation interviews and using other strands of data to validate, refine, enhance and develop emerging themes.

Ethnography often uses the term 'respondent validation' to refer to a researcher taking care to sense-check their findings with their research participants (Bloor, 1978). I used these techniques to check that I had an accurate understanding of a particular situation (Atkinson and Hammersley, 2007). Throughout delivery of the course, I discussed my thoughts with the participants, fellow teachers and other members of staff around the prison. With the participants, I asked about details of their lives inside prison, the way in which their society worked, and what they thought about different aspects of prison life. With staff, I reflected on my own experience of teaching particular individuals, discussing the difficulties and rewards of engaging this population. I also discussed with staff their view of current educational provision in the prisons, the wider regime and the general atmosphere of the prison environment.

Participants' voices

As the book progresses, I will relate a range of quotes and conversations that took place in the prison classroom. I endeavour to be clear how these conversations were recorded. In the case of direct quotes from people in prison, these either stem from interviews recorded via dictaphone (and then transcribed verbatim) or from written text from the participants themselves (in feedback forms, letters or reflections offered on the class). When relating conversations from the classroom, these stem from fieldwork notes. During my time discussing philosophy with the participants, I acted as a 'full participant', engaging in conversation and facilitating the class as a teacher. After leaving the prison classroom I would record the events of the discussion via a dictaphone on my long drives home followed up by notes taken directly after the class had finished. These will be somewhat less reliable than the quotes that stem from the interview recordings, but they offer an honest account of the conversation.

I have endeavoured to quote participants verbatim, being honest with their vernacular and choice of words. Occasionally, in transcripts, participants spent a lot of time saying 'um' and repeating words. In these cases, I have simplified the text with small edits but denoted any changes with '...' in the text. When relating discussions in the classroom, any direct quotes are those that have been recorded in the fieldwork as specific comments by individuals. Finally, all participants have been given pseudonyms – some chose their own while others let me assign a name. All descriptions of the participants are given in aggregate or are sufficiently altered so as to ensure they cannot be identified.

The opportunity to engage men in prison in philosophical conversation is not granted to everyone. The experience has focused the lens of this research onto the lives of prisoners, allowing them the opportunity to articulate the prison experience, their status as prisoner and the role of education from the dual perspectives of the prisoner-participants and the teacher-researcher. This research was informed by, and based within, the work of the Prisons Research Centre (PRC) at the University of Cambridge. As such, I draw on a range of techniques grounded in a fundamentally 'humanistic' approach that has produced accurate and careful description of the prisons, the prisoners and the communities of philosophical inquiry in which we engaged (Liebling, 2015). Liebling's descriptions of such work as 'emotional edgework' resonate with my own experience in the field – this research has been intimate, intrusive and emotionally demanding (Liebling, 2015), yet, at the same time, it has been informative and wholly worthwhile.

3

Survival, Plato and the Ideal Society

A desert island (Week 2, Stage 1)

Imagine you are travelling across the Pacific Ocean 2,500 years ago (around the time of the Ancient Greeks). Your transport is a large wooden ship that has been travelling for weeks across a featureless sea. A darkly powerful storm whips up and rages for days. The storm eventually capsizes your ship and you find yourself tossed about by the high waves. You manage to grab hold of a free-floating piece of wood and hang on to it for your life.

The following morning the storm has subsided and you find that you have been washed up on a beach of a tropical island. The sun is shining and the weather is beautifully calm. You stand up and decide to explore the island, which will be your home for the foreseeable future.

You discover that this island is not inhabited and seems never to have been. There is absolutely no sign of human life whatsoever. All around the perimeter is a golden sandy beach. The middle of the island is covered with a lush forest, full of animals and different fruits. There is a mountain at the heart of the forest from which run several fresh water streams that form a lake at the bottom, full of fish. There is plenty here for you to live on.

When you have returned from your exploration of the island you find that there are some other survivors from the wrecked ship. There are not many survivors, less than 20. You gather together and discuss what you should do.

Source: Taken from *The 'If' Machine* by Peter Worley

"We need a leader." Cady is the first to respond. A young man, in his mid-20s, with an extremely long sentence to serve, Cady's formative years were characterized by gang membership. Now, several years into his sentence, he has been in HMP Grendon for a few months.

Phil, in his mid-30s, with a history of drug abuse, disagreed. "There's only 20 people, we don't need a leader."

"People are selfish, we need structure to keep [a] check on behaviour," Michael chimes in. Phil disagrees again, and the conversation moves towards a discussion of democracy, ruling by consensus and class systems. Living, as these men do, in a democratic therapeutic community (TC), there is a clear understanding of constitutions, voting procedures and social responsibility. However, when I ask if any of them had actually voted when they were on the outside, not one of them had. When I ask why democracy was suggested as a means of choosing a leader, Cady admitted that he had got the idea from the TV show, Lost. They had done it on there, and so it seemed sensible to him.

Other than discussing how to choose a leader, the story of the shipwreck prompts discussion of the allocation of tasks. Having used this with a range of groups, most suggest using people's existing skills and allocating tasks accordingly. This, in turn, leads to discussions around choice – should people be allowed to choose their activities? Or should they do the activity to which they are most suited? Some groups focused closely on the specifics of the story – it's a dark and stormy night, it's 2,500 years ago – taking its contents more literally. Other groups quickly moved on to more abstract discussions of how work might be allocated, and how a society such as this could be structured.

One of the group discussions (at HMP Full Sutton) turns to the concept of power. How would power be wielded? Who would control the situation? Dave, a large self-conscious man who often made particularly insightful comments, pointed out that power might sit with the person who has the most prized skill. He gave an example of a community needing a blacksmith's skills but there being only one blacksmith. Then, he suggested, the blacksmith would hold the power within that community and could use his skills to leverage his position.

Power, leadership and social structure drive these conversations. These concepts take on particular meaning in the prison environment. Complex and varied interactions between participants in my philosophy groups meant philosophical conversation differed between prisons and between prisoners. Issues of hierarchy, power, trust and suspicion filtered into the philosophy classroom. To understand this,

I drew on the field of prison sociology. A range of other in-depth studies of prisons and the prisoner experience offer some key insights, considering questions of 'What is prison like?' and 'What does it mean to be a prisoner?'

Prisons, prisoners and the prison 'society'

Focusing on the 'communities' (Clemmer, 1958) and 'societies' (Sykes, 1958) formed in isolation, prison sociology concerns itself with the day-to-day reality of those restricted to this closed community. With prisoners confined within prison walls and watched over by prison staff, there are areas in which the prisoners' isolation is interrupted by positive social environments (education, the chaplaincy, visits). However, the bulk of an individual's time, while incarcerated, is within the 'Society of Captives' (Sykes, 1958).

When I am in conversation with friends about my work in prisons, discussion often turns to issues surrounding the physical threat of prison – the risk of being beaten up, physically intimidated, raped, or even murdered. I am regularly asked if I feel 'safe' in the prison environment, whether the prisoners are in the same room as me, whether there is a 'guard', and if I have ever seen violence in the prison. The perception of a prison as a place of violence and intimidation is not without foundation; in 2015 (the year my data collection took place) over 16,000 assaults and 7 homicides occurred in the male adult estate (Ministry of Justice, 2015).

However, figures related to incidences of self-harm surpass these, which, in 2015, stood at 20,409 and, eclipsing the number of homicides, 82 prisoners took their own lives (Ministry of Justice, 2015). These figures demonstrate that, although the risk of physical violence against a person is real, the effect of imprisonment on a person's psychological health is particularly acute.

Constituting a 'radical shattering' of continuity and routine (Liebling, 1992), on entering prison people are isolated from friends and family, excluded from participating in society and have the unenviable task of establishing themselves within the prison community. In one of the earliest sociological studies of the prison, Gresham Sykes, studying a prison in New Jersey (US) in the 1950s, argued that, despite the lack of corporal punishment, prison still involved equivalent 'pains and deprivations'. His initial study highlighted five key areas of deprivation: liberty, goods and services, heterosexual relationships, autonomy and security. In the years since then, prison sociologists have drawn on this framework and language to build an understanding of the effect of long-term imprisonment. Boredom, isolation, lack of activity, victimization, breakdown in relationships and poor living conditions all contribute to the difficulties of maintaining psychological wellbeing while in prison (Liebling, 1992):

> 'It's the same thing every day, same routine … we're still human beings, we're not sheep … open the gate, usher us forward through the gate, you stay up there for the day, and then the sheepdog comes, barks all you lot back into the little kitchen that you go in for the night or whatever it is, and that's it. And then when they come when it's feeding time, they come, put all the food, and everyone comes rushing, buzzing, get their food.' (Martin, Full Sutton, mainstream)

Prison exerts control over every aspect of a prisoner's life. Confined *to* as well as *within* the prison, prisoners are moved around, from location to location, from cell to work, from gym to education. Sykes argued that prisoners are reduced to a dependent state as they wait to be 'fed', to be unlocked, to be taken to work or visits. Toch (1977) argues that this loss of autonomy amounts to an attack on the individual's personal integrity, while Liebling (1992) claimed it left prisoners at risk of 'losing themselves' to the routine of the regime. The regime places a toll on a person's sense of self. Crewe et al (2020) argue that prison results in the individual losing a sense of who they 'had been', with the direct environment continuously stripping away their understanding of themselves.

In the philosophy classroom, prisoners in both prisons often discussed the difficulties of this loss of autonomy. Their studies would be interrupted by problems getting the materials they needed, their interests curtailed due to the lack of opportunities in prison, and their existing skills would often go unused. One of the participants said he would be happy if he could "just do a bit of gardening" (Paul, Full Sutton, VPU), with another saying he spent his days playing computer games to numb himself to the pain of being inside.

Beyond the routine of the regime, entering prison places expectations on the individual. To progress, to get parole, to be rewarded with a TV in your cell (rented, not given), you must comply, engage, show willing. In Grendon, although staff treated prisoners with respect, they were subject to the expectations of therapy. As members of the TC, they were required to engage in the process and to speak openly and honestly about their past, their behaviour and their feelings. To do this was a basic requirement. These expectations may have a benign intention – to help the prisoner understand what they may have done, how they came to commit their crime and to deal with their 'criminogenic tendencies', but they still constitute a lack of choice. There was pressure from their peers to conform to the ways of the community. The benefits of the system were, however, known to them all – for some on particularly long sentences, Grendon's TC offers a hope of eventual release that would otherwise have been unavailable.

The power of the institution over the individual underpins the loss of autonomy. In a seminal study, Sparks, Bottoms and Hay aimed to 'explore to what extent a stable and orderly form of life is achievable under conditions of confinement' (1996, pp 34–5). They spent extensive time in two prisons in England – Albany and Long Lartin – 'listening to staff, managers, and prisoners, and trying to understand the subtle dynamics of each prison's social life' (Sparks et al, 1996, p 113). The book, *Prisons and the Problem of Order*, entails a comprehensive overview of life inside these two prisons, focusing on, among other things, power and relationships within the prison community. The authors develop a typology of prison violence (interpersonal, protest and the informal economy), analyse the application of rules by governors and staff, and develop a set of dimensions to characterize staff–prisoner relationships (close–distant and flexible–consistent).

Sparks and colleagues focus particularly on social relationships, taking account of both staff and prisoner perspectives. They argue that maintaining control in a prison involves an implicit understanding that coercion, force and even violence can be used if necessary. Although I never felt a threat of violence in either prison, in Full Sutton I was conscious of being observed. If I walked from the classroom towards the staffroom engaging in friendly, casual conversation with one of the participants, I felt the gaze of suspicion from the prison officers who sat at their stations, silently observing but rarely interacting with the population. I discussed these feelings with teachers in the education department who candidly discussed the security concerns around conditioning or manipulation of staff by the prisoners. By way of an explanation, staff related the early history of the prison, characterized by a weak staff culture, with prisoners holding power and staff succumbing to the demands of the population. Having regained control, the staff had long memories and maintained a purposeful distance from the prisoners, and anyone who did not was subject to suspicion.

Beyond prisoners' lack of control over their day-to-day activities, they also have little say over the people with whom they socialize. As one of the participants in Crewe et al's (2020) study states, '...the "biggest problem in prisons today'" was that 'there's no outlet, no one to speak to, no one to trust, no one to share their thoughts with' (2020, p 166). Emotional distance and isolation typify the prisoner experience. Some long-term prisoners choose to sever all contact with the outside, focusing instead on their lives within the prison walls (Cohen and Taylor, 1972). However, isolation *within* the prisoner community is a result of there being a small pool of people from which the prisoner can choose friends (Cohen and Taylor, 1972). There is precariousness in these friendships. Having developed a bond with a fellow prisoner, there is always a risk of a sudden transfer, thereby ending the friendship. This, in turn, leads to psychological stress and some prisoners maintaining distance from their fellow prisoners to avoid such separation.

Cohen and Taylor's study in particular highlighted the issue of social isolation in prison. Their text, *Psychological Survival: The Experience of Long-Term Imprisonment*, represents one of the earliest studies of an English prison, one that is returned to regularly by those of us interested in the role of education in prisons. The authors spent several months in 1967 teaching in Durham's notorious E wing. Referred to as a 'prison-within-a-prison', E wing was where, at the time, some of the most high-profile and high-risk prisoners were kept, in full isolation from the rest of the prison. Cohen and Taylor delivered an educational class in this part of the prison. They worked with their students to develop a deeper understanding of the life of a long-term prisoner and the pains and deprivations of long-term imprisonment. The result was to compare the experience of long-term imprisonment to 'survival in extreme situations'. They drew on literature from adventurers, disaster studies and migration studies alongside written accounts of personal experiences of imprisonment in labour and war camps to articulate the prison experience. They justified their description of prison as an 'extreme environment' by highlighting a prison's physical characteristics, sensory deprivations, social restrictions and 'special psychological character as an authoritarian, punitive and relatively permanent regime' (Cohen and Taylor, 1972, p 58).

On the whole, Cohen and Taylor's participants experienced a greater level of isolation than those in my study, being segregated from the mainstream prison community in a unit of only a handful of prisoners. Despite this, their description of the wing resonated with my own experience of Full Sutton. One of the prisoners in their study commented, 'it's like living in a submarine' (Cohen and Taylor, 1972, p 60), a simile I have used on numerous occasions to describe my own experience of teaching in Full Sutton.

My route through the prison involved passing through numerous heavy doors (doubled with barred gates), down a series of identical corridors, passing prison officers waiting and watching at their stations. A lack of windows, either in these corridors or my classroom, resulted in an absence of daylight from the moment I stepped into the prison at around 8 am until I left again at 3 pm. With it being the long, sunny days of summer, this created a feeling of 'otherness' in the prison, that I was outside and separate from the surroundings while I was inside the prison walls.

I, too, often had the feeling of having been in a submarine, submerged from the outside world on entering the closed world of the prison and in leaving, emerging back into the light and out of the depths of such an environment.

Plato and the ideal society

Plato's *Republic* and the principle of specialization (Week 2, Stage 2)

Plato (born in 428 BC) said that each member of a society must perform the role that they are most naturally capable of performing; whatever you are naturally good at is what you should do. Once your role has been decided, you should not interfere with other people's roles. This is known as the principle of specialization. It keeps the farmer from carpentering, and the carpenter from farming. More importantly, it keeps both the farmer and the carpenter from becoming warriors and rulers.

A just society, according to Plato (Week 2, Stage 3)

The principle of specialization separates society into three classes: the class of producers (including farmers, craftsmen, doctors, etc), the class of warriors (who keep the law), and the class of rulers (who make the law). Rulers control the city, establishing its laws and objectives. Warriors carry out the commands of rulers. Producers stay out of political affairs, only worrying themselves about the business of ruling insofar as they need to obey what the rulers say and the warriors enforce. A city set up in this way, Plato contends, is a just city.

Following on from discussions of a shipwreck on a desert island, I introduced Plato's view of 'a just society'. This opened the door for conversations around authority and power, the class system, dictatorships, current politics and the importance (or not) of maintaining specific roles. Most of the participants disagreed with Plato's perspective, instead discussing the importance of individual rights, the need to have your voice heard and the importance of having opportunities.

"You could be the best ballerina in the world, but if you have never had the opportunity you will never know", Neil points out. A poignant comment from a man rounding on 60 years, who had served nearly his entire adult life in prison and whose opportunities had therefore been extremely limited.

Although all the groups offered interesting views on this topic, it is the content of the conversation with the VP group at Full Sutton that is perhaps the most interesting. Vulnerable prisoners (as they were called at the time of the research) are those who have been moved out of the mainstream population as it is not considered safe for them to remain on ordinary location. As I go on to discuss, these men are doubly rejected from society – first, by being sent to prison, and second, within the prison community. In this second session, I gained an insight into some of their views, learning more about their character and interactions. In particular, we had some interesting exchanges around the role of women in society. One participant argued that women going to work meant there were fewer jobs for men. To address this, I raised the question of fiscal independence. However, the conversation turned to discussing the need to have a 'place' in the world.

"Men don't have any purpose anymore", Keith claimed, before going on to say, "Now women are at work, we've got all these feral children running around."

In response, Dave took issue with Keith's claims. Through this, Dave demonstrated an ability to ask insightful and relevant questions, which impressed me, and he carefully challenged the premise of Keith's assertions and offered thoughtful counter-views to his ideas.

Earlier, I referred to some clear distinctions in the nature of the philosophical conversation between the groups. Initially, the contributions of the VP group in Full Sutton were guarded and careful. Throughout the Plato session, the conversation remained calm and polite, and some interaction between the participants came naturally. Compared with the conversations in other classes, however, many of these participants remained cautious in their contributions, carefully wording what they had to say, and often responding directly to me as opposed to their fellow participants.

Survival, adaptation and coping

When confined to prison, people find ways to cope with the deprivations. Furthermore, they find ways to 'survive', to maintain their identity and sense of self. Despite this, as Sykes says, 'The individual's picture of himself as a person of value ... begins to waver and grow dim' (Sykes, 1958, pp 78–9).

How do people entering prison cope with the prison environment? The simple answer is that some do not: risk of suicide and rates of self-harm peak in the first few weeks of imprisonment (Liebling, 1992), with prisons incorporating 'first night centres' in an effort to ameliorate the shock. The severity and reality of the prison experience mean that in order to survive undamaged, or even positively change and develop, individuals have to create 'adaptations' and 'coping' strategies. Prison sociologists develop 'typologies' to explain the different 'types' of prisoner and methods of adaptation. Prisons provide the opportunity to study power, order and resistance (Crewe, 2009). As such, these typologies of adaptation often relate to prisoners' relationship with authority (see Cohen and Taylor, 1972; Sparks et al, 1996, Crewe, 2009).

Resistance is often one way of coping with prison, as suggested by Cohen and Taylor. Some long-term prisoners in their study engaged in a form of 'self-protection', consciously making sense of the environment and actively finding ways of dealing with the slow passage of time. Others used more traditional forms of protest, engaging in campaigning, letter writing, plotting their escape, striking and confronting authorities. According to Cohen and Taylor, the prisoners had a variety of ways of dealing with their relationship with the prison regime: some actively resisted their adjustment to prison, resulting in a series of run-ins with prison staff; others maintained substantial relationships with the outside; others actively enjoyed the 'contest of wits' and the game of outward compliance.

Taking this theme further, Crewe's (2009) typology of prisoners in a Category 'C' prison discusses 'enthusiasts' who embrace the transformative experience; the 'stoics' who recognize the futility of resistance and bear the prison experience with dignity; and the 'players' who pay 'lip service' to the regime's rules while engaging in subversive activities and the prison economy. These studies highlight the fact that there are different 'types' of adaptation, engaged in by different types of prisoner. Individuals interact with, adapt to and cope in the prison environment in a variety of ways.

The term 'vulnerable' is synonymous with those convicted of sexually motivated crimes. In reality, within a VPU many prisoners are not convicted of sexual offences, having been moved to the vulnerable population due to difficulties not related to their offence (the label of 'snitch', for example). However, the participants of my philosophy course who acquired the label 'vulnerable' had, in fact, been convicted of sex offences or other crimes against women and as such, carried with them a stigma and shame directly related to their convictions.

In a more recent study, Crewe, Hulley and Wright (2020) distinguish between 'coping-survival' and 'coping-adaptation'. This work showed that adaptations to and reflections on prison life might vary depending on how far into a sentence the individual is. Adaptation to prison life seems to follow some broad patterns: early stage prisoners often defy the reality of the situation and spend most of their time reflecting on the past. However, those later in their sentences may start to find purpose in their time in prison. Further, Jarman (2020) argues that the age at which the person is sentenced also affects the way they adapt to their new prison life. Older prisoners' narratives tend to be highly retrospective, with the men seemingly trying to integrate their past '… with who they now recognized themselves to be' (2020, p 1469). For those who were younger, their narratives and reflections focused on the future.

Part of the process of 'adapting' to prison life, as opposed to simply 'surviving', seems to involve a process of meaning-making (Liebling, 2012; Crewe et al, 2020). Although popular discourse of the prison environment often focuses on issues of personal safety and loss of freedom, the overwhelming feeling among prisoners is that of boredom and stagnation. Cohen and Taylor's use of the term 'psychological survival' encapsulates the pains of imprisonment in that prison involves a mental struggle. Prison life is monotonous. Prisons are frequently grey, dull places with little daylight, and characterized by bars, locks and doors. Although staff often attempted to alleviate this by displaying paintings by prisoners, placing plants in corridors and adding colour to the walls, the lack of variety in a prison is starkly evident. Crewe et al (2020) report that coping with prison life involves a level of resignation to the situation. Prisoners learn to go with the flow in the prison, let go of some of the frustrations and accept the realities of their situation.

Cohen and Taylor (1972) also observe that individuals with consistent ideologies or philosophies are more able to maintain their integrity as human beings. Sykes (1958) argues that psychological survival involves developing a strategy for 'rejecting his rejectors' (1958, p 167), while Liebling et al (2011) argue that finding an interest or passion is often key. Crewe et al (2020) argue that prisoners engage in self-reflection throughout their sentence, but the nature, purpose and outcome of these reflections varies depending on how long they have spent in prison. Early stage prisoners are making sense of their circumstances, while later stage prisoners are more successful in understanding who they are in relation to the prison. For some, prison results in the finding of an inner strength and engaging in a search for meaning (O'Donnell, 2014). Crewe et al (2020) found that some later stage prisoners articulated a sense of finding an 'authentic self' in prison.

My research offers further insights into this. In engaging with a small group of prisoners over a period of time, I witnessed personal realizations, saw specific progress in the philosophy classroom, and developed an understanding of what is required. My findings demonstrate that engaging in philosophical dialogue, every week, for three months, allowed for relationships to emerge, trust to develop and deep *philosophical* interactions to take place. I got to know the participants and together, we engaged in meaningful dialogue.

In conducting this work, the lack of meaningful activities in prison is palpable. Ian O'Donnell (2014) articulates this as a feeling of being 'suspended in time'. In prison, there is simply nothing to do. Despite the focus on 'purposeful activity' in prisons in England, workshops are often characterized by too little to do and too many workers. My own observations of workshops in various prisons involved seeing men pacing aimlessly around the space or playing cards to pass the time. Among the prisoners in Full Sutton, the opportunity to engage in philosophical conversation provided the opportunity for intelligent conversation that they explicitly stated they 'craved' in the prison environment.

The work of Alison Liebling and the wider PRC at the University of Cambridge underpins much of my understanding of the prison environment. Much of PRC's work involves the use of a Measuring Quality of Prison Life (MQPL) survey in various prisons, which has informed my understanding of the penal landscape in England and Wales. Liebling and her team use an ethnographically led approach to their research, spending significant amounts of time in 'sustained observation' of various areas of the prisons in which they work. As my supervisor throughout this project, Alison provided important guidance and support. Widely considered to be a leading prison scholar, several of her studies proved invaluable. In particular, my fieldwork in Full Sutton followed on from Alison's project looking at trust in maximum security environments (see Liebling et al, 2016). In the year prior to my research commencing, Liebling and her colleagues spent significant periods of time conducting fieldwork in Full Sutton, Frankland and Long Lartin, all high security prisons in England. Some of their subsequent published papers around security in prison (Liebling and Williams, 2017) and the role of faith (Williams and Liebling, 2018) have offered important new insights.

However, it was Liebling's report (with Arnold and Straub, 2011) into staff–prisoner relationships at HMP Whitemoor (March, Cambridgeshire) that provided some of the most important insights into prison life for me. It provided a relevant and contemporary account of life inside high security prisons in England.

Liebling et al (2011) distinguish between those who can 'bear' the life and those who struggle. They highlight the opportunity for prisoners to take on productive roles such as a library or gym orderly as contributing to a 'bearable' prison experience. For others, often early on in their long sentences, coming to terms with the length of their sentences was extremely psychologically stressful. These prisoners described life as stagnant, boring, frustrating and unstable (Liebling et al, 2011). Liebling, Arnold and Straub (2011) confirm Cohen and Taylor's assertion that prisoners need a 'workable sustaining ideology in order to survive long-term imprisonment' (1972, p 120). Education, workshops, the chapel and the gym can be sources of 'hope, recognition and humanity' (Liebling et al, 2011, p 39). Many realized the need to change their lifestyles and had been forced to 'contemplate the meaning of their lives, the reasons for finding themselves in their current situation, and more existential topics like the finality and meaning of life' (Liebling et al, 2011, p 33).

Prisoners were often unsure how to proceed, however; with limited options for self-improvement, their self-reflection and search for meaning was stunted in the prison environment (Liebling et al, 2011). For some, religion and faith provided opportunities for reinvention and offered a method of finding meaning in prison.

The issue of faith and the use of religion to instil a moral framework among prisoners has a long history in prisons in the UK (Spalek and El-Hassam, 2007). In the 1700s, prisoners in England were kept in isolation to embark on a period of 'self-examination' (O'Donnell, 2014). Drawing on the Christian notion of 'quiet contemplation', prisoners were afforded space to have a 'moment with God' and reflect on their deeds (O'Donnell, 2014). For prisoners, faith can provide a route to finding meaning in life and an understanding of the reasons for imprisonment; it can provide a means of coping with the 'existential crisis' induced by the prison experience; or a source of care, protection and support (Liebling et al, 2011). Despite some alarmist groups focusing on the role of 'radical Islam' in violent extremism, scholars argue that Islam in prison '... does more good than harm due to the *structure* and sense of *identity* it offers ...' (Hamm, 2013, pp 48; original emphasis).

Although high rates of conversion to Islam have caused concern among policy-makers and media outlets, research indicates that religion, including Islam, acts as a coping mechanism by reducing aggression and engagement in illegal activities and increasing structure and self-discipline (Spalek and El-Hassam, 2007). Furthermore, religious conversion increases a sense of identity and belonging, and provides a 'brotherhood' of care and protection (Liebling et al, 2011). This theme is considered in more detail in Chapter 7, which focuses on the issue of trust in Full Sutton. As will become apparent, Full Sutton had a range of religious tensions that became central to the philosophy classroom in that prison.

More generally, issues of trust go beyond religious conversations. Prisoners describe the environment as 'fake' and can feel like there is some sort of 'game' between staff and prisoners (Liebling et al, 2011). Prisoners in the Whitemoor study discussed their inability to relax and be themselves for fear of being seen to be 'having fun' or being involved in gang-related behaviour. Echoing Crewe's use of the term 'players' to describe some prisoners, Liebling et al (2011) discuss the need for 'strategies and game plans' (2011, p 29) in order to survive everyday life. In such an environment, it is safest to be 'reserved' in one's interactions. Identities are thereby suppressed, as individuality is impossible and opportunities for self-expression rare. Liebling et al argue that loss of liberty goes far beyond physical liberty discussed earlier, and constitutes a 'deprivation of freedom of thought, action, and identity' (2011, p 29).

In such an environment, identity presentation and orchestration are tactics employed to survive the prison experience. Prisoners feel the need to build a reputation within the prison community (de Viggiani, 2012). Tested on a regular basis, manliness and machismo are part of the 'act' (Toch, 1977), which involves not appearing weak and standing your ground (Crewe, 2009). Research into high security prisons argues that prisoners are '... preoccupied with daily survival and unable to find contemplative space' in the prison (Crewe et al, 2020, p 142), despite prisoners articulating their need to come to terms with their situation.

Ben Crewe's study (2009) of a Category 'C' English prison argues that 'respect' among prisoners comes from bravery, stoicism, criminal maturity, intelligence, honesty and generosity, while stigma or dishonour comes from stupidity, naivety, cowardliness, disloyalty and instability. Prisoners who are either particularly persecuted or unable to live up to these expectations are separated (Toch, 1977). Research has demonstrated that men often engage in self-assessment and self-dialogue to reflect on their identity *before* incarceration, and then undergo a period of adjustment in their first few months, including altering the way they walk and talk (Jones and Schmid, 2000).

Developing strategies and personas that allow for safe navigation of the prison environment can lead to stagnation and, in the long run, have deleterious effects on the individual's sense of self. This leads us to the concluding concept for this chapter – Goffman's dramaturgical self and the construction of a 'front'.

Presentations of the self and 'survival'

Part of the reason for focusing on the idea of 'fronts' and presentations of identity relates to how the philosophy classroom confronts this. To understand the relevance of developing a space for a community of philosophical inquiry, we first have to understand how the prison environment shapes identities. The 'front' often relates to strategies of 'survival' (see, in particular, Cohen and Taylor, 1972).

Coping and adaptation strategies encompass a notion of survival, which means surviving with one's identity intact. The search for meaning, the description of prison as a 'radical shattering' of routine (Liebling, 1992), the mechanisms described here to cope with the environment, all point to prison being a place where a person's sense of self is challenged. Fundamentally, this emphasizes that the individual does not exist in a social vacuum. Identity is formed, at least in part, through validation of the self by interaction with, and the reactions of, others. This perspective of identity, often referred to as a person's 'social identity', maintains that the nature of identity and the true self can only be understood within a societal context.

Within prison literature, social identity is often discussed using the language of Goffman's dramaturgical self. According to this account of social interaction, the individual plays out a frontstage persona that is in accordance with the 'working consensus' of the nature of social interaction of the setting (Goffman, 1969). This frontstage persona is developed through (and as a result of) social interaction. The individual's backstage self presents only when they feel comfortable in the social setting and, according to Goffman, the individual presents a version of the self that is acceptable to the audience and the setting in which the interaction is taking place.

This characterization of identity has proved to be particularly relevant to the prisoner experience. Prisoners often discuss the need to put on a 'front' in order to survive. Goffman's theory argues that the choice of persona presented will depend on the motivations of the individual. Evidence from prison research suggests that men entering prison make a conscious effort to present a particular 'front' to the rest of the prison population. In particular, Jones and Schmid (2000) found that prisoners engage in a constant internal dialogue that attempts to reconcile their 'true selves' with their presented selves, with prisoners having awareness of their constant struggle to maintain their 'pre-prison identity'.

The language of 'presentations of the self' introduced by Goffman takes on a particular relevance in the prison context. In this chapter, we are discussing these 'presentations of the self' with respect to the need to 'survive' the prison experience. This is, in some ways, an artificial leap. A presentation of the self, in a broader context, speaks to the idea of taking on different roles and identities in different aspects of one's life – work, home, among friends, in court, in hospital, at school. We all, in everyday life, take on different personas suitable to different settings. These are not all necessarily about survival, but are often about understanding appropriate behaviour, and demonstrating an understanding of social expectations. For many, there will be a smooth transition between different personas that do not necessarily represent a disconnected identity or a step away from the 'true' internal self.

Prison, however, represents a very particular type of social environment. As discussed, prisons can be dangerous places, subsumed in a climate of distrust with threatening overtones and underpinned by a divided atmosphere. The dramaturgical perspective provides an important vocabulary for understanding the interaction between the individual's construction of the self and the environment in which they find themselves. In such an environment, survival of a sense of self is imperative.

Furthermore, this perspective can lead to the assumption that a person can consciously develop and outwardly project a specific personality suitable to a given situation. Jones and Schmid's work (2000), among others, demonstrates that, for some, this is true. However, to do this, a person must be capable of self-reflection with a reasonable level of self-understanding in order to consciously construct a 'front'. In reality, some people might not be capable of this level of insight, while others might construct a front more subconsciously. Furthermore, use of the terms 'frontstage' and 'backstage' self implies that the 'front' is not a true reflection of a person's character. In reality, the 'front' may be more of a true reflection of their personality than researchers suggest (see also Gergen, 2011, for a discussion of social constructions of the self).

Although Goffman's language is useful within a prison context, it is also an over-simplification of the way in which people manage presentations of the self. Research has demonstrated that prisons vary and different areas of the prison offer different types of environment. For example, Crewe et al (2013) discuss 'emotion zones' in prison and how prisoners can alter the manner in which they engage with one another due to the nature of these different zones. In particular, they highlight education, visits and the chaplaincy as places in which prisoners can drop their masculine fronts and engage in a level of camaraderie with one another. To use Goffman's terminology, these are not necessarily zones in which the 'backstage' self appears but rather, places where different fronts can be presented.

This draws on the work of Hochschild (1979) who discusses emotion management in the context of how people try to feel as opposed to how people try to *appear* to feel. Hochschild claims that Goffman describes two forms of acting: 'surface' acting and 'deep' acting. In the former, the individual is managing the direct expression of behaviour, while in the latter there is a management of the feelings from which an expression can follow. This goes beyond the scope of this book and begins to consider how behaviours are shaped and formed. However, Hochschild's distinction provides a subtle but important distinction, which highlights the point made by Crewe et al (2013) – to understand the prisoner experience it is necessary to recognize the complex human emotions and difficulties faced by an individual within the prison environment. Further, we must recognize that while prisons themselves vary, different spaces within a prison also offer distinct types of environment.

4

Kant, Bentham and the Question of Identity

> ### Compassion, Kant and the categorical imperative (Week 3, Stage 1)
>
> An example: It's wartime and two women volunteer to be nurses. Anne is motivated by compassion; by nature she is sensitive to the suffering of the wounded, and feels a mild personal satisfaction in helping someone's recovery. Sue, by contrast, lacks compassionate sentiments (she has lost a close relative and is consumed with grief). Nevertheless, Sue rouses herself and works just as hard as Anne because she can see that there are important reasons for tending the wounded that have nothing to do with her personal feelings (she has worked as a nurse before, and knows that anyone with her background would be useful to the community in this situation).

"Morality is behaviour", Toby asserts with certainty. A resident of a mainstream wing in HMP Full Sutton, Toby is older, well read, and very opinionated. I respond by asking whether some behaviours have a moral dimension while others do not. Toby moves on to discussing piety, and whether the fact that being more pious made one of the nurses more moral.

Gerry, the writer-in-residence who attended the philosophy session alongside the men, said she did not see the difference between the two women because they acted the same. Jonny, also older, confident and clear in his articulation of ideas, said, "It's the outcome that would matter – the one acting out of compassion, she might find it too difficult to do the job." We talk about the two nurses, about duty, about morality. What does it mean for something to be moral?

Discussing morality with people in prison involves some sensitivity. As Liebling argues, prisons have 'moral or relational climates' (2019, p 82), such that the experience of daily life is acutely affected by the values of the institution (see also Liebling, 2004). On this occasion, however, my concern over the direction of conversation related to Toby's contribution. He jumped in by saying "'morality' is a religious word". His assertion is loaded with meaning. In his pre-participation interview, when asked why he wanted to participate in philosophy, he responded by saying (in a loud, authoritative, somewhat over-the-top voice) that he wanted to "... rescue these young black men from the grapples of Islam." For him, a black man in his late 60s, the rate of young black men in the prison converting to Islam was of great concern. As a self-educated man with a seemingly vast knowledge of philosophers (he roundly chastised me for neglecting Mary Wollstonecraft in my teachings) and history, who was well travelled, and worldly-wise in his way, Toby felt that moving towards religion and, in his eyes, away from reason, logic and science, was dangerous. Philosophy, for him, was the answer. Philosophy was a means to help change this narrative.

This was the first moment that I came face-to-face with the underlying narratives in the prison. While I was there, religious identity seemed to permeate the prisoner hierarchy and somehow, I had managed to gather some people with particularly strong views in this area. In my classroom, I had Toby, alongside several Muslim prisoners, including two who held what many would describe as 'radical' views. As such, Toby's comment that "morality is a religious word" made me nervous. I did not want to get into a debate around religion. While I understood Toby's view of the role of philosophy in steering people away from dogma, this was not my aim. I had not entered to the prison environment to challenge people's religious beliefs.

In all honesty, I had not realized that the prison environment would involve such tensions. The need to carefully manage the conversation with the men in Full Sutton was not limited to religious discussion. As I came to find out later in this session, many of the participants were not as confident in themselves as their outward personas portrayed.

In this chapter, I will examine the issue of identity and persona more closely. Part of this will be reflecting on how people who have engaged in criminal activities find ways to develop a sense of self and a coherent 'narrative' self. In doing so, we will hear more from this

Intentions or actions, Which matter most?

session on Kant, and learn how I discovered the fragility of egos in prison, and how that affects identity.

On this occasion with the mainstream group, I steered them away from religious discussion by pointing out that morals can relate to non-religious ideas and encouraging them to return to the original story, and moved to talking about whether a person's intentions or the * outcomes of an action matter most. However, while I had managed avoiding religious debate, I did not maintain their focus for long. The conversation turned political and the participants ended up in a heated debate about Tony Blair and the Iraq War. Before the conversation strayed too far, and in an attempt to regain focus, I introduced Kant.

Different prison environments

Kant's response (Week 3, Stage 2)

Kant claimed that if you do something just because of how you feel, that is not a good action at all.

Therefore, although it is of benefit that both women have volunteered, only Sue can be said to have acted out of moral motive because her actions have nothing to do with her feelings.

The categorical imperative (Week 3, Stage 3)

Kant thought that morality should be based on rational thinking. As rational beings, we have certain duties. These duties are categorical, which means that they are absolute and unconditional; they apply at all times and in all circumstances and to all people.

This is what Kant called the 'categorical imperative' – moral rules that an individual is obliged to do as their duty.

Act only according to that maxim by which you can at the same time will that it should become a universal law. (Immanuel Kant, *Critique of Pure Reason*, 1781)

So Sue is acting morally because she has volunteered as a result of her duty to do so. In other words, she has acted in a way that all people should act, given the same situation.

In introducing Kant, the participants were able to see how the story of the two nurses related to a philosophical perspective. They had heard of Kant and were interested in what he had to say on the question of morality. Furthermore, this session, along with the subsequent session on utilitarianism, offered the participants the opportunity to discuss moral action. The men raised questions around how we, as human beings, ought to behave, and the moral principles we might draw on to make decisions on how to act. They used these sessions to discuss moral frameworks, which provided a basis for understanding the need to be consistent in one's underlying principles. On the whole, they felt that Kant was too absolute, that there was a range of ways of thinking about things and, to act morally, we have to take into account a range of considerations.

I delivered this material across all four groups (two in HMP Grendon and two in HMP Full Sutton). Comparing fieldwork notes, the content and nature of the discussion of Kant demonstrates some important differences. In the mainstream group in Full Sutton, the participants energetically engaged in conversation, offering hurried and decisive answers to the questions posed. They argued with each other and around the topic while I endeavoured to encourage focus. The conversation veered off at tangents and I struggled to maintain direction. Despite this, some interesting philosophical discussion occurred, albeit in an unstructured manner.

On the other hand, conversation in this early session with the other group in Full Sutton – the VP population – took a very different tone. In what became a characteristic of this group, they engaged carefully and politely, offering muted opinions on the topic. Rather than jumping in and talking over each other, it took some encouragement to get them to contribute. At first, all answers were directed at me, and I had to help them understand Kant's perspective and to develop genuine conversation *between* the participants. These men seemed more concerned with saying the 'right' thing and, in these early sessions, looked to me for affirmation.

In contrast, the men in Grendon had already begun to understand the requirements of *philosophical* conversation. My fieldwork notes state:

FIELDWORK NOTES
Grendon, 16 October 2014

At the end of the session we did a round of final thoughts and, for the first time, they all made a comment on the actual topic of the class as opposed to whether they enjoyed the class. They offered their

> own opinions on the philosophical question of "what is morality"....
> The full two-and-a-half hours was all on morality: what is morality?
> What makes something a moral action? How do you know how to
> behave?... Very very good, very interesting discussions.

In Grendon, the two groups were integrated, without the separation of VPs that occurred in Full Sutton. Both groups in Grendon understood that the session focused on the question of moral action. In response to the stimuli, and Kant's perspective, they considered the question of the role of compassion and duty. In particular, both groups considered how our emotions and feelings are relevant to our moral actions and the question of how to behave. One participant distinguished between 'moral feelings' and 'moral cognition' to articulate a situation where you might feel that something is wrong but not necessarily be able to articulate *why* it is wrong. Much of the discussion centred on issues of moral intention and motivation and whether it is the act, in and of itself, that carries with it a moral dimension.

Both of the groups in Grendon used these stimuli to delve into much bigger questions of philosophy. In one of the classes in Grendon, the discussion moved on to human rights. Kant's articulation of the need for everyone to follow the same moral principles naturally lends itself to a discussion about rights and how to behave. In one group in particular, the participants considered the issue of morally conflicted choices – how do we know which choice is right? On what principles might we base our choices? This led on to a discussion of whether there exists a 'hierarchy of morals'. In the other group, however, the discussion turned to the question of culture. Does our social environment and cultural perspective fundamentally shape our understanding of right and wrong? This moved us on to moral relativism. One participant claimed that for an act to be moral it requires some form of value judgement and as such, you cannot strip out emotions or compassion from the discussion on how to behave.

In Full Sutton, the participants either stated opinions without thinking them through (mainstream prisoners) or barely offered an opinion at all (VPs); in Grendon, the men launched themselves fully into philosophical dialogue. They went round in circles in their conversation, listening to each other and interrogating the issue at hand. Throughout, they contradicted themselves, changed their minds, listened to each other, and tested out different ways of considering the issue. They demonstrated an understanding of how to explore different ways of thinking about something, how to put forward ideas and hear other people's responses. They reflected and considered them and developed their own thoughts and opinions. They demonstrated both a willingness and an ability to engage with the philosopher's ideas.

By Week 4, philosophical conversation in Grendon was in full swing. The men arrived at the classroom enthusiastic and keen to engage. Looking back through my notes, the level of sophisticated exploration of ideas that the men engaged in here was impressive. In discussing utilitarianism and the idea of the greatest happiness for the greatest number of people, they discussed what happiness means, whether there are hierarchies or different categories of happiness, how to balance pleasure and pain, and how far our duty to minimize suffering might go. They appreciated and agreed with the principle that everyone's happiness is of equal worth, and debated the merits of balancing pleasure versus pain. One participant argued that our fundamental motivation in life is to be happy, and that this is what drives us as human beings. They then began to question the notion of happiness, and considered whether contentment is the attainable goal. These discussions took place in light of the discussion on Kant. They considered the use of consequences as a means of choosing how to act, and fundamentally concluded that there is a balance to be found.

Beyond the descriptions of the content of the discussion, what was apparent with both groups at Grendon was their ability to engage with the ideas. The introduction of the thought experiment (Stage 4) produced some particularly insightful conversations, as the following exchange denotes:

FIELDWORK NOTES
Grendon, 15 October 2014

Right at the end, one of the questions to me [was] "What if you could pick one of us and we would be allowed to be free and have our slates wiped clean? What would you do and how would you pick?" Tom responded, "Well, what if everyone could go free except for one person who had to stay in for the rest of their life?" In response to this and, I guess, in part to avoid fully answering the question, I turned these questions around and asked "What if you had to put your names in a hat and if your name is pulled out, you have to spend the rest of your life in prison, but everyone else goes free, would you do it?" Half of them said yes, half said no, but it really depended on how close to the end of their sentences they were. So it came down to how much you have to lose really.

In contrast, the events of Week 4 in Full Sutton highlight some important distinctions between the two prisons. In my fieldwork notes I wrote:

FIELDWORK NOTES
Full Sutton, mainstream participants, 8 July 2015

> I found this session so upsetting and difficult that I am typing these notes two days later. I couldn't bring myself to dictate or write anything about it afterwards at all … this is hard work and very emotionally draining. Maybe running a class like this in a maximum security prison just doesn't work … or maybe it needs more time to be established … or maybe I need to rethink my materials, do things a bit differently and think more carefully on the topics that I am covering. This requires reflection.

A particular incident in the first half of that week's dialogue highlights the fragile egos and complex interaction at play in a prison such as Full Sutton. This group, as already highlighted, were prone to going off at tangents, and I found it difficult to keep the conversation centred on the philosophical ideas at hand. During this discussion, one of the participants brought up the issue of Greek debt (at the time, Greece and the Greek economy featured heavily in the news). He managed to use the example to make a reasonably relevant point around utilitarianism – if the debt were to be forgiven, this may result in the greatest benefit to the most people so, in utilitarian terms, this might be the 'right' thing to do. Unfortunately, one of the other participants responded to his input by saying, "I could not disagree with you more." This led to a heated to-and-fro between the pair and, despite my best efforts, I struggled to get them back on topic.

Eventually, I raised my voice above their dialogue and asked them to calm down. I endeavoured to move the conversation on to a different topic. However, the person who had initially raised the issue of Greece seemed to be rather angry at the situation. It was at this point I made an error. I asked him directly if he would like to take a moment to step outside to gather his thoughts and calm down. In hindsight, this was somewhat patronizing, and his response was to walk out of the classroom and never return.

This incident constituted an important turning point in my understanding of the overarching atmosphere within the classroom and the prison beyond. Fundamentally, I had failed to recognize the fragility of egos in this prison. He was a towering figure of man, muscled and physically dominating. However, behind this outer persona lay a complex vulnerability hidden behind a veneer of machismo. In my naivety, I did not see this, and thought his outward confidence projected his true self. In reality, despite his size, he lacked confidence.

The other participants in the group let it happen, and continued with the conversation. We went on to discuss different aspects of utilitarianism. At the end they told me not to worry and, I think, one offered to speak to him to see if he would come back (I do not know if they did). Afterwards, the maths teacher asked me what happened. I explained, and he reassured me that it was not out of character and that these things sometimes happen. The following week I invited him back to the classroom but he declined, and that was the end of my interactions with him.

I learned a great deal from the incident. I realized that this world of bravado and machismo was a front, and that this front covered a complex social world that I scarcely understood. Incidences such as these pushed me towards the prison sociological literature in an attempt to understand the prison environment. It also encouraged me to speak more widely to staff in different parts of the prison so that I could begin to understand what was at stake for the participants in my philosophy classroom.

In hindsight, and with the benefit of a few years of distance from these discussions, there is an interesting distinction between the notes made in Grendon and those made in Full Sutton. I regularly described participants in Full Sutton as having a 'calm and controlled' manner. I did not use the term 'controlled' to describe the participants in Grendon. In Full Sutton, although the participants did engage in discussion, they did so in way that revealed as little as possible about themselves. Their opinions were often guarded, and although on the surface they seemed poorly stated, they were carefully stated. They struggled to work together but instead sat as individuals putting points across.

These examples indicate that the environment in Full Sutton did not encourage openness or allow for true explorations of the self. Instead, the need for survival meant that the men in this prison lacked trust; they could not relax and be themselves. This may seem unsurprising for some who would argue that prison is not supposed to be a place to call home, enjoy life and grow as a person. Even so, most would agree that it ought to offer opportunities for change, or rehabilitation, as it is often called.

Arguably, providing space for self-reflection and the opportunity to be open in self-articulation might be an important part of this process.

Narrative Identity - individuals form on identity by integrating their life experience into an internalized evolving story of the self which provide them with a sense of unity + purpose.

KANT, BENTHAM AND THE QUESTION OF IDENTITY

We shall see that Grendon, like Full Sutton, had issues of providing space for open conversation. Further, it was becoming clear that issues of trust, relationships and wellbeing were all relevant to the prison philosophy classroom.

What, then, do people in prison need to move beyond their survival identities? How can prison offer a space for personal development? What might growth look like?

These questions lead us into the next key area of literature to discuss: desistance. Desistance scholars focus on pathways out of crime, the process of moving away from a criminal lifestyle. In doing so, there has been a significant focus on identity, and this provided a starting point for me in thinking about identity. In particular, desistance research focuses on *narrative* identity and self-understanding. Prominently, the two seminal studies in desistance (Maruna, 2001; Giordano et al, 2002) both articulate the importance of self-reflection; that is, how individuals see themselves is fundamental to forging a new life. In the remaining sections of this chapter, I provide an overview of desistance research, using it as a tool to articulate what 'growth' might look like.

Desistance research

Desistance literature considers people's lives in a social context. Whereas criminology has traditionally focused on how people move *into* a criminal lifestyle, desistance scholars look at how people move *out of* criminal activity. Theories of maturation, developmental theories, life course theories, rational choice theories and social learning accounts offer both competing and complementary understandings of the desistance process (Laub and Sampson, 2001). For example, maturation theories suggest that individuals simply 'grow out' of criminal activities (Piquero et al, 2003). These theories stem from the work of Glueck and Glueck (1940), and reflect longitudinal data that showed a decline in criminal activity as people mature. Building on this, Sampson and Laub's social bond theory (1993) highlights specific life events (such as marriage or finding stable employment) as factors that can change the trajectory of a person's behaviour.

However, with their focus on factors external to the individual, these early theories of desistance have been criticized for their neglect of the agency of the individuals concerned. In other words, although data point towards maturity and developing social bonds, we must acknowledge that a person sits at the heart of these processes. We cannot simply encourage people who engage in offending behaviour to marry, or just provide jobs, and expect criminal behaviour to desist.

Instead, we have to recognize that there are processes and mechanisms at work that underpin or sit behind the data. For example, finding stable employment may be the (measurable) outcome that has occurred after several years of gradually working on the self, developing alternative perspectives, taking opportunities and being offered opportunities.

Two key pieces of empirical research developed theories of identity change. The first is Maruna's (2001) *Making Good: How Ex-Convicts Reform and Rebuild Their Lives*. The second is Giordano et al's (2002) 'Gender, crime, and desistance: Toward a theory of cognitive transformation'. Maruna's work emphasizes the role of developing a coherent internal narrative, or a story to tell ourselves, for successful desistance. Giordano et al's work outlines the need to develop a positive cognitive blueprint, or way of thinking, that provides a 'well-developed linguistic and cognitive guide to the change process' (2002, p 1035).

Both studies emphasize the relevance of 'identity work' in the change process, which relates to individuals modifying, or developing, their identity in response to their surroundings and their circumstances. As we saw in Chapter 3, in prison this can focus on developing survival identities or, in Goffman's language, a 'front' that helps the individual navigate their new-found situation. However, for desistance, research indicates that developing a positive sense of self, and an identity that allows them to move away from their criminal lifestyles, is essential. It seems, therefore, that the identity work required to survive prison might be at odds with the identity work required to grow and successfully desist from crime. First, we need to understand desistance and what it tells us about identity.

Narrative identity and desistance

Desistance literature, then, offers an insight into identity. By drawing on this work I am not considering whether philosophy can help in the desistance process – my research is based within prisons and concerned specifically with 'life inside'. Instead, I am attempting to understand identity and the nature of 'identity work' for those who have been involved in the criminal justice system. To that extent, the insights of desistance theorists help us think about personal identity in a way that is specific to the population with which my research is concerned. Further, as this section articulates, the focus of desistance on identity and the internal narrative holds particular relevance to philosophy. Desistance seems to be about understanding the self. This research suggests that spaces for personal exploration of philosophical ideas can enable such reflections.

people who have successfully desisted from crime have established a 'new' identity

Both Maruna and Giordano et al's studies clearly state that people who have successfully desisted from crime have established a 'new' identity. Furthermore, they indicate that the 'identity work' involved in successful desistance relies, at least in part, on a reframing of how the individuals see themselves. In interviewing current and former offenders, Maruna (2001) found specific differences between the life-story narratives of persistent offenders and those who had desisted. In particular, he noted the different ways in which desisters framed their past behaviour and the way they viewed themselves in the present. From this, he theorized that, in order to successfully desist from crime, individuals needed to reflect back on their lives, consider the positive things they had done, and re-establish their identity in this light. He termed this the 're-biographing' process, which led to a fundamental shift in identity.

Maruna's view of identity is based in the sociological theories of Giddens (1989) and McAdams (1993). Giddens claimed that self-identity is constructed through human experience and is mediated by language. McAdams' *The Stories We Live By* articulates identity as a self-reflective project involving examination of the inner self, engagement in self-improvement and the development of a coherent internal narrative. Maruna accepts the idea that we actively construct a sense of self by developing an internal life story. Further, he claims that it is the *nature* of this narrative that distinguishes successful desisters from those who persist with criminal activity.

Maruna conducted extensive analyses of life-story interviews with current offenders and ex-offenders. He concluded that desisters and persisters have distinct scripts to explain their past behaviour. Many persisters saw themselves as being condemned to a life of crime, revealing a lack of self-efficacy or belief in their capacity to take control over their own lives. In contrast, the scripts of desisters had an optimistic perception of the future, and were characterized by a desire to be productive (Maruna, 2001). Further, and perhaps most relevant to discussing philosophy in prisons, successful desisters had established core beliefs that seemed to characterize the core self. Maruna's theories therefore place self-understanding at the heart of the desistance process; how the 'offender' sees their past is of fundamental importance.

The second key study in this field was also published in the early 2000s. Giordano, Cernkovitch and Rudolph's (2002) research coined the phrase 'hooks for change'. Like Maruna's theory, Giordano and colleagues developed their theory through the analysis of the life stories of current and former offenders. The term 'hooks for change' highlights the need for the individual to actively take hold of opportunities that are made available to them. They are clear in stating that the environment must provide the 'scaffolding that makes possible the construction of significant life changes' (2002, p 1000). However, they place at the heart of their study the need for the individual to change the way they think about themselves.

Their model of desistance is based on phases of cognitive transformation. First, the individual must be open to change, and be exposed to the hook in the first place. The transformative potential of 'a hook for change' depends on how receptive the individual is, and the extent to which it can provide opportunities that help individuals develop the concept of the 'future self'. The final stage in cognitive transformation, which confirms the new identity, is for the individual to alter the way in which they view their past behaviour.

Giordano and colleagues place emphasis on the role of language in the desistance process. In using the word 'hooks' in a different context, they recognize that a person's life-history narrative will contain 'hooks' they deem as 'shorthand ways to describe what seems essential from the communicator's point of view' (2002, p 1000). These help organize the narrative into a coherent story. As they are analysing stories of change, they note that successful desisters can describe the change process using linguistic techniques that provide the opportunity for alternative self-definition. In their 'Suggestions for further theory building', they highlight the need to emphasize language, along with identity work and cognitive process, within any theory of cognitive transformation.

However, desistance theories should neither overstate nor underplay the role of identity work. As Giordano et al's research indicated, the role of cognitive transformation depends greatly on the social environment of the individual. For those who have a great deal of advantage (high social capital, good earnings), the transformations happen without much effort on the part of the individual – they play a very small role. Conversely, for those who are at an extreme disadvantage, the cognitive transformations are nowhere near sufficient to make a viable change to circumstances. For those somewhere in the middle, cognitive transformation plays the most significant role. In other words, if you have high social capital, the amount of 'identity work' required to desist is far lower than for those with low social capital. However, access to opportunities matters; for those with very little social capital, the identity work they undertake will go nowhere.

Desistance scholars draw on narrative accounts of identity. The narrative self is one perspective of identity among many. For proponents, the narrative perspective assumes that life is a form of 'narrative quest' (MacIntyre, 1984); part of our development requires us to provide ways to narrate the events of our lives (Schechtman, 2011). This perspective proposes that to understand ourselves and our place in the world, we develop 'stories' that help us understand our life and our life course. The life narrative perspective of desistance is based on understanding the self, on self-reflection and on coherently accounting to one's self for one's life story. This is primarily seen as a cognitive process whereby the person fundamentally alters the way they think about themselves. This allows them to consider who they are now and who they want to be in the future. Importantly, in doing this it allows the individual a means to articulate their self-understanding to themselves, and then to others.

Giddens (1991) argued that language mediates human experience. *mediate – bring about a result* He postulated that an individual achieves a stable self-identity when he or she has developed 'biographical continuity'. This involves being able to piece together life events and understand how these events have been relevant to personal development. Desistance theorists focus on internal self-reflection (Maruna, 2001), the need to 'craft a satisfying *replacement self*' (Giordano et al, 2002, p 1027; original emphasis), and the need to have a future 'desired self' (Bottoms and Shapland, 2016) to work towards. As a self-reflexive project, the internal narrative perspective of identity development recognizes the role of examining the inner self and engaging in self-improvement (McAdams, 2009). According to this perspective, developing a coherent life story involves making causal connections between life events (Habermas and Bluck, 2000); developing meaningful connections between past experiences and the self (Pals, 2006); and fostering an understanding of our own ethical views, and how they came to be established (McAdams, 2009). Those who are successful will be able to build a concept of the self that they can then strive towards, allowing them to forge a positive, pro-social identity.

Not all researchers and scholars accept this perspective. For some, the notion that the development of a coherent life narrative is essential to living a full life is objectionable (see, for example, Strawson, 2004). They question whether we really need to reflect on who we are to live a full life. Is it *necessary* to have a coherent life story to be able to develop and be happy?

Probably not. Here, however, I am not aiming to explain what identity is. Other scholars are far better placed for such conversations. Instead, I argue that the narrative perspective of identity is particularly relevant to people in prison. Extensive research has articulated the shock of entering prison leading to an 'existential crisis' and, within a range of literature, the importance of 'meaning-making' to those who serve long sentences (see, in particular, Liebling et al, 2011). When a person is sent to prison and handed a significant sentence, this seems to encourage a level of personal reflection. Essentially, people go to prison and end up wondering how they got there, what happened in their lives, and considering what this all means for who they are. Perhaps not introspecting, or not being required to constantly explain oneself to others, is a privileged position?

However, the narrative perspective also recognizes that we are co-authors in our own stories (Schechtman, 2011). The community within which we are based, and the people with whom we interact, all help write our stories by shaping our understanding of ourselves. The 'stories we live by' sit within a moral framework and a historical tradition. They reflect the communities in which we find ourselves, the communities that take our articulations of the self and interpret them, shape them, and, in some cases, constrain them. Different actors within the prison environment see the prison in different ways, but issues of right and wrong, of shame and belonging, of acceptance and regret, underpin many interactions. Prisoners' stories are fundamentally shaped by the prison system and the terminology employed to discuss their actions.

Both Maruna's theory and the 'hooks for change' theory emphasize the need for the individual to self-reflect. Both consider it important for the individual to frame their past behaviour in such a way as to be able to move forward. They also agree on the need for an envisioned future self to be crafted. However, they place emphasis on different areas. For Maruna, we must look to the past in order to understand our present. In re-biographing ourselves in a more positive light, we are able to move forward towards a newly constructed, desired self. For Giordano et al, crafting of the future self happens earlier, with the view of past behaviours coming as the final stage in the desistance process.

It is beyond the scope of my work to investigate which of these theories is correct or contributes more. Instead, it is sufficient to rely on that which they have in common to frame our understanding of the desistance process. Somewhere along the way, many of the people who have spent time in prison will need to forge a new self. This new self is important primarily to the individual, rather than to others. Desistance involves self-understanding.

The process of change and the context of prison

Identity change and, in turn, identity-related desistance, involve the individual asking, and answering, two key questions: 'Who do I want to be?' and 'How do I want to live?' Although these questions are, in reality, questions of philosophy (Socrates was, after all, the first to develop theories of 'the good life'), desistance scholars have much to contribute to the question of how an individual actually goes about answering them. In particular, by focusing on a process of change (from an offending lifestyle to a non-offending lifestyle) desistance theorists, and desistance research, make a significant contribution to answering the question of personal development and identity formation in general. As Graham and McNeill articulate,

> … desistance is not an outcome that can be produced by applying well-engineered raw materials; rather, it is an organic process; one that can be carefully cultivated or husbanded to enable flourishing – or neglected and trampled. (2017, p 440)

What, then, can desistance theory tell us about the process of change? The desistance process involves cognitive shifts (Giordano, 2016), developing a meaningful and credible concept of a future self (Healy, 2014), and the individual's agency and personal desire to change. However, it also relies on there being structural opportunities or 'hooks for change' (Giordano et al, 2002) that the desister can exploit. Further to this, Bottoms and Shapland (2016) discuss the role of reappraising life choices in the desistance process. They argue that such reappraisal is a key part of maturing into adulthood. This reappraisal leads to individuals taking greater responsibility in their lives, which, in turn, leads to a change in behaviour. However, it is important to note that presently there remains insufficient research into these processes to understand how or why the activity of reappraisal might encourage desistance.

That said, we have seen that there is a growing body of evidence that internal, personal self-exploration and imaginations of the self are key parts of the desistance process. However, as in the formation of identity, the process of desistance occurs within a social and structural framework. In developing a desire to desist, to articulate a desirable future self and gain an understanding of the self, the individual must do so within the context of their environment. Successful desistance, therefore, relies not only on identity change, but also successful renegotiation of this newly formed identity in a public sphere.

In this situation, the would-be desister is vulnerable to the structural situation in which they find themselves. The social and structural framework for the participants is the prison. There has been some, albeit limited, research into identity and change from the perspective of desistance in prison. In particular, the work of Soyer (2014), Healy (2014) and Schinkel (2015) all serve to highlight the different pathways to desistance prevalent among prison populations. Both Healy and Schinkel offer 'categories' of desister, while Soyer emphasizes the importance of opportunity. In addition to contemplations of the self, the individual needs to develop a 'credible and meaningful future self' (Healy, 2014) that is grounded in realistic expectations of opportunity.

Soyer's (2014) research into the subjective accounts of juveniles in prison leads her to coin the phrase 'imaginations of desistance'. This reflected her findings that prisoners might speak of desistance while imprisoned, but find they are unable to put their desires into action on release. She argues that the prisoners lacked the skills required to forge a new self on release. Healy (2014) builds on this work, attesting that the 'imaginations of desistance' are a necessary precursor to actual desistance. Healy puts forward three categories of desisters: imagined, authentic or liminal. Imagined desisters have not yet formed a credible, alternative self that they can work towards; authentic desisters have achieved the new self; while liminal desisters have forged an interim identity but have not fully realized their desired self. This formulation of desisters implies that successful desistance rests on the individual's self-understanding and their ability to envision a meaningful and credible future self.

These studies are somewhat consistent with Giordano et al's (2002) findings regarding 'hooks for change'. Reflected in Healy's emphasis on the need to 'imagine' a future self and Schinkel's discussions of 'moral transformation', at the centre of Giordano et al's theory is cognitive transformation – the person in question makes their own decisions regarding what paths to take, and what opportunities will allow them to flourish. These hooks are activities or opportunities that can act as sources of behavioural control, or as a gateway to forming relationships with people who are not engaged in offending behaviour. Furthermore, they assist the individual in developing a projection of possible future selves by providing a 'specific blueprint for how to proceed as a changed individual' (Giordano, 2016, p 21).

Modern desistance theories recognize the role of both internal processes and structural opportunity for change. The *interaction* between internal, personal understandings of the self, and the social environment in which they are enacted, are key to processes of identity work. While desistance involves a re-conceptualization of the self and a move towards compliance to social norms (see Bottoms, 2002), '… the extent to which ex-offenders can achieve their desires and goals is partly dependent on the availability of legitimate identities' (Farrall, 2016, p 201). In the prison, availability of different legitimate identities is sparse, as the following section discusses.

Defining 'growth' in the prison context

We have seen how desistance literature places identity work at the core of the change process. By drawing on desistance theory it is possible to develop an understanding of identity from the perspective of growth and development that we can now examine more closely.

Within desistance theories, criminologists have looked at a process of change – from a person committing offences to a person not committing offences, from engaging in anti-social behaviour to engaging in pro-social behaviour – but also recognizing the need for the individual to take control of their lives and develop a positive, pro-social identity in their own time.

This process can be seen as a form of personal growth or development, with the assumption that such change constitutes a 'bettering' of oneself, or progress towards a 'desirable' outcome. What it means to 'better' oneself, or what constitutes a 'desirable' outcome are often under-explored in the desistance literature. Working from the perspective of criminology, it seems self-evident that a desirable outcome would be a version of the self that is 'non-criminal' and a lifestyle that is offence-free. In reality, there is little to suggest that the process of self-reflection and identity change discussed in desistance literature *necessarily* leads to desistance (Vaughan, 2007). As Maruna points out, desistance only occurs when the new identity that develops is one that is incompatible with a criminal lifestyle. So what do we mean by 'growth'?

I consider a 'growth' identity to be one that is future-oriented. I state this in full recognition that a future-oriented outlook is not a necessary attribute for a person to live a life. However, in the context of working with prisoners, who often need to demonstrate some form of change or development in order to gain their freedom, this perspective is appropriate. In particular, desistance literature suggests that individuals need to develop 'meaningful and credible' future selves (Healy, 2014, p 873). These identities ought to be grounded in a coherent understanding of the self, developed through reflexive practice and a narrative of the self that provides autobiographical continuity from past experiences through to the present and into the future (Habermas and Bluck, 2000). Developing such growth identities involves a private and personal project that answers the question of who we wish to be and how we wish to live.

The process of constructing new narratives involves the opportunity to practise fledgling identities. Importantly, this involves developing language for alternative self-definition and the ability to communicate who we are to others through what we do and what we say. We confirm the possibility of new identities, and find potential for growth, through relevant and meaningful opportunity.

In discussing the idea of a prison environment that encourages personal development, transformation, and even human flourishing, it must be acknowledged, however, that the fundamental nature of imprisonment works against this. The aims of a prison service and of an education department are often at odds. As the discussion thus far has emphasized, prison removes autonomy, with prison culture underpinned by coercion and enforced loss of liberty. How far can development, progress and meaning-making (essential elements for growth) go when a person is removed from their friends and family and denied their liberty? The common environment of a prison is actively *disabling*, with some studies suggesting that overcoming the effects of institutionalization is a key part of the desistance process (Terry, with Cardwell, 2015). Prison engenders anti-social, hyper-masculine identity formation, promotes division and distrust, and is characterized by 'pains and deprivations'. In recognizing this, it is possible to discuss the ways in which the environment can have a different effect, and ameliorate the impact of incarceration on the individual's sense of self. Furthermore, we can at least consider how prison culture can be addressed to develop an environment that might allow for a different way of being.

In other words, we could consider this as a need for an 'enabling' environment that allows the prisoner to explore his or her interests. The term 'enabling environments' can be used as a generic term for approaches that look to put relationships at the heart of practice and take a more humanistic perspective than ordinary prison environments (Haigh et al, 2012). The notion of an 'enabling' environment stems from work in mental health and, in particular, from an initiative set up by the Royal College of Psychiatry (Haigh et al, 2012). It is used to describe what are referred to as 'psychologically informed planned environments'. A variety of prisons have such environments that are 'specifically designed, contained environments ... designed to enable offenders to progress through a pathway of intervention, maintaining developments that have previously been achieved, and supporting transition and personal development at significant stages of their pathway' (Turley et al, 2013, p 2). Both 'strive for greater psychological awareness of a setting, humane, and enlightened treatment, enhanced wellbeing for all involved, plus reflective practices and shared action learning in the staff team' (Jordan, 2011, p 1065).

Finally, it is important to note that I have assumed that development, or 'growth', is important to the individual, or even necessary to find meaning in life. However, this raises the question of whether it is necessary for human beings, in general, to 'move forward', grow and develop throughout their lives. Instead of continuously providing for growth, perhaps we ought to be more concerned with providing an environment for each person to live happy and positive lives.

In the context of education, and more specifically, prison education, framing identity change in the form of personal development is valid. People volunteer to engage in education while in prison, and there can be reasonable assumptions that they do so due to some desire to self-improve, or, at the very least, purposefully occupy themselves during their time in prison. Whether this is carried out with a particular goal in mind, or is intended to lead the participant on to the next step in their learning, is not relevant. For some, engaging in an educational course can be about personal enjoyment as opposed to being part of a programme of personal development. Furthermore, as was argued in Chapter 3, entering prison often leads to a form of existential crisis (Liebling et al, 2011), and surviving the environment involves processes of meaning-making. It is therefore appropriate to consider how and in what ways an educational course can provide the opportunity to facilitate prisoners in their personal development.

If we assume that the purpose of prison is to rehabilitate (and many would argue that it is not), then there is an expectation of transformation placed on people in prison. However, they are placed in a situation where survival involves projecting a particular persona, but growth and transformation involve deep and careful self-reflection in an environment characterized by fear, violence and intimidation. By distinguishing between the development of a future-oriented, positive, 'growth' identity and a defensive 'survival' identity, this contradiction is brought into sharp focus.

A 'survival' identity refers to the preoccupation of many prisoners to cultivate a persona that will allow them to psychologically survive the prison experience and maintain their pre-prison identity. However, for many this is an unrealistic goal as the length of their sentence means they will spend a significant proportion of their life behind bars. Instead, I consider the possibility of developing a 'growth' identity, and explore the role of philosophy in providing space for such personal development. In this chapter, I have highlighted the importance of narrative identity and its relevance to people convicted of offences.

Having now spent some time outlining the literature that has shaped my understanding of 'growth', we come to how it sits alongside my own work in prisons. My findings are arranged around themes – trust, wellbeing, relationships and open-mindedness – each of which is relevant to the prison environment that formed the setting of the research. However, perhaps more importantly, they relate to the individual and to the possibility of self-expression and self-reflection, which, in turn, relate to developing a 'growth' identity in such a setting.

In the chapters that follow, I focus more closely on my research findings, offering a rich description of the philosophy classroom, and necessarily feature the participants' words. The discussion around criminological constructs of identity highlights the role of self-reflection and self-understanding in the lives of prisoners. Goffman's (1969) work provides a vocabulary to describe the constructed 'front' prisoners often feel they are required to uphold as a means of survival. In contrast, desistance literature points towards personal and cognitive transformation as a key part of the process of identity development, while emphasizing the role of opportunity to put into practice these cognitive transformations. Self-reflection, developing language for alternative self-definition and the development of a realistic and credible future self are key mechanisms that can help the prisoner develop a positive sense of self. All are relevant to identity construction.

I will demonstrate the importance of having or finding space to engage in deeper conversation. Education departments have a distinct atmosphere within a prison, providing respite for prisoners and a place where prisoners take on the role of learner, work towards achievable goals and develop a sense of self-worth. As the discussions of Kant and Mill have illustrated, there is a thirst for intellectual conversation among prisoners. However, the importance of this type of opportunity (or 'hook') in the prison environment goes beyond notions of rehabilitation or encouraging change.

This is about being human.

5

'Why Do You Think That?' Descartes, Hume and Knowledge

I began the discussion on knowledge by presenting a set of optical illusions. The participants looked at them eagerly, examining each one and marvelling at the way the illusion tricked the mind. I brought the conversation back by asking the participants, "How do you know what you know?"

This was the third week in HMP Grendon, and the participants had already grasped the expectations of the philosophy classroom. In both of the prison's groups they seemed to bounce into the classroom, full of energy and ready to talk. There was some fluidity to the groups because of the integration of the prisoners, with no separate VPU. This meant I allowed some to switch days every now and then to accommodate other commitments they had in the prison.

In one group, the conversation went straight to the point: "Well, this is about doubt, isn't it?" Michael had had a troubled route through the prison system and a complex backstory. By the time I met him, he was half-way through a degree relating to politics and economics. He was thoughtful, often insightful, and always engaged.

The rest of the group joined in. They discussed the need to be cynical, about whether you could trust your senses, and how you ever know if anything is real. Michael was not the odd one out with his level of education. Most were studying Open University courses, with one having gained a degree prior to coming to prison. One had read a far greater amount of philosophy than I had, including texts such as Plato's *Republic*, which he casually dropped into conversation during his pre-participation interview.

In the other group, the conversation was more boisterous, although no less discerning. One of the participant's responses was to knock on the table, saying "It's here. We know it's real because it's here."

They followed this with a discussion about knowledge, with all participants chipping in with their thoughts. They interrogated the idea of facts and how we know something to be true. What do our senses tell us, and is it possible to trust our perceptions?

Hume's ideas on knowledge (Week 4, Stage 1)

David Hume (1711–76) claimed that knowledge comes solely from our sensory experiences. Basic knowledge of the material world comes from observation. We are also able to have knowledge of concepts or ideas, the basis of which he claimed are also in experiences. (This is known as empiricism.)

Hume said that every concept we have is ultimately furnished by experience. He divided the mind's contents into *impressions* and *ideas*. Impressions are perceptions we have when the world impacts on our senses. Hume said that concepts or ideas are copies of impressions. For example, I cannot have a concept of the colour red unless I have experience of it.

An example: When I see an apple sat on a table in front of me, it produces in my mind certain sensory impressions – of colour, shape, etc. If I were to bite into the apple, more impressions such as taste, texture and smell will develop.

We can combine our impressions to make ideas of things we haven't seen directly. For example, we can have a concept of a gold mountain because we have a concept of gold and of a mountain that we can combine to have an idea of a gold mountain. Without the concepts of gold and mountain, we cannot have an idea of a gold mountain.

In the following week in Grendon, in Week 4, I countered the discussion about knowledge. I realized the level of intellectual discussion these men were capable of; this was a group of articulate, educated men, who had a passion for learning and a desire to engage in intelligent conversation. We talked about what you can know versus what you believe, that you can believe anything you want but there is a difference between belief and knowledge. We discussed empiricism, what it means to have empirical knowledge, how these ideas relate to imagination, how you imagine 'stuff'. Tom asked whether these ideas would apply to quantum physics and maths, saying "Well, you're able to predict things in physics without knowing them, without having the experiences of them, so the maths would say it exists but we don't know what they are."

By Week 3 I was having fun. On entering the prison, I would pass through gardens into the building and down a few corridors to get to the classroom. I saw few bars, or gates, after the perimeter, and the place reminded my more of an old-fashioned municipal building of some kind. There was a lot of light in the corridors, and the classroom, despite being small, had a big window overlooking the grounds. The participants were superb – engaged, informed, intelligent. I was learning in every session. They pushed my thinking, helped me understand the ideas I was bringing into the classroom, and together, we philosophized. Not every class was as successful as these two, but all were enjoyable. Grendon had provided an excellent environment for this type of education.

As I would learn when I moved on to Full Sutton, this was a rare experience.

HMP Grendon

I begin my account of the research where my fieldwork started, in HMP Grendon. While I have talked in general about prison and the prison experience, I now offer a more detailed account of Grendon and the philosophy course in the prison. In doing so, we begin to develop a more concrete understanding of how participation of the prisoners in philosophical conversation progressed. In Grendon, the men engaged with the *content* of the course. The philosophy classes began with ease, offering a space for the participants to become more open about their own views and hearing the views of others. Unlike Full Sutton, the nature of the therapeutic community (TC) provided a space that allowed participants to explore philosophical questions in a deep and considered manner. First, however, we must understand the specific environment of a prison that operates as a democratic TC.

Unique in the UK, Grendon is the only prison to be entirely based on the principles of a TC. To go to Grendon, men must be recommended, and accepted, for the intense therapeutic work that living there involves. The prison offers a distinctive experience for an outside visitor with an environment quite different from the ones described in earlier chapters. This chapter, and the next, draws on the participants' own words to articulate the relevance of philosophical conversation. Chapters 6, 7 and 8 move into a discussion of Full Sutton, a place that resonated more specifically with the traditional descriptions of a prison discussed in Chapter 2. Each chapter discusses a different aspect of the philosophy classes organized around themes that emerged from the participants' own reflections on the classes. As my analysis progresses, and a deeper understanding of philosophy in the lives of the prisoners develops, we build towards a better understanding of identity and how a person, in the context of a prison, maintains a sense of self.

Grendon opened in 1962 and was the first TC in the prison service in England and Wales (Shuker and Shine, 2010). Since then, use of therapy and other psychological interventions has fallen in and out of favour. Throughout, Grendon's status as a TC has endured. The purpose of this section is to describe the TC regime in Grendon, as it was when I conducted my research, and to outline some of the outcomes members of the TC were expected to gain.

In general, prisons offer a variety of psychological therapies to prisoners (Harvey and Smedley, 2010). These range from short-term programmes based on the principles of cognitive behavioural therapy (CBT) (often enforced as part of the individual's sentence plan) to immersive TCs. In an immersive TC such as Grendon, prisoners are members of, and live within, a community and engage in *intensive* therapy. Such communities are used in hospitals, drug rehabilitation centres and prisons (Harvey and Smedley, 2010).

Grendon had six wings, each of which acted as an autonomous TC. At the time of the fieldwork, one of the six wings held prisoners whose crimes either directly involved sexual offences or had a sexual element to them; three of the wings held mainstream prisoners; one was for those prisoners with severe learning difficulties; and one was the induction wing. Each wing held around 40 members (prison capacity was 238), and was run independently. Each had its own constitution and tailored methods of adhering to the general principles of democratic TCs. Within the communities, members were expected to take on responsibilities, including acting as representatives and taking on work and education commitments.

The overarching aim of a TC is to provide an environment in which members are able to challenge one another's behaviour and explore actions through communal dialogue (Shuker and Shine, 2010). In the prison system, TCs focus on needs that relate specifically to criminal activity (Shuker and Shine, 2010). As such, therapy delivered within the context of a prison tends to focus on anti-social behaviour linked to the individual's offence. Although the primary aim in the more intensive therapy offered by TCs is to tackle offending behaviour, this is done by considering the wider context of prisoners' lives, tackling issues around identity, relationships and victim empathy.

The principles of a TC draw heavily on the work of Robert Rapoport and Maxwell Jones (see Whitely, 2004, for an overview of the history of TCs in the UK). TCs follow the principles of permissiveness (minimum rules to ensure safety of members), democracy (decision-making is a community responsibility) and communalism (as much autonomy is given to the community as possible) (see Genders and Player, 1995). By framing therapy within a community, members regularly interact, creating a sense of personal investment that develops ties, shared assets and a culture of collaborative activity (Toch, 1980). TCs are structured to place responsibility and authority with the community members, which includes regularly held community meetings in which prisoners conduct wing 'business' and therapeutic dialogue (Jones, 1980). Jones (1980) highlights the importance of an 'open' system within TCs that involves two-way communication between staff and prisoners. Problems are solved through interactions and the existence of shared goals and systems for shared decision-making.

Therapy is intended to be a 're-educative' process (Genders and Player, 1995). As part of this process, residents become:

> '… very used to getting in touch with personal issues, with their past, with their actions, why they behave the way they do.' (Tom, Grendon)

There are two key therapeutic tasks within a prison-based TC: first, to 'reintegrate' a person's personality so they have a coherent sense of self, and second, to establish the external and internal factors that led to committing a crime (Morris, 2001). In prisons, psychotherapy acknowledges the existence of prisoners who want to 'create alternative ways of being and relating to the world, to challenge their own beliefs' (Saunders, 2001, p 8). This leads to an emphasis on identity work, investigating past behaviours and understanding childhood experience as ways of understanding the current self.

To achieve this, TCs employ techniques of Socratic questioning (Kazantzis et al, 2014). As with philosophy, the therapy involves systematic questioning to facilitate independent thinking. The therapist serves as a 'guide, facilitating a self-discovery process' (Overholser, 1993, p 71). With both therapeutic work and the philosophy classes drawing on Socratic questioning, participants often compared the two endeavours. The therapeutic work of Grendon meant that some aspects of philosophical conversation were familiar to the philosophy participants; in therapy, prisoners learn the etiquette of group conversation. The participants were comfortable with discussing complex ideas with fellow prisoners, understood how to disagree, and had a clear understanding of how to build on each other's points.

This, in many ways, was problematic. I needed to understand the role of philosophy in the lives of people in prison. If the participants already had many of the skills philosophy develops, what role could it play for those in Grendon? If skills of conversation, self-expression and listening are already developed, is there a place for philosophical dialogue? If so, how does philosophical dialogue differ from therapeutic dialogue? Does it complement, enhance or detract from prisoners' therapeutic work?

I found that my early concerns were unfounded. As will become clear, philosophy had an important role to play in Grendon, and the participants took to it with a passion. I learned a great deal from these conversations and, with their skills of group dialogue well developed, I could sit back and engage as a co-participant. However, it remains important to have a strong understanding of the therapeutic work of the prison in order to appreciate the place of philosophy. In the following section, I focus specifically on the 'therapeutic conversation', highlighting the key points of departure from the work I was conducting in the prison.

The therapeutic community

> '[In therapy] we bring a subject ... "this is the way I saw what happened in committing my offence." So, you tell people a, kind of, version of events or something. And they [other group members] explore and they bring what they think and it helps you to understand things from a different perspective. It helps you see things what you may not have seen.' (John, Grendon)

Therapy in Grendon takes the perspective that identity is shaped by social interaction (Genders and Player, 1995). Accordingly, five mornings a week were spent in group therapy. Within these group sessions, community members explored the reasons for established behaviour patterns, with a focus on those behaviours deemed anti-social (Genders and Player, 1995). Three sessions a week involved small groups (of around eight people plus one member of staff acting as therapist or facilitator), which focused on historical exploration, clarification and reconstruction of past behaviours (Morris, 2001). Common themes addressed in therapy sessions such as these included self-esteem, identity, personal relationships, expression and control of feelings, interpersonal conflict and personal responsibility (Genders and Player, 1995).

The other two weekly group therapy sessions consisted of whole-wing meetings. I observed a session on each participating wing, three taking the form of 'wing business' and one a therapeutic session.

The wing business meetings all took the same form. All members of the community – staff and prisoners – attended and arranged themselves in a circle sitting around the edge of the room with staff sitting among the prisoners (around 30 to 40 participants in each). The prisoners were headed up by a chair and vice-chair who outlined the order of business, facilitated discussion and oversaw votes.

First were 'positive commendations' from prisoners to staff and staff to prisoners, followed by a request for 'backing' to proceed with a desired activity, and finally, 'negative commitments', which referred to breaches of community rules. In TCs, meetings such as these form the backbone of the democratic process. Issues are aired, problems raised and discussed, and several votes occur. Each meeting I observed involved over a dozen votes on a variety of issues. For example, a few of the men were asking for the backing of the community to go forward with a (prison-based) job application and one whether they could invite a staff member to family day. Each person making the request must explain why they want to do it and why they feel the community should back them.

In addition to the weekly 'wing business' meetings, each community held a weekly, whole-wing therapeutic meeting. These followed a similar agenda to whole-wing meetings. However, the bulk of the meeting involved a therapeutic session focusing on a specific individual. During the session I observed, the individual recounted in detail the offence for which they had been convicted, the events leading up to it, and their perception of why the offence had happened. The wing community then proceeded to ask personal and probing questions about the participant's motivations, truthfulness and actions. The individual defended his account to fellow prisoners who pushed him to reveal the truth of what happened. As an observer, I was both surprised and impressed at how the community conducted itself, and how the prisoners drew on their own experiences to encourage the individual to be honest with them:

> This work [therapy] is amplified by the therapeutic environment, providing the client with forty "therapists" (fellow inmates) who carry on psychotherapy in between

the formal groups; these fellow inmates are able to challenge
and ferret out evasions and dissemblings by the client with
a tenacity and vigour that far surpasses what therapists can
muster. As the inmates say "You can't con a con". (Morris,
2001, p 91)

During my time in Grendon, therefore, it became apparent that the
TC environment encouraged honest, open and reflective dialogue
among members. Prisoners discussed issues of a personal nature;
they aired grievances; they challenged each other's points of view;
they commented when members appeared to be inconsistent in
their views and behaviour; and they were comfortable in taking
issue with perceived unfairness in the way the regime was being run.
Most importantly, for my research, the participants were skilled in
disagreeing with one another respectfully: "People are more open
to discussion and discursive debates" (John, Grendon). In observing
these therapeutic sessions and wing meetings, it was clear that just as
a philosophical dialogue is built on the premise of a Socratic dialogue,
so, too, is therapy.

> 'Like I said on the group. I think we philosophize [in
> therapy] ... we have a small group where ... I've got a
> target. Say, like, I've got a negative relationship with my
> mum or had an abusive relationship with my girlfriend.
> I'll bring it in there and I'll say this is what happened – we
> used to do this and we'd take drugs.... People would bring
> a subject to the group and it is sort of explored.... I think
> the mindset and the nature of this place, it sort of fits in
> with the [philosophy] group anyway ... that doesn't happen
> in other prisons.' (John, Grendon)

This well-established norm meant that, in general, the participants
were ready, willing and able to engage in philosophical conversation
from the outset.

It is important, however, to distinguish between *philosophical* use of
Socratic dialogue and *therapeutic* use. In therapy, dialogue starts from,
and is about, the prisoner as a person in a therapeutic environment. In
philosophy, dialogue starts from, and is about, the prisoner as a person
in a learning environment. It may be that philosophy "fits in well with
the ethos of what we are trying to do here" (Charlie, Grendon), but
where therapy can be specific and personal, philosophy is abstract and
impersonal (see Szifris, 2016).

The participants understood that the purpose of the philosophy sessions was to "exercise your brain" (Samir, Grendon) or to discuss "what is reality and what do we know to be absolutely true" (Alex, Grendon). The atmosphere in the philosophy classroom was much 'lighter' than those in therapy, in part due to the intention of the philosophy activity to enhance the participants' knowledge. This stands in contrast to the focus of the discussions in therapy where participants are expected to discuss their past, their crimes and their problems. In doing this, therapy can entail '... the exploration and expression of painful material and disturbing emotions' (Greenwood, 2001, p 48) with the purpose of addressing participants' criminogenic needs (Shuker and Shine, 2010). In philosophy, the purpose is educational.

This focus on the whole person, as opposed to their crimes, and on broader conversations around how we 'ought' to live or act as opposed to specific offending behaviours provided a very different environment in the prison. As this chapter will go on to discuss, the men specifically stated that philosophy had opened their minds and broadened their perspectives.

Before going into this in more detail, the following sections provide an overview of who participated in the course, how they came to attend, and what it involved.

Participating in philosophy (in Grendon)

Twelve men agreed to participate in the philosophy course in Grendon. All 12 were engaged in therapy, but were at varying points in the process. At the point the course started, six had been in Grendon for 18 months or less; four had been there for between 18 months and 4 years; and two participants had been in for over 4 years. This meant that half of the participants were in the early stages of their therapeutic journey.

However, the outcomes for these men varied. Two of the participants did not go on to complete the therapeutic process at all. After my work in Grendon had been concluded, they were asked to leave the community due to behaviour considered to have breached the community's rules. A third participant did not find the TC to his liking and, throughout participation in philosophy, discussed finding therapy difficult and inappropriate for his needs. He subsequently left the establishment. One-third (four out of the twelve) were fully immersed in the therapeutic process throughout my time working in the prison. The final two participants, having been in Grendon for

4½ and 6 years respectively at the time of the course, were beginning to start the process of moving on from Grendon, usually to a lower security prison.

Each session was held in the afternoon and lasted 2½ hours with a 15-minute tea break. The prison assigned participants to either the Wednesday or Thursday session, but they were able to switch if the philosophy class clashed with other commitments. Participants attended, on average, nine sessions, with classes having around five or six attendees. Reasons for non-attendance included illness, other commitments (for example, work or a meeting relating to their sentence), lockdowns and, very occasionally, difficult personal circumstances that meant participants did not feel they were able to engage in the class.

Some of the participants already knew each other; however, many did not. Despite this, they quickly understood the purpose and expectations of the class. Due to the therapeutic environment that the men were used to, much of my time was spent engaging in the conversation as a co-inquirer. However, I led the discussion, and moved the conversation forwards to ensure it remained philosophical. Throughout, a positive and social discussion ensued, albeit in intellectually challenging discussions at times. I soon felt able to introduce more controversial topics, including issues around race, religion and human rights, which the participants (on the whole) approached in a thoughtful and reflective manner.

At this stage, it is important to note that some of the issues raised in Chapter 2, such as religious tensions, the hyper-masculine culture of maximum security and the need to develop a front for self-preservation, were not overtly present in Grendon. Although many of the participants had been in prison for some time, I worked with them when they were (arguably) in a supportive environment that encouraged self-reflection and growth (at least relatively compared to more traditional environments). For example, there were two Muslim prisoners among the participants in Grendon, one of whom had converted to Islam during his time in prison. However, they did not project their Muslim identity in the way they presented themselves, and faith and religion only became part of the discussion when appropriate. I detected a few underlying tensions within the groups but, in accordance with their behaviour in wing meetings, the participants were open and honest in the dialogue.

Grendon's environment meant that exploring the role of philosophy was less about feasibility and more about the content of the conversation. As facilitator, I rarely needed to actively manage the participants; they tended to check themselves when they interrupted, encouraged each other to speak up, and (usually) maintained focus.

Their listening skills and willingness to hear each other's point of view provided a comfortable environment in which to discuss philosophy and, within a matter of weeks, we had established a sense of community. Consequently, I spent the majority of my time actively participating in conversation rather than managing the dialogue. As a group, we were able to have some complex and in-depth philosophical discussions.

The participants in Grendon emphasized the role of these discussions in broadening perspectives and opening their minds. Consequently, I began to organize the data around this theme. In the following section, I explore how the specific subject matter, and the orientation of the programme towards abstract, impersonal concepts, broadened the participants' thinking.

Defining 'openness'

> '… the philosophical point of view is to stay open-minded,
> to look at both ends of an argument, to look at both sides
> of a coin and try and work out what is the best outcome,
> if there is a best outcome.' (Charlie, Grendon)

In interviews after the course had been completed, the participants made reference to "becoming more flexible in the way I think" (Samir, Grendon), "opening my eyes" (Phil, Grendon), and "thinking more openly" (Michael, Grendon). The notion of having an 'open mind' is a familiar concept that conjures up ideas of tolerance, acceptance and understanding. It is, however, a somewhat 'loose' term that requires exploration. Concepts of 'openness' have been defined elsewhere (see, for example, Costa and McCrae, 1992). As I analysed the interviews, the term became increasingly common in the way participants viewed the philosophy course. But what does it mean to have a 'more open mind' and, more specifically, what does it mean to, and for, people living in prison?

A range of research offers explorations of 'openness'. Perhaps most relevant to this research, the term 'integrative complexity' is employed by scholars interested in the psychology and sociology of religious extremism. Having high integrative complexity includes the ability to perceive multiple viewpoints, to incorporate a wide array of values into moral reasoning, and to understand why others hold different viewpoints (Liht and Savage, 2013). Openness is discussed in terms of 'openness to change', and the ability to engage in more complex thinking (Williams, 2013). This perspective of openness is often studied from a political psychology perspective and as such, has been used in the study of radicalization, religious extremism and interventions that address these issues.

Beyond integrative complexity, other perspectives also discuss 'openness'. For example, in positive psychology, the idea of broadening mindsets relates to building enduring personal resources (Fredrickson, 2001). In other areas, openness is described as being 'characterized by curiosity about the inner and outer worlds, an active imagination, aesthetic sensitivity, and wide-ranging interests' (Romero et al, 2003, p 66). Others state that 'openness represents a tendency to be intellectual, flexible, and broad-minded, and involves divergent thinking and unconventional attitudes' (Butrus and Witenberg, 2013, p 291). However, none of these definitions 'fit' with the way in which the participants discussed the philosophy sessions.

Having read around the literature on the topic of open-mindedness, I turned to my research data and the participants' words. In analysing the interviews, I developed a range of 'codes' to draw out the points the participants discussed that related to becoming more open-minded. These 'codes' offer shorthand for participants' words that allow for themes to develop. Under the theme of 'open-minded', the codes included statements such as 'becoming more thoughtful', 'examining what you believe in', 'hearing other people's ideas', 'learning that you can change your opinion', 'philosophy's relevance to the world', 'abstract thinking', 'learning to listen/question/evaluate' and 'thinking beyond offending behaviour'. Using the participants' words as a guide, I defined 'open-mindedness' as follows:

> Being willing to critically reflect on your own opinion; being able to listen to others and incorporate new knowledge into your own understanding of the world; to appreciate different ways of thinking; being willing to change your mind; taking account of the wider society and community of which you are a part.

Having defined openness in the context of my research, we now need to understand why developing a more open mind is relevant to being a person in prison. Why did the participants discuss this so universally in their post-participation interviews? In what ways does philosophical conversation provide a means to develop openness? Why is this meaningful to the men in Grendon?

Open-mindedness: in their own words

> '[Philosophy is] looking at why I'm thinking the way I am
> and being able to realize that I am able to change me mind.'
> (Phil, Grendon)

Philosophical dialogue encouraged openness by exposing participants
to a variety of points of view. All 12 made some reference to their
enjoyment of hearing new ideas and other people's perspectives. Some
discussed how looking "at other philosophical ideas and different
thinkers and the way they saw things" (John, Grendon) improved
their understanding of philosophy, providing access to an area of
thought previously unknown to them. For others, "the discussion,
hearing people's ideas and … what they're saying" (Tom, Grendon)
proved the most enjoyable aspect of the course. The participants
understood the purpose of the dialogue was to "… try and build on
other people's arguments…. Instead of dismissing theirs, it's about
seeing what they're saying and seeing if I can add to it" (Michael,
Grendon).

The participants articulated how philosophy encouraged them to
recognize that issues can be complex and multifaceted. Furthermore,
although many of the topics focused on complex issues, the dialogue
made the subject matter accessible:

> '… there are a lot of options to things rather than just one
> solution.' (Charlie, Grendon)

> 'When we actually discussed it, although I realized how
> complex it is, at the same time I realized you could get
> your head round it.' (Samir, Grendon)

> 'The ability to actually say "what did that person really
> mean when they say that?"' (Tom, Grendon)

> 'Taking other people's views, their perspective, not seeing
> things with tunnel vision, slowing down, keeping it logical,
> going away, calming down, playing out scenarios in your
> head, this way, that way and then you come to a resolution.
> It enhances your thinking, it enhances knowledge.' (Cady,
> Grendon)

'... now I can sort of, as we were having a discussion or whatever, and we say something my mind is thinking why are they saying that? What's that sort of angle kind of, what is this argument they are coming at and it allows me to ask more questions – why do you think that? Is it because of this?' (Michael, Grendon)

Through participatory dialogue, ideas are considered, discussed, analysed and developed. I found that the participants learned the value of stepping back and taking a moment to consider the underlying principles of an opinion. Both the ideas of the philosophers and the contributions of the members of the community of inquiry created an environment of learning and inquiry that demonstrated the value of listening to what others have to say and being open to examining an opinion before accepting it as true.

Several participants reflected on how this might affect their behaviour in day-to-day life. One explained:

'... if it broadens people's thinking, then people might be able to understand their behaviour; how they interact with society ... have a broader range of feelings, responsibilities, to what you do in life – to be aware more. A lot of people, from what I see, their thoughts don't usually extend beyond one, two, three people. If you go moving out from the centre – a bit like a chess player – just as a casual player will only think one or two moves ahead, a good chess player ten, twelve moves ahead. A thoughtful person will think more moves ahead in life and probably have an awareness of their behaviour and the impact it has on other people. And that might improve decision-making and that is what this place [Grendon] is all about. There's a direct link between listening to alternative ways of reaching decisions and having substance to reaching that decision.' (Phil, Grendon)

Another participant, when asked whether they felt the philosophy classes might help them in their rehabilitation, said,

'Yeah. Analysing situations, because that directly links to my index [offence] ... thinking I'd read a situation right and whether I did or didn't, I'm never going to know, but definitely looking at things, whether it's an argument or a situation from all different angles and then trying to assess the most appropriate approach, the best approach. That's probably the biggest impact.' (Simon, Grendon)

Beyond understanding how to listen, and how to consider other people's points of view, the topics covered allowed for reflection on philosophical ideas. They developed insights and opinions on the 'big' questions in life around society, human rights and how to live, and demonstrated an ability to reflect on their own thinking:

> 'An understanding that a "perfect" society arrived at by consensus wouldn't be any more workable than all the others if the masses weren't on board.' (Neil, fieldwork notes, Session 2)

> 'It seems that most often when people discuss rights it's only their personal rights that are affected or of concern, ie, my rights and not the rights of all people.' (Tom, fieldwork notes, Session 9)

Fundamentally, philosophical discussion allows participants to engage in Socratic dialogue on topics that are of interest to all people wishing to develop knowledge. As such, philosophical conversations tend to focus on topics that are abstract and impersonal, rather than focusing on specific and personal events in the participants' lives. The participants recognized that the aim of discussions was to "explore philosophical theory" (John, Grendon) and "openly discuss the topic of a philosopher" (Peter, Grendon). In doing this, in the company of others, the participants reported becoming more open.

The next question to consider, then, is how? How might philosophical conversation, developed on the premise of a community of inquiry, encourage openness in the participants? The following section begins to develop our understanding of this process. To do so, instead of focusing on one particular philosophy session, as I have done in previous chapters, I consider a range of sessions. In particular, I draw on comparisons – between Hume and Descartes, and Kant and Mill – to illustrate how the course helped the participants understand different ways of thinking.

How philosophical conversation develops an open mind

> 'I understood that I am expected to put my point of view across in a way that allows me to get involved with the discussion.' (Matt, Grendon)

In this section, I explain the course materials. In Chapter 1 I provided an overview of philosophy education and the pedagogy employed for this research project. Part of the pedagogy relates to how a facilitator makes use of a stimulus to start, and maintain, dialogue within a group. The unusual aspect of working in a prison is that the educational sessions are long (between 2 and 3½ hours).

To keep the conversation focused for the length of time required, the course materials (or stimuli) had to be carefully developed and thought through. I developed all of the materials myself, drawing on my training in Philosophy for Children and my years working as a teacher and tutor in various settings. As the research progressed, the data (from fieldwork notes, feedback forms and interviews) began to reveal the importance of philosophy in shaping the outcomes the participants described for the philosophy course. In particular, both the *structure* of the materials and the *content* of discussions were crucial to the participants becoming more open-minded.

In what follows I provide an overview of four sessions, two that focus on identity and knowledge (Hume and Descartes) and two that focus on moral philosophy (Kant, Bentham and Mill). All of the philosophy sessions were structured in three or four stages with each progressing from the last, building arguments and offering different perspectives. In this case, both pairs of sessions were designed to mirror each other by asking similar questions but offering different perspectives on the answers.

The sessions on Descartes and Hume offered distinct perspectives on knowledge and identity (Descartes' dualism vs Hume's bundle theory of the self). The stages of each session drew the participants through the philosopher's arguments, beginning with a discussion on the nature of knowledge. For Descartes, I presented participants with a series of optical illusions and asked whether our senses are reliable sources of information. In the case of Hume, I introduced the notion of empiricism. The sessions then proceeded to take the participants from first principles to the philosophers' perspectives on identity. For Descartes, I introduced his famous 'evil demon' scenario:

Descartes – Dualism distinction between the mind + the physical self

Descartes and the 'evil demon' scenario (Week 5, Stage 2)

Descartes analysed the basis of knowledge. His first observation was that our senses sometimes deceive us. He went on to ask 'How do I know I am not dreaming?' Taking this thought further, he considered the following scenario:

> Suppose there exists an evil demon, god-like in its power that is intent on deceiving you. This demon might place all sorts of ideas and experiences into your head. It might cause you to think you are surrounded by physical objects when in fact nothing exists apart from you and this malevolent being. How can you know anything for certain?

Descartes notes that even if there is such a demon, this demon cannot deceive him into believing that he, Descartes, exists, when he does not. Descartes hits on 'the cogito'. *Cogito, ergo sum*: I think, therefore I am. Even if the demon deceives him, still Descartes continues to think, and if he thinks, then he must exist.

Over the duration of these two sessions, the participants engaged in discussions of the difference between knowledge and belief; the purpose of gaining new knowledge; what empirical knowledge means; how this relates to imagination and creativity; and what it means to have doubt (fieldwork notes, Sessions 5 and 6). The participants grasped these ideas enthusiastically, and took a great deal of interest in comparing "what we believe, what we know exists, and all we can say is that we personally exist" (Alex, feedback form, Grendon, Session 5).

Both of these sessions moved on to questions of identity. By starting with questions of knowledge, the participants were able to see the premise of the different perspectives on identity and understand how philosophers build their ideas from first principles. While Descartes believed in a distinction between the mind and the physical self (known as dualism), Hume conceptualized the self as a 'bundle' of thoughts and experiences. Both philosophy sessions introduced ideas of personal identity as a logical extension of the two philosophers' perspectives on knowledge.

Hume – the self as a 'bundle' of thoughts + experiences

Descartes' and Hume's ideas on knowledge (Week 5, Stage 3)

Descartes' other great insight along this line is that, while he could imagine himself in some strange situation existing without a body, he could not imagine being a body without a mind. Therefore, his mind or consciousness is fundamental to who he is, with the body being secondary. His assertion of 'I think, therefore I am' led him to the belief that the thinking mind must be the fundamental essence of the human being.

This led him to state that the mind and the body are entirely separate beings. A human being consists of an immaterial mind united, somehow, with a material body. The mind does the thinking, feeling, desiring, perceiving, and so on. The body does the moving around. This is known as 'dualism'.

Hume rejected the notion of there being a single unitary self. Instead, he claimed that we are a bundle of thoughts, experiences and perceptions. He came to this conclusion based on his own beliefs regarding knowledge. He did believe that introspection was a valid sensory experience, but claimed that when examining the inner self, it wasn't possible to 'catch sight of the soul'. All you see are thoughts and experiences running through your mind, therefore, that's all the self is – a bundle of thoughts and experiences.

The final stage of Session 6 brought in a modern philosopher's adaptation of Hume's ideas and introduced a third perspective on personal identity:

Arendt's perspective on personal identity (Week 6, Stage 3)

Arendt agreed somewhat with Hume's bundle theory of the self. At the very least, she agreed that there is no fundamental essence of the self. Instead, she claimed that each individual is born with the freedom to choose how to act; each new birth is a new beginning, and each person has the capacity to change the world. However, she also stated that we do not act in isolation, and that it is important that we are part of society. We need our actions to be observed and approved of by others.

It is in action and speech that the individual discloses who they are. Identities are developed through narratives that emerge from actions of the individual.

She claimed that an individual's identity is self-constructed through representation of the self in society. This constructed identity is constantly renegotiated and developed through the individual articulating and defending different conceptions of themselves.

The structure of the sessions started at first principles before leading the participants through the logical steps of Arendt's argument. This meant that the participants not only reflected on their own point of view of personal identity, but also considered where these views came from: what do they believe knowledge is, and what does that mean for their view on personal identity? Are they consistent and coherent in thinking through these ideas? Importantly, instead of asking the participants directly about their own views, they were asked to think about a *philosopher's* point of view. Presenting two competing theories of knowledge, and three ways of thinking about identity, provided the participants with a space in which they could think about these ideas for themselves:

> 'Looking at Descartes' theory seems a bit nuts now after working through Hume, Arendt and then Baggini. The mind and body can't be separate as the "ego", sense of self, et cetera, influences our identity and embodiment happens, identity is portrayed through the body and the body influences our mind, ego, sense of self, personality et cetera.' (John, Grendon)

Both of these sessions were intellectually challenging, for the participants and for me. The participants challenged Arendt's notion that everyone was free to act; they debated the question of knowledge; they appreciated the competing arguments around identity, the soul and truth. By allowing two sessions to mirror each other, they could see how each stage built on the last. The participants began to develop skills in understanding the foundation of arguments, and the structure of the sessions allowed for an accessible introduction to complex philosophies:

'I think that a lot of thought processes and a lot of thinking, in my view, has gone into the whole scholar's work.... I mean people don't just wake up one day and have an idea, a philosophical idea, they must have to work through that theory and kind of test it as well to some point.' (Charlie, Grendon)

'... the way you structured it as well, to look at one thing and then to expand on it with a recent idea from an old idea or whatever. You know, you sort of progress through it.' (John, Grendon)

This had been the intention of these sessions – to carefully illustrate how philosophers build their arguments. By introducing ideas and premises in stages, the participants had the opportunity to reflect on each stage and consider what their own opinions were before progressing on to the next step in the philosophical line of reasoning. They developed a strong understanding of the philosophical arguments being introduced because they themselves followed the same process, analysing and critiquing the arguments as the sessions progressed.

The two sessions on moral philosophy followed a different structure. In these sessions we tackled the question of morality by looking at Bentham and Mill's utilitarianism and Kant's categorical imperative. Although these sessions were paired and offered competing philosophies for the foundation of moral actions, each presented arguments for and against those particular philosophies within one session.

The first stage in discussing utilitarianism presented Bentham's consequentialism. This states that the extent to which an action is morally right or wrong is determined by its consequences, with decisions being made according to that which creates the most happiness overall. The second stage presented Mill's extension of utilitarianism and included a discussion around the notion of happiness and the greater good. The participants discussed questions including 'What is happiness?' 'What is pleasure?' 'What is pain?' and 'What is suffering?' Overall, they broadly agreed with the principles of utilitarianism, although with some reservations. However, the session concluded by employing a classic counter-example of utilitarianism known as 'framing the innocent man' (McCloskey, 1972).

Bentham's consequentialism (Week 4, Stage 4)

Suppose a black person kills a white person in an area torn by racial strife. As a result there are daily riots and escalating levels of violence leading to increasing levels of unhappiness. As a visitor to the area, you know you could secure the arrest of an innocent black person for the original crime simply by testifying against them. The riots would immediately stop and further bloodshed would be avoided – a much happier outcome. A utilitarian calculation suggests that, morally, the right thing to do is to frame an innocent black person. But surely that would be very wrong indeed, whatever the consequences might be for happiness overall?

The purpose of using such an extreme example was to 'shock' the participants into appreciating how far philosophical arguments can be taken. Again, mirroring the structure of the session on utilitarianism, the session on Kant began by introducing his ideas around moral action before countering it with an extreme example. Kant's categorical imperative states that we, as people, should act in a way that we would wish others to act. In contrast to the utilitarian perspective, Kant emphasized duty and principle in his arguments around moral action. The final stage of the discussion described an illustration of this perspective:

Kant's counter-example (Week 3, Stage 4)

There's a knock at the door. You answer. It's your best friend who looks pale, worried and out of breath. He tells you someone is chasing him, someone who wants to kill him. He's got a knife. You let your friend in, and he runs upstairs to hide. Moments later, there is yet another knock at the door. This time it's the would-be killer and he has a crazy look in his eyes. He wants to know where your friend is. Is he in the house? Is he hiding in the cupboard? Where is he? In fact, your friend is upstairs. But you tell a lie – you say he has gone to the park. Have you done the right thing?

According to Kant, you have not done the right thing. It is morally wrong to tell a lie, and this is always the case. Therefore, it is morally wrong to lie to the would-be murderer. This is an example that Kant himself used, and demonstrates the length to which he took his 'categorical imperative'.

In both of the sessions on Kant and utilitarianism, as the discussion progressed through each stage, the participants changed their minds in light of what they heard, they turned over ideas, considered them from different angles and took account of a variety of factors and perspectives. The first half of each discussion focused on the arguments of Kant, Bentham and Mill resulted in the participants raising objections and criticisms, but ultimately recognizing the value in each of the philosophies. However, the final two stages introduced key counter-arguments that often shocked the participants. As such, they developed more nuanced opinions:

> 'There are basic principles one must rely on to guide your life but consequences matter. You have to think about consequences as well because if you don't, you can end up committing a large wrong because you don't want to commit a minor wrong. Sometimes, the right thing to do is commit a small wrong in order to ensure a greater wrong does not occur.' (Alex, Grendon)

The ideas of Kant and Mill encouraged the participants to consider the fundamental principles on which to base a moral framework for actions. These ideas raised a multitude of questions for the participants – is it our intentions or our emotions that make something a moral act? Or is it the act itself that is inherently moral? Does morality depend primarily on consequences?

At the end of each of these sessions, there was a buzz or energy in the room, and I felt the weight of heavy intellectual discussion. The philosophy classroom provided the opportunity for stimulating conversation around a variety of issues. The participants made contributions and formed opinions, received feedback from their peers, and gained new knowledge as the sessions progressed.

The freedom to disagree

As I have said, philosophy literally means 'a love of wisdom' (Butler-Bowdon, 2013). This seems appropriate when reflecting on how philosophical inquiry enthused the participants in Grendon, encouraging them to think about why they held an opinion, listen to new ideas and learn alternative points of view. Through philosophical dialogue, the participants learned how philosophical ideas are developed. The carefully planned stages of each session meant that they were able to grasp complex ideas and begin to consider questions such as 'What is morality?' 'What is knowledge' 'What makes us who we are?' These questions were posed in a dialogic forum. By presenting counter-arguments or other ways of thinking about things, they were able to form their own views on these important questions.

The participants formed more 'considered' opinions as a result of the philosophical dialogue. During the course of the discussions, they developed an understanding of the strengths and weaknesses of taking a particular standpoint, and became more willing and able to defend their own point of view. During the course of a philosophical inquiry, their points of view had been subjected to questioning, had been amended in light of new information, and had emerged after they had heard, and often incorporated, a range of others' opinions and points of view. They left the course with an opinion on how society ought to be, on how people ought to behave – or if they did not have such an opinion, they were more open to having a conversation about it.

The focus of this chapter has been on 'openness'. Through the words of the participants I have developed a specific definition of openness relating to the ability to critically reflect, listen to others, change your mind and take account of the broader picture. The work in Grendon demonstrated that philosophy provides a space for open conversation, a place where the participants can think about issues from different perspectives and develop their own, nuanced views. In the philosophy classroom, the participants not only considered different perspectives, but they also verbalized their own views. They questioned the perspectives of philosophers, changed their minds, agonized over contradictions in thinking, and whole-heartedly engaged in conversation with their fellow participants. Further, they discussed how the content of the stimuli encouraged them to reflect on the foundation of their opinions and beliefs; how the process of dialogue had developed their appreciation for hearing a wide range of views before settling on an opinion; and how the abstract and impersonal nature of the discussion gave them the freedom to disagree.

This final point – the freedom to disagree – takes on particular relevance in the context of a prison. Even in Grendon, a place ostensibly about openness and self-reflection, the participants argued that the philosophy class provided an opportunity for different types of reflection and openness. In the context of a therapeutic environment, where prisoners spend their time engaging in deep and complex explorations of the self, the suggestion by the participants that *philosophical* conversation can lead to more 'openness' is interesting. It indicates that there are some meaningful differences between the conversations and personal explorations that are rooted in psychological interventions, and the conversations that are rooted in education.

In pulling these strands together, providing these forums for conversation, philosophy caters for a perspective that the participants themselves suggest is omitted from other courses available in prisons. Rather than focusing on the prisoner as an offender, philosophical discussion focuses on how we, as people, as members of society and a community, should behave, on how we might want our society to be in an ideal world, and how we, as individuals, play a role in achieving that. In the following chapter I discuss the relevance of philosophical conversation to the whole person, focusing more closely on the participants' experience of philosophy at Grendon.

6

Not Just an Offender, But a Person

'The subjects, I've never in my life ever thought about ...
even the most famous questions, I think therefore I am and
all of that lot. Actually knowing where that came from, and
the fact that even something that I believe in very strongly
can be flipped within a sentence.' (Phil, Grendon)

Over time, the philosophy classroom became a place for genuine,
exploratory conversation. We have seen how, being in HMP Grendon
with participants who were already willing and able to engage in
conversation in a group setting, establishing the ethos of safe community
inquiry proved relatively straightforward. To illustrate this further, I
return to the example presented in Chapter 5 that focused on Hume
and Arendt's perspectives of identity. In this session, philosophical
conversation flowed, conversation was deep and meaningful, and the
participants were engaged and insightful.

However, at the end of the session, an incident happened that served
to remind me that this was still a prison. Despite the emphasis in
Grendon on personal development, on therapy and democracy, I was
still working in a restricted environment.

The session on Hume and Arendt in Week 6 proved to be a 'deep
dive' into the concept of identity and the core self for the men with
whom I worked. By this point we had touched on identity through
Theseus' ship, moved to society through Plato, and discussed moral
action through Kant, Bentham and Mill. In the previous discussion,
we had considered Descartes' famous phrase *Cogito, ergo sum*. This
time, however, we looked at an alternative perspective of identity,
considering the role of identity, experience and culture in shaping not
only *who we are* but also *how we perceive ourselves*. Further, the work of

Arendt, in particular, allowed us to explore the relevance of *how others see us*, an issue that is of particular relevance to people in prison.

Only three men attended this session. The Open University was hosting an event in the prison at the same time, and several of the participants needed to attend. Despite this, the conversation was rich and insightful. By this point we had been discussing philosophy together for six weeks; we had begun to know each other, and the men had developed a clear understanding of what to expect in the class. During this discussion, I was able to act as a 'full participant', engaging with the conversation as a philosophical enquirer alongside them. To illustrate the discussion, the following is an extract from fieldwork notes taken following this session. The aim here is to illustrate the depth of discussion and introspection we achieved. The notes have been edited slightly for flow, but the content remains the same:

FIELDWORK NOTES
Grendon, 19 October 2014

In the second half [of the session], we looked at Hannah Arendt. They [the participants] were really taken by the idea that we develop our identities through our actions.... We talked a lot about how "who you are" will be influenced by the way others see you and the way you behave.

Then we looked at the word "narrative" ... what does it mean? They said this is what they do in therapy, looking at your past in order to understand your present to alter your future and understand who you were then vs who you are now. You develop a story which helps you better understand where you are today. The narrative identity, the story that we live by, is quite key. It helps their [the participants'] self-perception and I pushed them towards thinking about how this internal self-perception effects the way you behave. In turn, we then think about how this effects the way you portray yourself. [The participants] said that they are not two separate things – the internal and the external – the way you perceive yourself will impact on the way you act.

During this session, the walls of the prison melted away and the gap between us seemed to narrow. We were neither student-teacher nor prisoner-civilian; we were simply co-inquirers. I explored the notion of identity with them, a concept I find fascinating myself. Not coming from a religious background, Hume's ideas appealed and, as a direct result of these sessions, Arendt's ideas became central to my own thinking. The following extract demonstrates how these sessions were not only relevant to the participants' thinking, but have also been an invaluable source for my own understanding of what it means to be human:

FIELDWORK NOTES
Grendon, 19 October 2014

We talked about actions and behaviour and how people interpret who you are according to the way you behave. We talked about the re-negotiation of the self. We talked about what it means to act out of character.... Some people will seek to do certain things, others will never do those things, people will do those things if circumstances allow and encourage them to do those things. And they used this phrase "they haven't got it in them". I said if you are going to start talking about this idea of whether you've "got it in you" or not, then it goes back to this concept that we do have a fundamental sense of self. Tom said that he doesn't disagree that there is a fundamental sense of self, it's just that we don't know how to define this fundamental sense of self, this core self, that it does exist but we don't know how to define it. Some people say [the core self] is the "soul", some people say the pearl of the self, some people say it's located in a certain part of the brain. However, we don't know what it is and maybe it is [referring back to Hume] a "bundle" of things.

We then discussed the composition of an onion: onions have layers but do not have hearts. And the guys said yeah, but just because an onion is made up of layers doesn't mean it's not an onion. I think that's an interesting point that Phil said that just because a person is made up of thoughts, ideas, experiences and memories doesn't mean it's not a person, you don't need to have this core at the centre of the self. We also talked about traits, there are certain traits that will always carry through.

This session was deep and meaningful, both for me and for the participants. We 'dug deep' into these issues and worked together to understand what Hume and Arendt's ideas meant to our own understanding of ourselves. Of all the sessions I had teaching philosophy in prisons, this session has stayed with me the most. Our dialogue around this topic has shaped my understanding of identity. Furthermore, it demonstrated how offering the time and space to engage in philosophical conversation can provide some form of escape or safe space for the participants, and allow us the opportunity to overcome difference.

Unfortunately, at the end of the session, we were brought back to the prison environment with a thud. Somehow, somewhere in the education wing, a teaspoon had gone missing. The men were prevented from leaving the area and held up for close to half an hour while they were thoroughly searched for the offending item. I made no note, and now cannot recall if the item was found. However, for the 2 hours that we had discussed the question of what it means to be human, I had forgotten that we were in a prison. I do not know if the men ever really forget that they are prisoners, but I often forgot that they were. I was brought back to reality when I realized that these men, who had discussed identity at an intellectual level that far outstripped most conversations I had had in 10 years of higher education study, could not be trusted with a teaspoon.

How did this affect the participants' experience of the philosophy class? For a time, they had sat as 'non-prisoners' – with me and with each other – as philosophers and inquirers joining a conversation that humans have had for thousands of years. In an instant, they had been returned to the status of 'untrustworthy prisoner'. At the time, the men were unfazed. Most of them had been in the system for some years; they knew how things worked. Their prisoner-identity was so ingrained that they just calmly milled around and chatted to each other, waiting patiently before being allowed to move back to the wings. For me, I was less used to being prevented from going as I please. I had to ask them what was happening and what it meant. It was me who was surprised by the loss of a teaspoon being so important. They understood the system, accepted it, and went on with their day.

Abstract conversation

Thus far, we have developed an understanding of a range of literatures. I have discussed philosophy education, describing philosophical dialogue and its use in the prison classroom; provided an overview of prison sociology, highlighting some key research into prisons and the prisoner society; and I have introduced the concept of identity.

Much of the discussion in this book centres on the dichotomy of survival versus growth. In Chapter 3, I argued that prisons encourage a survival identity, with prisoners developing a 'front' that protects them both physically and personally. In Chapter 4, I moved the discussion on to the possibilities of growth in this environment; what might this look like and how does this relate to self-understanding? I rooted my understanding of identity in the 'narrative' perspective, and considered how the environment of a prison shapes a person's way of thinking about themselves. In Chapter 5, I moved on to the prison environment, focusing on Grendon.

Now, I move the discussion on to the specifics of this research, focusing more closely on the words of the participants. In particular, I focus on the abstract nature of the philosophy sessions. Maintaining the focus on Grendon, this chapter has discussed how the philosophical conversation was 'de-personalized' for the participants. Unlike therapy, philosophy did not focus on their 'offending behaviour'. This led to meaningful personal realizations. Through philosophical dialogue, they were able to develop ways of articulating themselves that were meaningful to them, and expressed how they saw themselves. As this chapter progresses, we will begin to build a picture of philosophy as a means of breaking down barriers and developing both a sense of self as well as a sense of community.

Each of the participants had the opportunity to provide feedback for the course in a range of ways. Throughout, they were encouraged to complete feedback forms after each session (some of them took the opportunity to write mini-essays on the back, reflecting on the philosophies discussed in the classroom), and I spent some time speaking with them after the class, or going to their wings to seek out specific participants' opinions. Most importantly, each was interviewed, in depth, after participation.

Having spent three months engaging in philosophical conversation, these post-participation interviews took a conversational and casual tone. I had developed relationships with the participants by this point, and we had developed a form of camaraderie (more of this when we come to discuss Full Sutton in Chapter 7). They were open and candid with me, as I was with them. Here is an overview of their views:

> '... nothing's just black and white, nothing's just straightforward, you have to, like, analyse it to, kind of, some degree, to get a better understanding of it.' (Charlie, Grendon)

By ensuring that I presented different points of view, either within a session or across sessions, the participants learned to appreciate nuanced arguments:

'... the way you were putting things together ... it kind of made you think, even if you agree with one thing you end up disagreeing with another thing or agreeing with one thing at the end of the session....' (Samir, Grendon)

'There were a few times when I was sitting and listening to people put their argument forward, when I thought, it makes a lot more sense than what I was thinking. So I get clearer understanding of the arguments which were put forward.' (Simon, Grendon)

The nature of a philosophy session encouraged open dialogue, with opportunities to put forward ideas and gain responses. The course allowed the participants the space to listen to each other and develop their own understanding of a topic:

'It's not just about the philosophy, it's about other people's perceptions and views ... we all digest and analyse what other people have said and think, "well, that's actually quite good, why didn't I think of that?" or "I can use that later on in life".' (Peter, Grendon)

The pedagogy encouraged the participants to "actually try to break it down" (Samir, Grendon) and think about *their* philosophy of, for example, moral action. What do they base their decisions on? How do we – or should we – decide what is right or wrong?

'I've been considering how consequences may not be the only considerations in a decision. The motive can also be a deciding factor, but this can be mollified by the "road to hell is paved with good intentions". Ultimately a balance between the critique of pure reason [Kant] and purely consequences [Bentham and Mill] based on decisions is what I favour.' (Neil, Grendon, Session 6)

Although the participants reflected on their own opinions, beliefs and ideas, they were asked to do so in the context of the 'ought' – what ought we all to be doing to make society work, and how ought people to behave more generally? Using the established ideas of Descartes, Hume, Kant and Mill, philosophy provided "a more structured approach" (Alex, Grendon) when thinking about issues of morality and identity. Instead of just asking 'What is your morality?', the stimulus asked, 'Here's what this person said. What do you think about that?' This provided the participants with access to ideas that they could use in everyday life and, more importantly, to develop an opinion on what *they* themselves thought.

For some, these reflections were personal and relevant to their therapeutic work in Grendon:

> 'After taking part in this session, it made me think about my own life experiences, especially the early trauma I suffered as a child and how this has impacted on my life. When doing some work in my therapy group "The ship of Theseus" became part of my reasoning and influenced my thinking about letting go of the past, and whether I can. Will past experiences always plague me, have power over me?' (Michael, Grendon)

This indicates the relevance of abstract discussion around an ancient philosophical problem to an individual's self-reflection. For Michael, the discussion around Theseus' ship (introduced in Chapter 1) helped him consider his own life experience and identity in a different way. For others, philosophical conversation encouraged them to think about their behaviour in the context of wider society:

> 'In philosophy you're standing back a bit more and looking at how your behaviour fits in with other people's behaviour and how it fits in structurally rather than tactically. It gives you a sense of perspective that you wouldn't get from anything.' (Tom, Grendon)

Many of the participants discussed how the classes provided an "… opportunity to involve discussion in a non-adversarial arena" (Neil, Grendon). Part of the process of developing more nuanced opinions was related to the safe space the class cultivated. There was a *freedom to disagree* with each other. Employing Socratic questioning placed an emphasis on asking each other questions as a means of exploring a topic. As a result, the participants developed each other's ideas as opposed to trying to prove each other wrong.

The session on freedom of speech provides an illustration of how abstract conversations can lead to personal realizations. In this session, I used Salman Rushdie as an example.

do we have the right to cause offence?

> ### Rushdie's freedom of speech: A counter-example (Week 10, Stage 4)
>
> Salman Rushdie famously said:
>
>> What is freedom of expression? Without the freedom to offend, it ceases to exist.
>
> In *The Satanic Verses*, Rushdie wrote on topics that many people in Muslim countries found offensive. This resulted in a *fatwa* being issued and Rushdie going into hiding for nine years. He himself escaped harm, but a translator and a bodyguard both died as a result. Further to this, several people died in the violent protests that resulted from publication of the book.
>> This has led some to ask whether freedom of speech in a case such as this is really worth it.

This topic came in Week 10 of the course. By this stage, the participants had a clear understanding of the expectations of the philosophy classroom. They were able to discuss Salman Rushdie in an open and in (what I felt to be) a positive manner. They focused on the principles that this scenario presented instead of the politics that surrounded this controversial individual. Do we have the right to cause offence? Does a government have the right to ban a book? What is an appropriate reaction? What was the purpose of writing something that caused such offence? Are all topics up for debate, or is it not appropriate to discuss this?

FIELDWORK NOTES
Grendon, 4 December 2014

> They enjoyed it, everyone joined in. It was lively and animated. But it was intelligent and constructive, albeit a bit heated, it was still respectful.

All but one of the participants engaged in a lively debate from the outset. Cady, a Muslim who had converted while in prison, initially said, "Nah, I'm not going to debate on that", citing his religion as a basis for his refusal. However, he respectfully listened to the conversation and, towards the end, started to engage in the dialogue. I suspect he was encouraged by the full participation of another Muslim in the group, Samir, who happened to be of Iranian descent and offered a fascinating insight into this discussion. During his post-participation interview I asked Cady, "Did any of the topics we covered particularly impact you?"

'Just the Salman Rushdie thing. For me, that was the only one, that was the only thing you know.... A few weeks ago I would have [a] different thing to say, I would either have got up, walked out of class, not wanted to partake because of religious beliefs. I would shut down other people because I would've thought they were being derogatory or disrespectful to my religion. Whether that was because of my immaturity or masculinity, bravado, vulnerability I don't know. Whereas now, I was more comfortable sitting in a class. I'm having open debate ... about something which, in my mind, goes to show the level of maturity that I'm at now, compared to where I come from, that I can discuss the topic that ... I find offensive. But I can be professional in a classroom.' (Cady, Grendon)

It is important to note that Cady does not attribute this change to the philosophy classes – in all likelihood it was a direct consequence of being in a therapeutic community. However, the philosophical space had allowed Cady the opportunity to discuss controversial topics with his peers. The discussion around Salman Rushdie gave him an insight into how he had changed since arriving in Grendon. Similar to Michael's use of Theseus' ship to reflect on his progress in therapy, Cady's engagement in philosophy provided him with an opportunity to reflect on his progress and growth.

The structure and content of the stimuli, combined with the pedagogy of a philosophical inquiry, provided a space for personal exploration and abstract thinking. The sequential nature of the stimuli illustrated the structure of philosophical arguments and allowed time and space for the participants to reflect on the foundations of arguments. Hearing a variety of perspectives – of philosophers and the participants – encouraged the participants to consider different ways of thinking. This meant they had the opportunity to reflect on their own views and opinions, leading some to gain insights into their own way of thinking and the progress they had made in Grendon. The participants were also clear on the role of philosophy in encouraging them to recognize their place in wider society; they reflected on their

(margin note, handwritten: What is different about philosophical conversation?)

behaviour, choices and opinions by taking account of what these meant for society as a whole.

Philosophy, like therapy, engages participants in an open dialogue. However, philosophy broadens their perspectives by asking them to consider questions of identity, society and morality from the perspective of how we should all behave, or how society ought to be structured. The following section turns to the question of how adding this broader perspective relates to the therapeutic environment in Grendon, and asks, 'What is *different* about philosophical conversation?' Perhaps, more importantly, it asks, 'What does this mean for the participants themselves?'

Therapeutic conversation

Philosophy focuses on the individual as a person who is part of society. Instead of asking people how they would behave, they are asked how they, as people and as members of society, ought to behave. This means the participants have to "take a step back and think more widely about things" (Michael, Grendon). The focus of philosophy on the person rather than the prisoner was a new experience in prison for Neil:

> '… prior to this philosophy course, all my understandings and enquiries have been [as] an offender in various environments. Now I can see some of my decisions being selfish, not taking other people into consideration, and actually linking it in with philosophy.' (Neil, Grendon)

The participants valued the opportunity to move away from the label of 'offender' and engage in abstract philosophical conversation. For example, through the work of John Stuart Mill and Immanuel Kant, they reflected on morality and moral action. Instead of "looking at how you respond to things on a day-to-day basis, to this event, that event" the participants considered "What, about your philosophy of life, has led you to behave in certain ways throughout your life?" (Tom, Grendon). In philosophy, the participants were encouraged to reflect on their philosophies of life rather than specific situations:

> 'The ethos of a therapeutic community … [is] about exploring what you already know, trying to break it down and to get a bit of understanding. Exploring things that have led to a lot of decision-making, some of your beliefs, some of your values, and I've actually realized that in [the

philosophy] course ... we were talking about beliefs, values and some of the things that have led us to making certain decision based on what we believe ... this is exactly what we do in the [therapy] group but from the philosophy thing, it just comes from a different angle.' (Samir, Grendon)

I asked some participants directly about the use of the word 'open-mindedness' and how this related to their therapeutic work:

Interviewer: 'With respect to the idea of being open-minded, do you think you have been able to get that from philosophy in a way that you haven't been able to get from the therapy that you do?'

Charlie, Grendon: 'I wouldn't say that. I would say that it's like we just discussed, it's enhanced that; kind of like, reinforced it and kind of put a bit of whipped cream and sugar on top. It's made it a little bit more appealing to go that way about things. It kind of reinforced it, to say, you know what, maybe you do need to kind of, like, look at things from further away before and let them hit you in the face.'

As opposed to philosophy being 'better' or 'more effective' than therapy, it was complementary and enhancing:

'In the [therapeutic] group discussions we have, things are very intense and personal, whereas in the philosophy you tend not to bring in the personal as such. You tend to look at it from a much more constructive way, a much more distant way than you would in the discussion groups. It complements, I think it does complement it, I think it helps to give it perspective.' (Tom, Grendon)

Importantly, philosophical discussions focus on people, as individuals, as members of society, thereby providing a space for thinking through an issue. The abstract nature of the discussion provided a different perspective, one of contemplation of the personal:

'It's helped me look at things from different point of view, it helps you see both sides of an argument, it helps you see sometimes a bigger picture that you are looking at rather than yourself ... there are many dimensions ... something

[handwritten marginalia: philosophy - focused on the general rather than the particular + not on the offender as a person who needs to be corrected]

that might just seem too deep at the start may have lots of different aspects that I tap into and think about.' (Charlie, Grendon)

Although the participants emphasize that therapy is the major factor in the changes that they have experienced since being in Grendon, they are clear that philosophy has contributed to their thought processes:

'[Philosophy is] not a major factor – I think being in therapy is a major factor but it's definitely had an impact and it's definitely added a bit more momentum to it [therapy].... It's sped things along a little bit and it's given me the ideas of the people to go on and it's got me more used to thinking about myself in a more analytic way.' (Charlie, Grendon)

'The thing is, it's useful because in Grendon, you tend to talk about your feelings more, that sort of thing. But in the philosophy group you're more likely to end up talking about more abstract things than your feelings, rather than personal. Looking to and talking about things in the abstract can help you to actually look again at the personal from a different point of view.' (Tom, Grendon)

In philosophy, this is achieved through dialogue focusing on the general rather than the particular:

'With the philosophy thing, I think is more focused on life ... and not just one aspect of your life. I think you can take the stuff that you learn in your discussions and you think outside the box into all aspects of your life, not just your offending.' (Matt, Grendon)

This focus – considering the general rather than the particular, the person as a member of a society rather than the offender who needs to be corrected, and on principles of moral action as opposed to how to behave in a given circumstance – is what provides the broader perspective. Philosophy develops open-mindedness by encouraging the individual to consider themselves and their place in the world through a philosophical lens.

The period of fieldwork in Grendon provided opportunities to explore the role of philosophy in developing participants' thinking. It built on the findings from the pilot work in HMP Low Moss in

Scotland, where participants discussed philosophy as a means of accessing wider conversations in society that had previously seemed obscure (see Szifris, 2017). These conversations provide a space for the participants to break down barriers, and consider themselves and their environment in a different way. From this, we begin to see how philosophy might provide the opportunity to develop the self, even in the prison environment.

Beyond openness, themes of community, coping and self-reflection emerged from the data. These themes become particularly relevant to the work in Full Sutton to come later. First, however, we maintain our focus on Grendon.

Developing community

Philosophy focuses on the participant as a whole person, as a member of society and a community. The question remains, however, why is philosophy important to prisoners in particular? Why is a class, such as the one under discussion here, relevant to their incarcerated lives and their future, either post-release or as they work their way through the prison system? Beyond philosophy's relevance to participants' ways of thinking, three further themes emerged from the fieldwork in Grendon: community, coping and identity. All three feature heavily in the findings from Full Sutton. Here, I introduce some of the findings around philosophy's role in community, coping and personal identity as a starting point for a more in-depth analysis of these themes later.

As I have discussed in Chapters 1 and 2, I delivered the philosophy course in the form of a *community* of philosophical inquiry that encouraged communal dialogue. I emphasized the ease with which this community aspect of the course was established in Grendon, highlighting the similarities between therapy and philosophical inquiry in their use of Socratic dialogue. However, the developing communities of inquiry provided a shared purpose for the participants. Hans Toch, a well-known criminologist who has written extensively on prisons and therapeutic communities, provides a clear outline of the definition of 'community'. He asserts that therapeutic communities are characterized by face-to-face interactions, personal investment, shared assets, collaborative activity, solidarity and egalitarianism. Further, he states that communities must provide 'an accepting, reliable, and supportive milieu' (Toch, 1980, p 10).

Philosophy, therefore, complemented the community aspirations of Grendon by providing a "chance to meet different people and discuss things with people that I don't normally talk to" (Tom, Grendon).

Some participants suggested that philosophical dialogue classes could play a role in giving people the chance to be more "involved" (Charlie, Grendon) in Grendon's community, and get people "talking to a wider group" (Alex, Grendon). The participants developed "a working friendship with other people in the class" (Cady, Grendon) that helped them move beyond their initial judgements of other people:

Interviewer: 'Why didn't you interact before?'
Cady, Grendon: 'Different wings, stereotypes views, opinions on both parties. So once we get into a working environment, you work together, you build things, you build a bond and a trust and a relationship with a group that you worked with. I kind of think that I've gone away judging them differently. And I prejudged them and they've gone away judging me differently to have prejudged me because we've worked together on a topic.'

This went beyond the classroom and onto the wings, with the participants often discussing the topics in between sessions and passing on what they learned to others:

'He weren't in this jail when you were signing people up, it was a real shame. I've took all the pieces back in the class I've took them out to him and he's read them all.' (Phil, Grendon)

Face-to-face interactions within a community and an emphasis on respect and shared interests do not necessarily lead to individuals liking each other. Several members of the philosophy class did not get on, with specific individuals "clashing" (Phil, Grendon). However, due in part to the environment of Grendon, the participants remained polite and respectful during conversation. The nature of philosophical dialogue, in particular, developed their skills in learning how to argue and how to put their point across. For one participant, this translated into tolerance:

'It was about tolerance … he got under my skin, he really did. You have to use tolerance – learn to be tolerant – so the class wasn't brought down to my level of anger or frustration.' (Peter, Grendon)

He went on to discuss how philosophy "helps me understand [him] and his behaviour." The participants had the opportunity "to get to know guys ... and to actually find out what their opinions and ideas were and how it, kinda, formulated the basis for ... people's beliefs" (Charlie, Grendon).

In philosophy, the collaborative activity of the shared dialogue meant the participants worked together to develop understanding of a topic and their own opinion, as well as the opinions of others. In doing this, they were not only able to understand themselves better, but also accepted other people's flaws:

> 'I think being able to sit with my own contradictions had helped me to be less frustrated with other people's. Some people can say one thing, they can say this is the right thing to do and then not do it and do the wrong thing. I can sit with other people's contradictions more and I am more comfortable being able to explain to other people about their contradictions.' (Alex, Grendon)

Through such collaborative activity, the participants developed respect for other people's opinions:

> 'What I've got [from philosophy] is every opinion, no matter how crazy you may think it is in your mind, it's exactly that – it's someone's opinions. They're entitled to that opinion whether or not it fits that way of thinking about things or not. I think that's really important as well though, I think there's a way to say to people "Okay, I understand where you are coming from, but I disagree".' (Charlie, Grendon)

> 'So, I suppose, doing philosophy, it gives you a chance to think about others, think about what others may be thinking, why they may be thinking that, why people may appear a certain way, it gives you more understanding.... Prior to being on the course, I judged them and I was surprised to hear some of them talking and some of their ideas. It kind of shocked me, which I suppose has kind of helped me in not judging people, talking to people more, letting people talk, working with them, that collaborative kind of thing, so that's helped me a lot as well.' (Michael, Grendon)

The participants discussed how they might previously have judged another person as being "not the sort of guy who would come down here [to education]" (Phil, Grendon). However, philosophy seemed to be a 'leveller'; the participants realized that, despite their different levels of educational qualifications, everyone had something worth saying. For those with university-level education, they realized that those with little or no formal qualifications "had positive, strong contribution[s] to make" (Tom, Grendon):

> 'You've got, like, you've got a Master's student in there and you've got some with minimal skills, but we all manage to interact.' (John, Grendon)

Further to that, they collaborated and worked to ensure everybody was able to access the discussion:

> 'I think people were trying to bring people up ... to be batting on the same pitch.' (Matt, Grendon)

In developing new social networks, based on a positive, pro-social premise and a shared experience of philosophical dialogue, the participants could be helped in moving away from their established friendships:

> 'If certain people are away from their circle, then they become different people ... it gives people the chance to grow as individuals, rather than as a collective where you feel like you have to be someone and you are really not and you never have been.' (Charlie, Grendon)

For example, one of the participants, an ex-gang member, discussed how participating in Grendon and the philosophy course was about re-indentifying himself as an individual rather than as a member of his gang.

In general, providing opportunities for self-expression encouraged the participants to reflect on how others received their ways of expressing themselves. They enjoyed the "good, open debate, structured conversation" (Neil, Grendon). Several mentioned "being able to communicate" and gaining "good communication skills, listening skills" (Michael, Grendon) as one of the key benefits of the course:

'I think I'm more thoughtful as far as social interactions go, I think a lot more about the content of what I am about to say and whether or not it is relevant … to kind of articulate myself a lot better and to think about how much water my argument actually holds, or my opinion actually holds, before I say it. I think in the philosophy class there were a couple of times where I mentioned a couple of things and people looked at me like I'd just fallen out the sky. So I thought, even though what I was saying was relevant, the way I put it was a little bit mis-understandable. So I could've structured my response a lot better. I think that's one thing I got from it, to kind of work out what I'm saying and deliver what I'm saying to an intelligible standard so people actually get what I'm trying to say.' (Charlie, Grendon)

'My intention always was for philosophy to give me the ability to speak in groups again.… I was struggling in the wing and … just after I had started philosophy I actually used a wing meeting, an open wing meeting, to discuss me and my whole childhood leading up to the crime. So, I sort of got the confidence from the philosophy, speaking in philosophy to put my words, my thoughts into words and vocalize them rather than just sit there nodding my head, perhaps, or just looking at the floor. For me it really was a good turning point.' (Peter, Grendon)

For this participant, the abstract, impersonal content of a philosophical conversation provided the opportunity to practise the skills required in the more difficult and personal dialogue in group therapy. For the more long-standing members of Grendon's TC, the philosophy sessions provided the opportunity to "put some of my skills into practice" (Samir, Grendon). For these members, the philosophy class had a much more moderate impact. For them, the intellectual activity was primarily enjoyable. It served as a novel diversion where they could get to know new people and engage in lively and interesting discussions with people they would not necessarily know in normal circumstances.

However, the collaborative nature of philosophical inquiry enhanced the sense of community among the participants. The pedagogy "gives the guys a chance to be able to feed off each other" (Charlie, Grendon) in order to build understanding. The participants enjoyed the unusual situation of having the freedom to disagree with each other as "just sitting down having a debate with people, it's something that you really miss in jail" (Phil, Grendon):

> 'Being able to actually talk about something that is sensitive to some more than others. Being able to, actually, be mature about it and have an open discussion without insulting anyone's belief or, that was actually, to realize that this could be done, that was good.' (Samir, Grendon)

The philosophy class provided a bit of 'light relief' from the heavy therapeutic work. As a group, we had fun. Although some of the topics were complex and difficult to understand, the purpose of the sessions was simply to understand what Descartes meant when he said *Cogito, ergo sum*, to join in the 2,000-year-old discussion around Theseus' ship, and to learn about philosophy:

> 'I went in with my eyes wide shut, I didn't really know at all what it was about, philosophy. So it was very intriguing for me to find out that there were people out there with these ideas that are actually, kinda like, the cornerstone of thought processes.' (Charlie, Grendon)

Where therapy 'entails the exploration and expression of painful material and disturbing emotions' (Greenwood, 2001, p 48), philosophy entails the exploration of other people's ideas. There is no expectation of revealing personal details beyond what one might wish to disclose in the course of the discussion, no requirement to explain the past or delve into deeply personal topics. However, although the philosophy classes did not set out to encourage personal self-reflection, for many, the philosophical content did encourage this:

Interviewer: 'What role do you think philosophy can play in Grendon?'

Alex, Grendon: 'Application to identity. That is something that strongly links into this place because of the work that we do in our groups. [In Grendon] we don't go in and look at the whole part of ourselves … [philosophy's] given it a more structured approach. Particularly Hume's identity, that really struck a chord with me, about being different points of people.'

In therapy, although there is a focus on a person's past and attributes beyond the offending behaviour, the reasons for participating centre on the criminal activity of the individual. Philosophy, on the other hand, considers the whole person:

> 'What sort of person would I like to be? Again, I would like to be putting the majority of people first, but would I do that at my expense? At our family's expenses – would I protect a family member if I done something wrong? What would I do if someone paid money into me house, if someone was ready to kill them?... Just this simple thing about lying, telling lies. When is it okay, when is it not okay? They are just the sort of things you do automatically, the sort of thing you do spur of the moment as and when they come up. But now [having been in philosophy], I think it's slightly more aware of what you are doing. It just, if your thinking process was a yard wide, mine's about a yard and a bit now so it's just added more to the thought processes. Which is good.' (Neil, Grendon)

It is clear that the skills required to philosophize are very similar to those required for therapy. Philosophy is much more light-hearted, however; it is abstract and impersonal, and therefore easier to engage with. The participants discussed the role philosophy might play in Grendon, arguing that it could be complementary to therapy, initially serving as an enjoyable, non-threatening way of learning the skills required to engage in therapy and then later, as a means to practise those skills in a more educational setting and in life generally.

The community aspect of philosophical inquiry had a clear impact on this group. The men widely discussed their pleasure at being able to participate in discussions and self-reflect in a safe environment. Philosophy provided an opportunity to develop positive, pro-social relationships that could serve to help people break away from their usual circle, to learn skills, to improve therapeutic engagement, and as a positive intellectual diversion from the heavy work of therapy.

Thinking about the self as a whole

Although there are similarities between therapeutic dialogue and philosophical dialogue, philosophy asks participants to think in a different way. In philosophy, participants discuss issues such as morality, 'the good life' and identity in the abstract and impersonally. In doing this, philosophy lends itself to 'opening minds' and 'broadening perspectives'. In making such claims, it is important to be clear that there is no evidence that philosophy is necessarily 'better' or 'more effective' or, indeed, 'preferable' to therapy. Instead, the evidence here is that philosophy might offer something different: complementary, but distinct.

In therapy, dialogue is underpinned by the fact that the participants are in prison. Although the discussions may not always focus on criminal behaviours, therapeutic work in Grendon was conducted with an underlying understanding that the aim was to reduce offending tendencies. As a result, therapy starts from the point of an offender with 'criminogenic tendencies' and anti-social behaviours that require addressing. In the philosophy classes, the participants entered the dialogue as people, members of society, ready and willing to discuss what that meant to them. By starting from this perspective, they were able to reflect on themselves without needing to reflect on their offending behaviour, although this could, conceivably, be an outcome.

Philosophy encouraged reflection on the 'big' questions in life. In so doing, the participants were asked to think beyond their immediate circumstances, to the wider perspective. By keeping it impersonal, I was able to broaden perspectives and open minds to new ways of thinking. Importantly, we conducted our philosophical dialogue in the context of a community. As such, the participants were able to forge positive pro-social relationships. They got to know new people, not because they were in their therapeutic group or had a cell next door, but because they had a shared experience in philosophy.

Initially, in Grendon, the philosophy classes were an intellectual diversion. The participants attended because they wanted to. This was an intellectual exercise engaged in for its own sake. In some cases, bringing people together in such circumstances served to break down stereotypes; in others, it served as a means of equalizing participants. Despite different personal and educational backgrounds, they were able to develop mutual respect for one another. In particular, they began to understand each other – where another person was coming from, and why they thought the way they did.

Finally, the participants enjoyed the course. This might seem a trivial observation; however, the value of this in the context of a prison should not be overlooked. In Grendon, the participants were engaged in difficult and complex therapeutic work. Providing a space in which they could engage in something similar – to either practise or learn skills – that was interesting, and enjoyable, gave them an important break in this context. For some, the classes highlighted how far they had come; for others, this served to help them engage more fully in therapy; and for others still, learning of the teaching of philosophers served as an interesting framework in which to think about their own therapeutic journey.

Fundamentally, my time spent in Grendon demonstrated the role philosophy can play in developing understanding. The men articulated, in clear terms, how the classes had helped them develop a better understanding of themselves, of those around them, and of the wider world. By encouraging more open attitudes, the philosophy class not only encouraged the participants to reflect on their own positions, but also provided opportunities to be more open with other people. They developed relationships and a sense of community with their fellow participants, which, in turn, could help shape their understanding of their place in the world. Through communicating with others, some realized that they could be something other than that which they had been, and something other than that which the prison system suggested.

Where Grendon was a story of philosophical exploration, Full Sutton was a story of perseverance. In Full Sutton, I had to work constantly to establish trust and respect in the classroom, with the participants challenging my skills at every turn. Even so, despite the difficulties of trying to establish a safe, non-adversarial environment to discuss philosophical ideas, Full Sutton proved rewarding in different ways. The backdrop of a maximum security prison allowed for exploration of different aspects of philosophical inquiry from those explored in Grendon. Trust, relationships and wellbeing emerged at the heart of the data. The divisive and suspicious atmosphere of the prison meant the process of delivering the philosophy course focused on developing the *community* aspect of a philosophical inquiry.

7

Trying to Find a Community of Philosophical Inquiry

My time in HMP Full Sutton provides a clear narrative of progress. The development of the dialogue, the changing attitudes towards philosophical content and the growing sense of community provides a means to understanding why philosophical dialogue might be relevant to the wider issues of a prisoner society. However, Full Sutton is, perhaps, best understood through the lens of community. Underpinning this, we begin to 'set the scene' for understanding the wider themes that emerged from this research – trust, relationships and wellbeing. Chapter 8 goes on to focus on trust and relationships, with Chapter 9 then articulating the relevance of wellbeing and self-expression.

Full Sutton prison was divided in two – one half consisted of the 'mainstream' population 'on normal location'. The other half, the vulnerable prisoners (VPs), were held in the vulnerable prisoner unit (VPU). The two populations rarely met and, in many ways, the prison operated, and felt like, two separate communities – co-existing, but never interacting, making use of the same physical environment, but occupying different wings, and attending the same workshops and education, but at different times.

The experience of teaching in Full Sutton was also a story of two halves. Each side of the prison had a different atmosphere, presented different challenges and involved very different types of philosophical conversation. However, despite the differences, the themes that emerged from the data cut both ways: trust, relationships, wellbeing and self-expression were relevant to all the participants, regardless of the population they resided in.

The journey here, so different from what happened in HMP Grendon, provides a means to understanding why philosophical dialogue might be relevant to the wider issues of a prisoner society. To understand the relevance of trust, relationships, wellbeing and self-expression, we first have to understand the prison. Fundamentally, in spite of the prevailing atmosphere in the prison (or perhaps because of it?), the philosophy classroom provided a rare space to develop a sense of community. As with the Grendon community of philosophical inquiry, philosophy and the use of dialogue provided the participants in Full Sutton with the same means to encourage them to listen to each other. Common ground was sought and found, understanding of each other grew, and relationships began to form.

The following account of one of the early discussions returns us to the work on utilitarianism. I have already recounted some of the events of that week's session in Chapter 4. One of the participants left the group, walking out after an altercation with another, and choosing not to return despite my best efforts. Week 4 was a difficult week in Full Sutton and the following articulates what happened.

"Look, most people don't like it, but I like a bit of gambling. But, on the whole, you might say it's bad for society, how's that work?" Jonny asked, immediately seeking a concrete example to help frame the issue. Jonny was in his 50s, had been in an out of prison since his early 20s, and seemed to cope with the prison environment. For him, a stint in prison was part and parcel of his lifestyle. He was often the voice of reason in the class, although not without his own challenges.

We focused on the idea of 'every person's happiness is of equal importance and all types of pleasure hold equal weight'. Toby pointed out that, at the time, this was quite revolutionary – that the happiness of a pauper should have the same merit as the happiness of a prince was not the common opinion in the 1700s (he claimed). We discussed whether we agreed with this as a group and, on the whole, we did. There was a clear appreciation of the historical relevance of Bentham's ideas.

Mill's adaptation (Week 4, Stage 2)

John Stuart Mill was a pupil of Bentham's, and broadly agreed with the idea of utilitarianism. However, he disagreed with the idea that all pleasures held equal weight. Famously, Mill asked whether you would rather be a 'happy pig' or a 'sad human'. For Mill, you are better off being a sad human because the pleasure that humans can derive from life, even if in small amounts, far outweigh the primitive pleasure a pig might enjoy.

> Mill categorized pleasures as being lower or higher – lower pleasures are those that can be enjoyed by animals and humans alike (such as food, warmth, etc), while higher pleasures can only be enjoyed by humans (such as music and literature).

As we moved into Mill's adaptation, the conversation shifted into a discussion of the afterlife and the differences in religion and belief in the group. Two of us believed in it and two did not. I was nervous of the direction of this conversation. This was not a topic I was particularly well versed in, having neither practised nor studied religion. This conversation was also happening after the argument between two of the participants that resulted in one storming out of the classroom (as described in Chapter 4). I had only three participants left at this point from the mainstream classroom and, in the back of my mind, I was worrying that my research was falling apart.

Despite the earlier argument, it was a calm and controlled discussion. Peter, a young Muslim who had been convicted of terrorist-related offences, was thoughtful and composed when he spoke and gave little away about his religious beliefs – only bringing them into the conversation when it was relevant. Jonny was also very calm and controlled in the way he spoke. He was very helpful when the others "go off on one a bit" and seemed to understand the topics better.

However, the peace did not last long. Stage 3 of the discussion caused some problems that were more typical of this group.

The pleasure machine (a critique) (Week 4, Stage 3)

Utilitarianism insists that happiness is what we ought to aim for. But is happiness what we do, or should, value most?

The following thought-experiment is used to test the suggestion that happiness alone is what ultimately matters. Suppose a new machine is built – the pleasure machine. The device can replicate perfectly any experience you like. Do you want to know what it is like to climb Mount Everest, to converse with Aristotle, or to enjoy a romantic evening with a supermodel? The pleasure machine can now show you. Just strap on the helmet, and a vast computer will stimulate your brain in order to induce any experience you desire.

What if you were given the opportunity to permanently immerse yourself in the pleasure machine's virtual world? Would you do it?

Peter, Jonny and I started having an interesting conversation about why we did not think spending too much time in the pleasure machine would be a good thing. Was this what we want out of life, over and above happiness? We discussed ideas of truth, fulfilment, purpose and meaning. The conversation was rich and insightful.

Unfortunately, however, Toby refused point blank to 'play the game'. He kept on insisting life is a pleasure machine and that he gets pleasure out of everything. He did not seem to really listen to the points being made, despite Jonny, Peter and I trying a variety of methods to explain the problem. It was quite difficult. Eventually it was Jonny who managed to get him to answer the issue, and interestingly he said that he wouldn't want to be in the pleasure machine because he "wouldn't be safe when everyone else is around outside." We were not really able to explore this discussion much further.

This type of difficulty was common in the first weeks. The small number of participants intensified their personalities. Peter seemed to enjoy winding Toby up, who would occasionally have outbursts that he later described as "pantomimic". He had a booming voice and a passionate desire for people to understand truth, reason and logic. However, his manner could be aggressive, and he would occasionally say outrageous things in an attempt to make his point. In reality, it often served to undermine as opposed to emphasize what he was saying.

Later, as the weeks progressed, I found ways to get more participants into the classroom, which helped to broaden the conversation. The participants developed a better understanding of expectations. That week, however, I left the classroom exhausted, ending my fieldwork notes with the following:

FIELDWORK NOTES
Full Sutton, mainstream, 8 July 2015

It was a very difficult session today and I did feel that I could have done a better job. This is a tumultuous group, though, and I could really do with a few more voices in the mix – it is a shame that I only have four. That being said, if I had a couple more like these it might be too much to handle.

HMP Full Sutton

Full Sutton is a high security prison in the Yorkshire and Humberside region. At the time of the fieldwork, the most recent report from HM Chief Inspector of Prisons (from 2013) described the atmosphere in the prison as 'calm', with low levels of violence and drug use, and a 'range of good quality, well-managed purposeful activity available' (2013, p 5). The report uses terms such as 'innovative' and 'effective' to describe the regime structure and services on offer.

Full Sutton had the capacity to hold 616 prisoners on six main wings (three for mainstream and three for VPs), a small close supervision centre for persistently disruptive prisoners, an induction wing and a drug treatment unit. To be sent to Full Sutton, a prisoner had to have a sentence of more than four years, with 64 per cent of the population serving life and a further 28 per cent serving 10 years or more (at the time of the 2013 Inspectorate report). The VP population made up around half the prison population accommodated in three separate wings, with round 60 per cent of them having been convicted of sexually motivated crimes or crimes of a sexual nature.

In 2012, the education department in the prison had been praised for its range and quality of delivery. In 2014, a study conducted by the University of Cambridge's PRC spoke positively of the attitude of staff towards educational opportunities, and highlighted prisoners' praise for the work of the education department, despite limited funding and reduced provision. During my time in the department, the education staff (along with the writer-in-residence and the library staff) demonstrated enthusiastic attitudes towards prisoners' learning. However, by the time I arrived, the staff were only able to deliver courses up to Level 2 (equivalent to basic secondary school qualifications or GCSE Grade C or above) due to changes in funding, and were clearly frustrated. Even so, the education department was doing all it could to maintain an interesting range of courses and, beyond basic numeracy and literacy, there were art, cookery and woodwork courses available, as well as a writer-in-residence who delivered book groups and held a chess club, who also attended the philosophy class alongside the participants. Staff expressed their disappointment in the limited opportunity to deliver higher levels of education, supporting the observation by Liebling's Cambridge team that those men in prison who wished to move on to more advanced qualifications were left without the support to do so (Liebling et al, 2014).

The mainstream half of the prison was closer to the classic descriptions of the prison environment outlined in Chapter 3. On the whole, the mainstream population consisted of prisoners convicted of violent offences, and was characterized by a divisive and macho culture. My experience echoed the notion of 'hyper-masculinity' described by other prison scholars (see Jewkes, 2005a). Men projected a macho 'front', prison officers watched the prisoners from a distance, and power, authority and distrust flowed through the prisoner society. Liebling et al's (2011) descriptions of HMP Whitemoor offered the most useful point of comparison due, in part, to their research being one of the few studies of a maximum security environment reporting in a risk-averse, post-9/11, political climate (see Liebling and Arnold, 2012). Full Sutton's mainstream population included overt and distinct religious groups, and, evident from the outset, the strained relationships between Muslims and non-Muslims formed the undercurrent of relationships in the prison.

In contrast, the VPU had a more compliant population, with quiet and more 'unassuming' prisoners. I observed that VPs, particularly those convicted of sexual offences, often behaved as though they were attempting to shrink into the shadows and stay 'under the radar'. Despite their outward compliance, the nature of their crimes led to suspicions among staff around grooming and manipulation. When commenting to a member of education staff on the cooperative nature of the VPs compared to the mainstream prisoners, it was quickly pointed out that they were "much more manipulative, though", with staff stating that they would much prefer to work with the "mains" because at least "you know where you stand" (education staff member).

Staff were, overall, supportive of my work, and seemed to appreciate the importance of providing activities for prisoners. At the same time, I always felt under surveillance. The systems and structure of a maximum security environment required staff to be on constant watch over the prisoners, with the risk-averse culture meaning that interactions between prisoners and staff were seen as a potential opportunity for prisoners to 'groom' or condition staff. As I will go on to discuss, my presence in the prison was received with some suspicion. While I was outwardly well received by the staff, uniformed officers seemed suspicious of any vaguely friendly encounter I had with prisoners as I walked with them to my tea breaks, or received them into the classrooms from my door. The prisoners, too, did not seem to know what to make of me. They made assumptions about my background and my motives.

These issues were not unique to my experience. In general, staff–prisoner relationships were relatively strained. While Inspectorate reports indicated that there were 'good' relationships overall, there were also mixed reports of staff–prisoner relationships. Discipline or uniformed staff (officers), who maintained order and supervised movements and activities, indicated a lack of trust in the prisoners, and doubted that they could be rehabilitated, while prisoners had little faith in official procedures in the prison (Liebling et al, 2014).

Liebling and Williams (who conducted research in Full Sutton in the year before my own) described Full Sutton as follows:

> Security and other staff had an overbearing presence. Prisoners were subject to all forms of non-disciplinary actions (that is, disciplinary action taken that is not subject to the adjudication process) such as being sent to segregation under rule 54 for good order and discipline, being subject to warnings that could lead to the removal of prisoners' Incentives and Earned Privileges (IEPs, which includes access to television and more visitations permitted per month), random and overly frequent checks of prisoners, their personal artefacts, and cells (eg "bolts and bars" checks, mandatory drugs tests, or volumetric controls, which means that prisoners have to pack up their possessions to fit them within a predefined volume allowance for X-ray purposes). Prisoners also could be removed from meaningful roles and positions such as being a wing cleaner or a "listener; without knowing the reasons why." (Williams and Liebling, 2018, p 278)

Black and minority ethnic prisoners, and Muslim prisoners, felt their treatment was worse than the treatment of white prisoners. Evidence suggested a 'lack of cultural sensitivity', with clear evidence to support the relatively negative perceptions of black prisoners regarding their treatment (Liebling et al, 2014). Relationships between the Muslim population and prison staff were described as 'hostile', with communal activities among Muslim prisoners being treated as 'suspicious' by staff. Racial and religious issues in Full Sutton had also been affected by a hostage-taking incident in 2013 involving three Muslim prisoners taking a non-Muslim member of staff hostage (Liebling et al, 2016).

These issues came to bear on the atmosphere of the philosophy classroom, particularly on the mainstream side. Issues of religion and faith were not, however, only discussed within that population, as the following describes.

Religious tensions in Full Sutton

In entering Full Sutton, religious identities (most notably, Muslim religious identities) were explicit and evident from the moment I stepped into the corridors. There was a high percentage of Muslim prisoners in Full Sutton, many of whom had converted in prison (see also Liebling and Williams, 2017). Prisoners and staff casually discussed 'forced' conversions to Islam and articulated clear concerns around the Muslim group. I did not investigate, and cannot verify, their assertions around conversion, but their perspective highlighted the concerns staff had around the issues of faith.

There seemed to be a kind of religious 'fervour' when I was there (see also Liebling et al, 2020). Men dressed to display their adherence to the Islamic faith, and I regularly saw prisoners intensely studying a religious text at the table during breaks in the education department. In the pre-participation interviews, one man dropped out in case he 'learned anything that went against his Islamic beliefs', and at least two others asked if I was Jewish (I am not, although I have Polish-Jewish heritage, and it is not unusual for me to be asked this question). As such, I entered Full Sutton somewhat unbalanced, with a growing realization that I would have to try to understand these issues.

Propaganda and misinformation about different religions circulated within the prison. The chaplains (which included both Imams and Christian ministers) openly discussed the difficulties of working in Full Sutton, and their experience largely reflected my own. The Imam revealed how some members of the Muslim population's interpretation of scriptures differed from his teachings. However, the prisoners would not raise this with him but instead, returned to their wings to discuss issues they had with his interpretations among themselves. This meant he had difficulty openly challenging alternative interpretations.

Non-conventional interpretations of scriptures were not limited to the mainstream Muslim population. A member of the VP philosophy group brought a series of pamphlets to my attention that were being circulated on the wings by a number of Christians. These pamphlets outlined the 'lie of evolution' and the 'myth' of carbon dating. Where these leaflets had come from was unclear. On one occasion, when discussing the idea of a philosophy group for the over-60s with one of my participants while in his workshop, a different resident of the VPU overheard and said that he was not interested in the teachings of philosophers because, as he understood it, "philosophers are largely Godless people".

Despite there being evidence of other groups, studies suggest that the most dominant group in high security prisons in England is the Muslim group. A recent report by the Ministry of Justice in the UK (Powis et al, 2019) states that the majority wanted to 'practice their faith peacefully' and immerse themselves in Islamic scriptures to '... elicit change in their life and to cope with custody' (2019, p 10). However, within this group, a small subgroup operated as a gang with a clear gang structure (leader, recruiters, followers, foot-soldiers) who controlled the majority of the contraband in the prison and used religion as a way to victimize others. Importantly, in interviewing a wide range of Muslim prisoners, they reported that the leaders of these gangs gained their legitimacy from their faith. Those higher up were those who were born into the faith (or they had, at least, converted a long time ago, prior to coming to prison), could speak Arabic, and had often been convicted under the Terrorism Act (and were known as TACT prisoners).

Furthermore, in a post-9/11 world, the issue of radicalization has become more acute. The Muslim population in prison has disproportionately grown since 2000, leading to an increasing number of conversations about in-prison conversion (see, in particular, Hamm, 2013). I discuss these issues in far greater detail in Chapter 8, as they relate in particular to the issues of trust. However, relevant to the broader experience of working in Full Sutton, issues of religion have led to what Liebling and Williams describe as a particular 'security threat group':

> Religious identity, ideology, and practice have become subject to intense scrutiny by security departments ... disproportionately the case in relation to Islam. (2017, p 1198)

Consequently, engaging in research that involves the Muslim prison population is inherently tied up with the political climate and public opinion (see, for example, Quraishi, 2008). British national newspapers highlight forced conversions and Muslim 'protection rackets', and talk of 'terror gangs' in prisons (see, for example, articles from the *Daily Mail* [Beckford, 2015] and *Express* [Burman, 2015]). Quilliam, a counter-terrorism think tank, produced a report entitled *Unlocking Al-Qaeda: Islamist Extremism in British Prisons* (Brandon, 2009), and claimed that British prisons were 'incubating' Islamic extremism. They outline conflict between Islamic and non-Islamic prisoners, arguing that radicalization occurs through extremists 'gaining the sympathy and respect of other Muslim prisoners' (2009, p 3). They claim, like others, that the prison service has mishandled the situation. More recently, a Civitas report, entitled *'The New Syria?' Critical Perspectives on the Deradicalisation and Reintegration of Islamist Offenders* (Webb, 2020), begins by outlining the threat of 'prison leavers', articulating the 'mounting challenges from extremism within the prison system' (2020, p 1).

The purpose of recounting these issues is not to offer a view on whether there is a problem of radicalization in the prison system in the UK. My research did not focus on this, and I do not have the insight or data to offer a view. Instead, it is to place my work in a wider political context. Research has indicated that prisons often fail to distinguish between genuine faith conversion as part of a process of meaning-making and personal development, and conversion for protection (Liebling et al, 2011). However, a key issue, as is so often the case, involves the labelling of all Muslim prisoners as being part of this process. Being a Muslim can mean being tacitly treated as being a 'risk', while conversion to other faiths is seen as a positive part of the rehabilitation process.

The point, therefore, is that while staff tension around the Muslim population is clear, religious identities within the prison population were obvious and apparent. These identities were tied up with power, hierarchy and risk, all of which resulted in a tense atmosphere at the time of the fieldwork. These tensions led to a very 'risk-averse' security department in the prison, and even getting people into my classroom was not easy. A number of hurdles had to be overcome, and a number of checks had to take place, as the following describes.

Recruitment and participation

From the outset, Full Sutton presented a range of problems, the first of which involved advertising the course and encouraging some men to come along. In some ways, the process of recruitment in Full Sutton followed a simpler process than the one in Grendon. There were no community meetings, no votes and no backings required. Instead, once I gained security clearance (a long and slow process of form filling, background checks and in-prison training), I met with two members of the senior leadership team at the prison who provided a tour, and who introduced me to the education department. I then supplied a poster to advertise the course, and an information sheet for those who might be interested. Any interested men would complete my sheet and an 'app' (used across the prison estate in England and Wales for prisoners to apply for programmes and courses), and the prison then organized the class lists.

However, in a maximum security prison, getting and maintaining a group of participants for a 12-week course is never straightforward. Attendance in the philosophy class varied between the two halves of the prison. Among the VPs, attendance remained stable, with five (out of six) attending all 12 sessions, and the sixth member of the group being transferred after attending seven sessions. However, among the mainstream prisoners, attendance fluctuated. The volatile nature of the mainstream philosophy class, and incidences of participants walking out halfway through, severely limited the number of participants from the mainstream wings in the first few weeks. Taking this into account, I took a more flexible approach to attendance, allowing prisoners to 'sit in' on the philosophy class (with the permission of their teachers and the prison officers) if they showed an interest. Among the mainstream attendees, half of those who completed the course came to attend in this manner.

For those who did not just 'wander in' to see what was going on, attending the course involved a process within the prison of application and acceptance into the classroom. A staff member advertised the course around the prison with posters and, I discovered later, the writer-in-residence had encouraged many of those who attended to sign up. She asked to attend the course alongside the participants for her own interest. She mostly sat and listened, and gave me support to continue when things were not going well.

When prisoners had applied, a variety of checks took place: the education department checked whether the course would affect the prisoner's learning plans; security checked that the applicants were 'safe' to be in a room together and with me; and the prison checked that the participants were free to be in the classroom at the time specified. If the individual prisoner 'passed' all of these checks, they could join the class list.

Initially, across both halves, I had a class list of 18 prisoners, nine of whom went on to complete the course. A further three participants joined the course halfway through, having taken an interest from hearing about it around the prison. This meant that in total 12 prisoners completed the course (six from the mainstream and six from the VP population) and nine prisoners 'dropped out'. However, only one of these nine attended any of the sessions. The other eight dropped out between recruitment and the start of the course. Most of those who did not turn up when the course commenced had completed the pre-participation interviews with me (leading me to wonder whether it was something I had said).

On further investigation, I found that one had decided against participation due to concerns around the impact it might have on appealing his conviction, and another chose not to participate because he felt philosophy might involve learning things that went against his Islamic beliefs. Sadly, one of the prisoners in the VPU (generally an older population) had a heart attack and passed away between the interview and the start of the course. Another member of the VP population did not attend without providing an explanation. In the mainstream group, two decided they wanted to stay in cookery and two were sent to another prison. The final participant to 'drop out' attended three-and-a-half sessions, walking out of the fourth after an altercation with one of the other participants and my mishandling of the situation.

In addition to the 12 men who took part in the research and the course, several others attended a few philosophy sessions on an ad hoc basis. Within a couple of weeks of the course running, several men from the mainstream population enquired about attending the course. Due to low numbers, and having checked with security staff in education and the other participants in the group, I allowed several of them to sit in on a philosophy session. In total, 10 passed through the mainstream philosophy classroom over the course of delivery, with six engaging fully in the research. Although there was a core to the group from the outset, others came and went, which meant the classes varied in conversation and atmosphere from week to week.

The 12 participants who took part in the research are included in the following analysis. Despite the small number of participants, both of the classes were ethnically and religiously diverse. Ethnically, five described themselves as 'white', one as 'black', three as 'dual heritage/ mixed race', one as 'Asian' and two as 'other'. Three of the participants were Muslims, three had no faith or were atheists, four were Catholic/ Christian, one was Buddhist and one was 'spiritualist'.

Cultural diversity also ensured a range of views was represented in both halves of the prison. For example, one of the participants among the VPs was Eastern European, highly educated, and had been raised behind the 'Iron Curtain' under the Soviet Union. A second participant, although raised in England, also had Eastern European roots, while a third had mixed-race heritage and had spent much of his adolescence in the US. Several discussions were enriched by the breadth of the experiences of living in different cultures and societal structures.

In many ways, allowing an unknown researcher inside a maximum security prison to deliver philosophy classes was bold. The prison administration did not know me; I did not have a reputation with them, having never been in the prison prior to starting the research. During my time there, I engaged in conversation with the participants without a prison officer present. As per prison protocol, I locked myself into the room with them while the class was in session, and I was generally left to get on with it. I was specifically given a classroom directly opposite where the prison officers sat in the education department, so they could always see into the room. I carried my own keys, sat near the wall alarm and was obliged to attend a week of training that covered security issues, prison rules and so forth. After my course started, however, I was largely left to my own devices.

I have no doubt that such a level of access and the trust placed in my professionalism stemmed from the reputation of my supervisor. Alison Liebling is widely recognized as one of (if not *the*) leading prison scholar in the UK with an international reputation. Furthermore, my work directly followed on from her extensive piece of research around trust in the prison (discussed at various points throughout this book). It was her relationship with the prison, and their trust in her judgement, that allowed me the opportunity to be there. Access to such spaces was not given lightly, and the people with whom I worked were not easily reached.

The diversity in the group meant that a range of perspectives and ideas were represented in the discussion. However, due to the racial and religious tensions in the prison, as described, it also meant that underlying issues between participants proved both difficult to understand and complex to mediate. Although I consciously avoided raising issues of religion or God directly in my teaching materials, religious topics came up in the conversation as the participants drew on their own life experiences to make sense of the philosophical content.

In Full Sutton, I had a rare opportunity to bring together groups of people who, in other circumstances, may never have interacted, or may have even actively avoided each other. Each of the philosophy classes became a microcosm of the issues that prevailed in the wider prison community. In the early stages, raising issues around religion and politics was often the catalyst for aggressive contributions and personal comments. However, as the participants' understanding of my expectations and the purpose of the inquiry grew, discussions became more respectful and cooperative. This was hard work.

What happened in the Full Sutton philosophy classroom

'It was great last week miss, really enjoyable, one of the best days I have ever had in prison.' (Jonny, Full Sutton, mainstream, Week 1, 17 June 2015)

FIELDWORK NOTES
Full Sutton, mainstream, Week 1, 17 June 2015

I am clearly tired, frustrated and a little worn out after this session.

To understand how a philosophical conversation is relevant in a maximum security environment characterized by distrust, division and poor relationships, it is helpful to understand what happened in the two classes. The experience of teaching in Full Sutton's two distinct communities highlighted the importance of trust and relationships in the successful development of a community philosophy group. However, in the case of a philosophy group in a prison, those who are incarcerated do not choose to be part of the prison 'community'. Rather, they are there because they have to be – membership is enforced. So developing such principles takes on a different and particular meaning.

This was particularly true in Full Sutton. Unlike prisoners in Grendon, those in Full Sutton have rarely progressed in their sentences. To go to Grendon, prisoners have to demonstrate some willingness to cooperate with the regime before they can attend. Further, they can be de-selected and sent elsewhere if they contravene Grendon's rules. Full Sutton, on the other hand, was where people were sent if they were found to be causing problems in other prisons, or were deemed a security risk.

In fact, I met one of the participants from Grendon in Full Sutton, a young man on an indeterminate sentence who, after many years of struggling to make progress, had managed to get into Grendon. However, he had been bounced back to Full Sutton for some contravention of the rules. I recall that I spoke with him and discussed what had happened, but cannot recall the circumstances of his move. However, to go from a Category 'B' prison back up to a high security Category 'A' prison was certainly a step backwards in his prison journey.

Despite the different circumstances and the much more complex population I was now working with, my time in Grendon had set me up well. I had practised and developed my materials, and I had had time to work on my skills as a facilitator. I had become comfortable with wearing the belt, complete with tiny whistle, key chain and pocket for keys, and now had a broader understanding of how prisons work. I had also been in a range of other prisons as part of different projects, having run the two pilots for this project by this point (see Chapter 2). While prisons vary, the language of the prison system now made sense to me, and I was comfortable with the prison environment as a whole. All of this experience gave me confidence as I began my research in Full Sutton. However, I immediately found that both classes involved drawing on significantly more skills to encourage philosophical conversation.

Among the mainstream population, early discussions were characterized by aggressive outbursts, confrontational dialogue and boisterous conversation. Further, as the classes progressed, the nature of the challenge also changed. The mainstream class went from being personally challenging – with the participants testing my views and skills as a facilitator – to being intellectually challenging – with the participants questioning everyone's views and interrogating the subject at hand. Unlike the VPs, who took some encouragement to engage, the participants in the mainstream class were quick to offer an opinion and confident in participating. However, the conversation would take unpredictable, and sometimes confrontational, turns as the participants expressed an opinion without listening to or engaging with the statement made by the previous contributor. Some participants were prone to aggressive outbursts, passionately stating their case without taking heed of the nuanced arguments under discussion, and demonstrating a clear lack of respect for their fellow participants. Some seemed to enjoy 'needling' others, undermining their statements and fostering discord. Power relations and masculine 'fronts' flowed through the conversation, and I found myself in the middle of (or, more accurately, on the outside, trying to find a way into) a battle for authority and intellectual superiority that I scarcely understood.

Standing in stark contrast to the atmosphere in the mainstream philosophy class, VPs engaged in calm and respectful dialogue from the outset. The class had a positive, cooperative atmosphere, with the participants eager to comply and make a good impression. As with the mainstream prisoners, VPs engaged in the dialogue from the beginning. However, they required more specific encouragement to contribute. Initially, the participants answered the questions I posed, when directed at them, and looked to me to find the 'right' answer. As they developed an understanding of what was expected of them, and of the purpose of the discussions, they grew in confidence. The sessions became more lively and interactive, with the participants engaging with each other, challenging both their own and each other's contributions.

In Full Sutton, the majority of the participants had little experience of Socratic dialogue or collaborative conversation. As facilitator, I took an active role in managing the discussion and emphasizing the purpose and nature of philosophical dialogue. In doing this, I encouraged the participants to listen to each other and explain their point of view in an articulate and succinct manner. Whereas in Grendon group dialogue came quickly, and the community ethos we established reflected the wider prison community, in Full Sutton I had to work to establish a safe space for dialogue.

To do this, I drew on my experience as a teacher and returned to the pedagogical principles of philosophy education in which I had been trained. In such circumstances, the process of facilitation, along with the content of the material, became more relevant to the experience. For example, participants from both sides of the prison initially had difficulties in engaging with the broader philosophical questions the topics posed. The unpredictability of the conversation among the mainstream population in particular indicated inexperience in engaging in abstract thinking among some of the participants (or, perhaps it would be more accurate to say, that they were inexperienced in *articulating* their abstract thinking). To tackle these issues, I focused on the purpose of the underlying philosophical conversation. I tried not to be drawn into specific or unrelated arguments, which sometimes proved difficult when the participants expressed prejudiced and controversial views.

Week 2 involved a particularly tangential conversation that caused me to have a period of reflection on the ultimate purpose of the philosophy class. During the session in which the participants discussed Plato's *Republic* (see Chapter 3), I asked what it meant for a society to be 'just'. In response, they began to discuss the question of what a government can or cannot tell their people to do – a theme that was largely relevant to the question. However, within a couple of sentences, they had strayed into a debate around whether it would be acceptable for a parent to smoke in a car with a child – a topic some distance away from the original question around how society ought to be structured.

To address this, I reflected on my role as facilitator. When I got home, I returned to the fundamental principles of philosophical inquiry, going back over notes and texts I had previously learned from, and making clear in my own mind what was meant by *philosophical* conversation. Fundamentally, as I drove home, I asked myself, 'What exactly am I trying to achieve here?' I knew that I was not achieving philosophical discussion with either side of the prison, but this meant I had to work out, in clear and applicable terms, the specific attributes of collaborative, philosophical dialogue.

Ultimately, philosophical dialogue relates to interrogating the underlying principles of an argument. As articulated in Chapter 1, engaging in *active* philosophizing means examining our own perspectives and involves considering not simply *what* we think, but *why* and *how* we think. As such, I had to find a way to encourage the participants towards this way of thinking and responding to the stimuli. This meant recalling the method of Socratic questioning. I reconstructed my role so that it involved a constant, careful method of posing questions in an attempt to draw the participants back to the stimuli and develop *philosophical* conversation. I asked questions such as, 'What does that example tell us about our identities as people?' 'What does that tell us about how to decide if something is right or wrong?' 'How would a utilitarian respond to that example?' Drawing on the principles of Socratic dialogue, through systematic questioning, I gradually encouraged the participants to engage in philosophical conversation.

Battling towards community

Over the course of the 12 sessions, in both groups, we made clear (albeit slow) progress towards a safe, non-adversarial dialogue. VPs became livelier and engaged in the conversation, and we became more 'equal' as a group of people (as opposed to them always looking to me for answers and for approval of what they had said). With the mainstream group, in the first few weeks I often stayed outside their adversarial and complex conversations, desperately trying to encourage them to engage in cooperative and respectful dialogue. Even in the final two sessions there were moments of volatility, but gradually, the participants began to understand the process of philosophical dialogue, and of engaging in rational and calm discussions often involving controversial and personal topics.

In both groups, the inquiry served as a means of developing not only the dialogic skills of the participants, but also the relationships between them. In post-participation interviews, the men in both groups discussed their enjoyment of the social aspect of the course. For the VPs, this seemed to be more about inclusion and acceptance, while the mainstream group discussed issues around building bridges, learning "to be more tolerant" and to "exercise more patience" (Jason, Full Sutton, mainstream) with their fellow participants. They enjoyed hearing other people's views, recognized the need to be understanding of people whose views differed from their own and, importantly, the dialogue helped them recognize that not everybody thought the way they did. Part of this shared experience relied on the participants recognizing their own biases and intolerances.

Interviewer: 'So do you think you can apply what you've learned
                 to your everyday life?'
Martin, Full Sutton, mainstream: 'Yeah, of course.'
I: 'In what way?'

M: 'As in sometimes you've got to agree to disagree and keep it moving.'

I: '... Do you think that's something that you weren't able to do before the philosophy class?'

M: 'I could do it before, but now, like, sometimes it's good to do certain things that make you experience it a bit more often, 'cause then it gives you a bit of a reminder.'

Another said,

> 'I think I'm pragmatically learning through these sessions ... learning more tolerance. Because for me, [another member of the group] really pushed my tolerance level at times.... I have to broaden my horizon[s] even more, understand people more, why, who, how, feelings, all of them stuff, which I, kind of, closed off.' (Jason, Full Sutton, mainstream)

Over time, with emerging trust and developing relationships, the ethos of a community began to emerge. The participants gained a shared experience of philosophical exploration and began to have a stake in the group (recall Toch's description of a community discussed previously). The mainstream group made clear progress towards more positive relations and a community atmosphere. Although in Weeks 10 and 11 my fieldwork notes still include comments on their 'sniping', and the need to remind participants of respectful discussion, there were some clear indications of a sense of community.

Week 7 constituted a turning point, particularly among the mainstream participants. By this stage, the participants seemed to be laughing 'with' each other as opposed to 'at' each other, and contributions became less adversarial and more cooperative. Some clear evidence emerged that the participants were learning from each other and beginning to respect the insights of their fellow participants. One of the participants had entered the classroom and told me how he had written down the points of another participant because he had found them so interesting. He complimented his fellow participant, saying that he came up with some "really good ideas".

There was even a development of a shared terminology that only those in the class would understand. In an early session, during a particularly tangential contribution by a fellow participant, one of the participants said that "some questions are not worth considering ... [we] may as well ponder the existence of our own thumbs" (Toby, Full

Sutton, mainstream), pointing at his thumb as he spoke. In later sessions, this became shorthand for contributions or tangents that were deemed irrelevant to the core questions. Participants would comment, saying, "Well, it's the thumb argument again, isn't it" or just pointing at their thumb. When others saw this, they understood and it often brought the conversation back to the topic without my need to interject.

Through these shared interactions, the participants established the ethos of a community; the philosophy classroom provided a rare, safe haven where they had invested time and energy in a project with others. As the 'thumb argument' demonstrates, they had not only developed a shared terminology, but they had also begun to support the idea of philosophical conversation. By the end of the course, several of the participants had begun assisting with facilitation by respectfully encouraging others to précis their points and to stay on topic.

However, a true philosophical conversation involves *collaborative* exploration of an idea. This involves participants working together to develop knowledge and understanding of a particular concept. This is a key characteristic of the community aspect of philosophical inquiry and, although both groups progressed towards it, collaborative conversation was always somewhat lacking on both sides of the prison. Among the mainstream prisoners, although the discussions did become less egocentric, adversarial and personal, it was rare that they actually managed to work together to build understanding.[1] Among the VPs, there was more evidence of collaboration. They were more willing to listen to each other and, as the course progressed, they became more skilled at questioning each other's statements.

Fundamental to the development of philosophical dialogue that occurred within both groups was the participants' changing attitudes towards me. In the first few weeks, the participants on both sides of the prison challenged my background and my beliefs. Some struggled with my admission that I am a feminist, while others aggressively challenged my lack of belief in God. This was more vociferous among the mainstream prisoners:

> [While pointing a finger at my face and openly mocking me] 'You're an atheist? Ha. Believe me, when you are on that plane, and it comes down, believe me, you will pray to God, you *will* pray to God.'

---

[1] It should be noted that although this was achieved at points in Grendon, even in an established therapeutic community, this kind of sophisticated philosophical discussion was not achieved in every discussion.

Such challenges felt personal and challenged my fundamental sense of self. I had stated explicitly from the outset that I would not debate religion directly with the group and, although when relevant religious beliefs and teachings could become part of the philosophical discussion, I would not try to persuade them that there is no God if they would not attempt to persuade me of God's existence. In this, I was clear throughout. I responded to the challenge described above by saying "I won't question your beliefs if you won't question mine", highlighting the need for them to respect me for my lack of religious belief if they wished me to respect them for their faith. By maintaining this attitude, I demonstrated to the participants that my aim was not to get them to change their beliefs or opinions, but instead to explore different ideas as a means of understanding the range of beliefs and opinions more fully. Over time, they accepted this.

The style of the challenges differed between the groups. Where the VPs asked questions in a polite, enquiring manner, the mainstream prisoners could often be aggressive, accusatory and confrontational – although I, myself, did not always maintain a calm and professional manner. For example, when one of the participants aggressively argued that homosexuality and paedophilia were the same, I lost my cool and stated outright that such an opinion was unacceptable, bluntly disagreeing with the point of view and failing to model philosophical, non-adversarial dialogue. The participant, to his credit, seemed to notice he had touched a nerve, and backed down (we did return to the issue of homosexuality at a later date, and engaged in a much more thoughtful discussion that allowed them space to air their objections and those of us who disagreed to counter them). In general, I endeavoured to respond to these confrontations by being open and honest with my opinion, reminding the participants that this space was intended to be a safe environment.

In teaching the mainstream group, the first half of the course felt like a battle. The lack of cooperation from the participants as they pushed the pedagogy to its limits and tested my boundaries meant that I left the prison at the end of each day feeling exhausted and emotionally drained. My supervisor supported me emotionally throughout my time in Full Sutton (knowing the prison as well as she did), and the education staff in the prison were extremely supportive; they encouraged me not to worry about mistakes, and helped me understand the dynamics of a prison education classroom.

Despite this help, I found these first few weeks difficult. For the first time in delivering philosophy in prisons, I was not enjoying the experience, and fundamentally doubted my ability to establish a *community* of philosophical inquiry among mainstream prisoners. Self-doubt in the early weeks was compounded by my mishandling of a couple of situations that had undermined some individuals' egos, which were more fragile than I realized, and I had failed to take into account the particular environment in which I was working. In total, three people walked out of the mainstream sessions halfway through, with one choosing not to return. However, the turning point came in Week 7.

Progress ...

In my final few weeks in Full Sutton, I found myself on one of the mainstream wings, waiting to speak with one of the participants. During the 12 weeks of teaching, there was some evidence that the philosophy class had been discussed beyond the education department, and I was often approached by other men asking to take part, or inquiring as to whether I would run it again. On this occasion, I spoke with a Muslim man in his mid-30s. He was articulate and approachable in his manner, and knew several of the participants from the mainstream half of the prison. He spoke with me about what he had witnessed with those who attended the philosophy classes with me. He told me,

> 'They used to come back from philosophy separately, but now they come back together, like a unit. You have done something here.'

This observation from a non-participant prisoner, with no reason to give feedback, and who had approached me unsolicited, gave me a sense of hope. If what he had observed was true, perhaps there was some power in the process that could help overcome some of the wider issues within the prison. Is it possible that a space for dialogue and conversation could be truly transformative? Could philosophical conversation be a means to develop a more pro-social environment in a prison?

In reality, answering these questions goes beyond the scope of my research. I worked with 24 men across two prisons in England. This is no basis for demonstrating a measurable impact across the board. However, the small numbers and extended periods of time I spent with these men meant I gained an in-depth insight into some of the complexities of living in prison and some of the ways philosophy can encourage growth.

In particular, understanding the interactions within the philosophy classroom proved challenging. Consequently, during my time in Full Sutton, I occasionally sought the advice of the chaplaincy and teachers in the prison. I also discussed my experience at length with my supervisor and returned to the prison sociology literature, which could now be read in light of personal experience. Rather than having a *theoretical* understanding of how prison culture encourages hyper-masculine fronts and aggressive macho culture (and having seen it only in Louis Theroux documentaries and fictional TV programmes), I had now seen it first-hand. Not only that, I had sat in the middle of it, attempting to encourage a group of men – including some hyper-masculine, macho characters, alongside some of the more pious, calm and careful prisoners – to sit in a circle and discuss Kant's categorical imperative and Plato's notion of philosopher kings in a calm and sensible manner. There were moments of surrealism in this situation where, if I thought too much about who these men had been or what they had done, I would wonder what I thought I was trying to do.

In the midst of these complex hierarchies of power and fragile but well defended egos, I had to develop some form of collaborative working relationship with and among the participants. This began with, and developed through, the establishment of trust between us.

8

Finding Trust and
Developing Relationships

On a June day in HMP Full Sutton, I returned from my tea break to the classroom. There were no windows in the room, the carpet was a dark grey, and the classroom was lined with ancient computers, rarely used. A small group of tables had been moved into the centre of the room to form a sort of circle, and six men from the VPU were sat at the desks, waiting for my return.

Before the tea break, we had discussed Kant's categorical imperative. We discussed compassion, duty and moral choice. The conversation was thoughtful, and the participants had engaged in polite conversation. They had also been for a tea break, usually in another classroom, where they could mingle with others from the VPU who were attending education that day.

As I entered, they fell silent and looked at me nervously. This was my third week working with these men and we had developed a gentle rapport. Prior to the tea break, they had engaged in the conversation with ease, having relaxed now that they understood what was expected in the philosophy classroom. However, as is often the way with this particular population, they were not always forthcoming in their opinions, and I could tell that they wanted to ask me something.

"What?" I ask, "Come on, what is it? What do you want to ask me?"

They were shifting in their seats and glancing at one another conspiratorially. Eventually, one piped up, "Er, Miss, are you a ... *feminist*!?!" The word was spoken with a sort of awe (tinged with disapproval), as though a feminist was some kind of rare creature that they had never come across before.

I sighed inwardly, and smiled to myself. Carefully, I responded.

"Well, I think the word 'feminist' can take on a range of meanings, but on the whole, yes, I would be happy to give myself that label."

Another retorted, "But, doesn't that mean you *hate* men Miss!?"

This time, I sighed outwardly. I am pretty sure I failed to prevent myself from rolling my eyes. Calmly, and with patience, I explained that it did not mean that I hated men, but instead, that I wanted there to be equality between men and women. They pressed me, arguing that if it was about equality, "Wouldn't that mean you are a 'humanist', not a feminist?"

The conversation continued for some minutes. They seemed to enjoy the opportunity to ask a woman about feminism, reminding me of a conversation I had had with the men in HMP Grendon who wanted to hear my views on abortion. The men in Grendon deferred, rightly so, to my experience as a woman, but did not hold back, pushing their views to hear my responses. On this occasion, some of the participants felt that feminism had "gone too far" and that "women had everything" while "men were losing". They listened, and appreciated my perspective as I offered some responses to their points.

One of the participants, Dave, surprised me with his insightful contribution to the discussion. In attempting to assist me, he said, "I tried to explain to them, miss, the ideas of feminism, that it's not like that." He even went as far as recommending a journalist for me to read who, he said, "had some good ideas around this."

Afterwards, I wrote the following in my fieldwork notes:

FIELDWORK NOTES
Full Sutton, VPU, Session 3, 30 June 2015

It is difficult to assess whether this view of women and feminism is common specifically among sex offenders or just more generally. It is also interesting that Dave seemed to be the most clued up about feminism ... [as] he is the one in for a series of sexual offences against women across decades. It is interesting considering the feminist narrative about sexual violence against women in the world that the one in my class who is most understanding of women's rights and the feminist movement is the one who would come under that banner. I wonder if these two things are linked or whether this is a coincidence? I wonder if work he has done elsewhere in the prison (other courses perhaps?) has helped him try to understand the role of women and redevelop his view of them....

I might try to discuss this with him at a later date. Too soon right now – need to build up the trust first.

Developing trust-relationships

This chapter explores issues of trust directly. I begin with the trust-relationships that emerged within the philosophy classroom. I also consider the definition of trust, and provide some insight into what these trust-relationships looked like, and how they developed. To explore the issue of trust and relationships, I draw primarily on Liebling's definition. She describes it as a 'reliance on honesty, reliability, and good sense of a person; the level of responsibility or confidence invested in and experienced by individuals' (Liebling, assisted by Arnold, 2004, p 248).

In the philosophy classroom, three types of 'trust-relationship' became apparent: trust by the prisoner-participants in me and in my motivations; my trust of the prisoner-participants; and trust between the prisoner-participants.

Trust, and the lack of it, underpins social relationships in prisons. Prison researchers have often described the lives of prisoners as being in a constant state of suspicion and distrust (see, in particular, Toch, 1977). Working in Full Sutton, it became apparent that understanding wider issues of trust and relationships in high security prisons would be central to the findings of the research. 'Trust' and 'relationships' emerged as key themes from the interview data, which (alongside openness and wellbeing) formed the basis of the theoretical framework I used to interpret the data.

Working in Full Sutton was challenging and it took significant perseverance to, eventually, develop a space for philosophical conversation. However, it was in analysing my data (fieldwork notes and interview transcripts) some months later that the story of emerging trust and developing relationships transpired. While in the prison, I was too immersed in the environment, too focused on making it 'work', to notice what was happing.

Throughout delivery of the course, there were clear indications that teaching philosophy was believed to have an ulterior motive: to undermine religious teachings in the prison (particularly for Muslims, but there was also some evidence of other religions having these concerns); to gather information and provide information to security; or to push some form of feminist or other political agenda. The participants informed me that some prisoners had declined to apply because they were concerned about philosophy being 'anti-religion' and 'pagan', or that it was really a 'ruse' to establish an accredited course relevant to conditions and parole. Teaching philosophy constituted a suspicious move in the context of the prison.

Issues of trust in my motivations, and in me, although present in both populations, were particularly acute among the VP population. They seemed to be concerned about my judgement of them as people (exemplified by the fact that some did not wish to state their index offences, unlike those not convicted for sexual offences). For the first few weeks, the VPs maintained a guarded attitude towards the discussions that belied their uncertainty regarding my place in the prison and my motives in the course. As a 30-year-old, smartly dressed female in the prison, I was easily mistaken for a prison psychologist (a group particularly distrusted in the prison environment) and the participants, particularly the VPs, seemed to suspect that I might be passing on information to the governor or other areas of the prison.

Prison security departments are acutely concerned with issues of 'risk'. A recent article by Jason Warr (2020) articulates the impact this has on the individual. He argues that prisoners have to constantly manage their prison identities that are imposed on them by the bureaucratic process of the prison. All prisoners are categorized according to their risk ('A' being the highest, 'D' the lowest), and part of their progress in the prison estate involves working their way down the risk categories. This is a complex, frustrating and difficult process (see Liebling and Williams, 2017). Early on, in some of the feedback forms, the participants would make comments such as, "This has really helped me reflect on my offence and my future" (Bruce, Full Sutton, VPU), as though I had some role in prison and that their comments might form part of some record relevant to their sentences.

Further to this, one participant pulled out of the programme because he was concerned that he would learn something that would be "contrary to his religious beliefs". A possible explanation for this (apparently not uncommon) attitude from Muslim prisoners only came during my feedback session some months after delivery of the course. One Muslim participant explained that his branch of Islam taught that philosophers between the 6th and 11th centuries had "taken Muslims away from the teachings of the Prophet" and were therefore not to be trusted. The truth of this assertion is not relevant here. What is relevant is that within the prison, Muslim prisoners were particularly uncomfortable with the *idea* of philosophy. Despite these early concerns, he and two fellow Muslims successfully completed the course and engaged enthusiastically in the conversation, with several others coming in for odd sessions on an ad hoc basis. 'Background' perceptions of philosophy and its purpose, circulating in some high security prison circles, contributed to the prisoners' suspicions of me and my motives.

It was not until the 11th week that I realized that the required level of trust worked in both directions. In Grendon, because the class was comfortable in the dialogic environment and used to dealing with controversial topics in a community setting, I had confidence in their ability to discuss sensitive topics. Due to the difficulties in creating a calm and controlled dialogue among the mainstream prisoners in Full Sutton, I had been quite sure that I would not discuss a topic such as human rights with this group of participants.[1] However, in Week 10, the class had engaged in an excellent dialogue around the role and purpose of art that had been deep, exploratory, considered and respectful. After this discussion, I decided that I could trust these participants to handle a potentially controversial discussion around rights. On reflection, it seemed that I had not only earned their trust, but they, too, had earned mine.

The issues of trust and respect underpinning the mainstream prisoners' discussions related to the complex social world within the prison. The distrust of each other went far deeper than the suspicion that is part of the 'normal' prisoner experience. Issues among the mainstream prisoners related to the complex position of being a Muslim in British society, and the issues that circulate around being Muslim in prison (see Powis et al, 2019). The issue of trust among the mainstream population can be tracked through the fieldwork notes that, on reflection post-delivery, provided a clear story of the development of trust over the period of the classes.

Week 9 represented a defining moment in relations with mainstream prisoners. The session focused on identity, with an aim of building on understanding of Hume's 'bundle theory of the self'. I started the session by asking the participants to complete a 'Diamond Nine' task. This involved the participants being given nine diamond-shaped pieces of paper, six of which had something already entered on them

---

[1] In my experience, discussing human rights with prisoners often becomes heated. This is perhaps because their rights have been stripped from them by the state and, within prisons, prisoners often have to argue for what they perceive to be their rights within the establishment. However, I did not investigate reasons for this formally.

– culture, upbringing, genetics biology/DNA, social environment, experiences, memories – and three left blank to allow the participants to add their own contributions. The participants were asked to consider what factors they felt had been most important in making them who they were today, and to rank them in a diamond shape. This meant they had to choose one for the top, two for the second row, three for the third and then two and one again for the least important factors. This is a common teaching tool, used to encourage learners to consider their own point of view, and to engage in a dialogue to justify their positioning of different pieces of the 'Diamond Nine'. In both Grendon and the VP group in Full Sutton, this task had been very successful, with the participants quickly going about the task with enthusiasm. In fact, among the VPs, this allowed for an extremely personal session. Each participant took time to explain their rankings, and seemed to use it as a time to explain who they were, and to tell the group a little about their background.

However, the mainstream prisoners in Full Sutton were immediately suspicious of the task. They said that it was like "something you'd do in psychology", and they seemed uncomfortable discussing personal issues with each other. I explained the purpose of the exercise, reiterating my own motivations and background to reassure them that this was not an exercise intended to psychoanalyse or psychologize their way of thinking. After some reassurance, they agreed to take part in the task, and the dialogue that ensued was engaging and positive.

On reflection, this incident represented an interesting moment. On the one hand, it demonstrated the participants' scepticism and wariness about engaging in philosophical discussion. On the other, it demonstrated the progress we had made as a community in developing a level of trust in the process and purpose of the class. Whether they would have agreed to take part in the 'Diamond Nine' exercise in an earlier session cannot be known, but the fact that they did can be taken as an indication of trust having developed.

In general, then, my experience of the course at Full Sutton was strongly underpinned by this suspicion of me, and of my motivations. On the one hand, for the VPs it was concern about being judged and ostracized. On the other, for the mainstream prisoners, it was much more closely entangled with the religious narrative within the prison. However, these issues also relate to broad issues of trust and the difficulties of developing relationships that allow for self-expression in the prison environment.

Over time, relationships changed and the participants in both groups seemed to relax and trust the process. For the VPs, this happened gradually. However, there was a specific turning point with the mainstream half of the prison. In Week 6, I still thought it would not be possible to get philosophical dialogue going properly. However, in Week 7, things changed.

Changing relations

FIELDWORK NOTES
Full Sutton, mainstream, Session 6, 22 July 2015

This was a very draining session for me and ... I am tired. The "attacking" of myself from [the participants] really bothered me and it was hard to shake off that day.

FIELDWORK NOTES
Full Sutton, mainstream, Session 7, 29 July 2015

This was a really nice session. For the first hour and half everyone did really well at having a really positive conversation.

In the seventh week of teaching at Full Sutton, I chose to cover a different topic to the one I taught in the same week in Grendon. In the last few weeks of teaching at Grendon, we covered topics such as free speech, human rights and the famous trolley problem.[2] However, I was not yet comfortable covering such complex and potentially personal topics with these participants. Instead, I chose to look at Socrates, asking the participants to consider questions of 'the good life'.

---

[2] The trolley problem has a range of variations, but the most famous involves asking someone whether they would 'pull the lever' on a train (or trolley, as they say in the US) that is heading down the track and would certainly kill five people. If you pulled a lever, it would change course and, instead, kill only one person.

Socrates and 'the good life' (Week 7, Stage 1)

Unlike the philosophers before him, Socrates was primarily concerned with how we *ought* to live. (As such, he is often considered to be the father of the branch of philosophy known as 'ethics'.)

The greatest good is to reason every day about human excellence.

He believed that reason, when properly cultivated, will make us virtuous and happy, that once we truly know what is good we will do it, that anyone who acts wrongly does so through ignorance. His supporting argument is as follows:

We are all hedonists. That is, everything we do is prompted by the desire to experience pleasure or to avoid pain. This means that all this talk of "good" and "bad" ultimately boils down to considerations of pleasure and pain. Whatever leads to pleasure we call "good" and whatever leads to pain we call "bad".

Clearly, no one knowingly chooses pain over pleasure. But this is equivalent to saying that no one knowingly chooses bad over good. Therefore, anyone who chooses the bad in preference to the good must do so in error: because he mistakes it for the good.

The first stage of this session asked the participants to discuss knowledge and wisdom, how to know how to act and what it means for something to be 'just'. Both sides of the prison discussed the relevance of reason and logic, the need to understand definitions and underlying principles. Following on from this, in coming to discuss 'the good life', knowing how to live, both halves of the prison responded by engaging in meaningful discussion. They discussed the importance of reason, considered the role of pleasure and pain, moved smoothly on to conversations around knowing the 'right' way to behave, the relevance of introspection and your environment to these choices, and considered the meaning of happiness.

Although the discussion in the mainstream group still involved tangents, the participants engaged more fully with the content. By Week 7, my self-doubt had disappeared and, although there were still people failing to listen to each other and being disrespectful in their contributions, the underlying atmosphere had changed. The classes became much more manageable and enjoyable. The participants seemed to gain a level of respect for each other, and me, and comments and personal attacks disappeared. By Week 11, I was feeling 'supported' by the participants in my endeavours to maintain a philosophical atmosphere, and the final two weeks involved some excellent philosophical conversation. I felt at the time (and still do) that the participants from the mainstream group had somehow tested me and, without anyone explicitly saying anything, I had finally 'passed'. They relaxed, taking the classes for what they were meant to be – a place to engage in open, philosophical conversation. The negativity had gone, and the lack of trust in me, the process, or each other, dissipated.

Among the VPs there was also evidence of changing relations. Although always polite and respectful towards me, they were guarded in their opinion, and there were indications that they, too, were suspicious of my motives. However, particularly after my open attitude towards sharing my own views and opinions around feminism, they relaxed in my presence. Dialogue became open and often personal. In Week 9, we had a clear indication that we had developed a safe space in which the participants felt comfortable in airing their views. One of the participants openly discussed how uncomfortable he was with homosexuality, despite the rest of the group clearly being accepting of it (another contrast to the mainstream group). He knew we would all disagree with his point of view, but proceeded to explain his standpoint and why he felt the way he did. The group accepted this view without judgement, and discussed with him the reasons why they disagreed. A safe, comradely conversation ensued, free of accusation or insult, instead characterized by reflective input and careful choice of language.

For both groups, the philosophy classroom had evolved to provide a space to develop a shared interest. In Week 1, barely any philosophical conversation occurred, the participants did not engage in collaborative explorations of ideas (the mainstream group argued with each other, the VPs sought approval from me), and underlying tensions of the wider prison affected the atmosphere of the philosophy classroom. By the end, there was a sense of shared endeavour and, through perseverance, a community of philosophical inquiry had begun to emerge.

Although work with the mainstream group was particularly difficult, the battle (and at times it felt like a battle) that I had to develop philosophical inquiry meant more to me than the work with any of the other groups. As a group, we had overcome the complex characteristics of the participants, the division between some of the men, and had discussed difficult and sometimes controversial philosophical ideas. Although the mainstream group was made up of two Muslim TACT prisoners, an aggressive anti-religious individual, a Muslim convert, a Catholic and a 'spiritualist' career criminal, plus me – a liberal, left-wing, feminist, pro-LGBT, pro-choice, non-religious female – we eventually found some common ground. The philosophy classroom provided the space to achieve this, despite the prevailing atmosphere in the prison.

Trust and hierarchy

To understand trust and relationships, we also need a better understanding of the complex hierarchies and strained relationships that occur within maximum security prisons. I therefore return to the literature and provide a more in-depth discussion of prison sociology. This literature proved invaluable. It helped to articulate the issues I observed in the philosophy classroom and the particular way trust and distrust operates around the Muslim population and the VP population.

Early studies of prisoners and prisons highlight the role of relationships and prison culture in shaping prisoner experience. Clemmer's (1958) *The Prison Community* introduced the term 'prisonization' to refer to the individual becoming 'assimilated' to prison culture. Sykes' (1958) *The Society of Captives* outlined the 'inmate code', implying that prisoners form a cohesive group with a sense of solidarity. Other titles such as Toch's *Living in Prison* (1977) and, more recently, Crewe's (2009) *The Prisoner Society: Power, Adaptation, and Social Life in an English Prison* focus on prisons as a place in which people live, socialize, develop and change over time.

Developing and maintaining relationships in prison is complex. In Chapter 3, I highlighted the issue of social isolation in prisons, drawing, in particular, on Cohen and Taylor's study of life in Durham's E wing. Crewe's study (2009), a follow-up from Sykes' work (albeit in a Category 'C' rather than a high security prison), demonstrated that social relations are often a defence against loneliness and lack of safety, with prisoners reporting that they only made one or two 'proper friends' during their time in prison. The participants in Full Sutton confirmed this when I asked whether there was anyone in the prison they could trust. One participant responded with a trace of incredulity in his voice, "What, you mean prisoners I trust? No." The population turnover within a prison – although less rapid in high security prisons – means that friendships are constantly having to be renegotiated.

The community structure of Grendon, with its emphasis on open dialogue and shared responsibility, meant that prisoners could share, discuss and resolve grievances. The participants lived in wings of small communities of around 40 men, all of whom were part of a shared project of personal exploration. They knew each other intimately as they were expected to speak openly about their index offence, their childhood and their behaviours. In Grendon, because of this, there was no 'fear of the unknown', no concern that you might have befriended the wrong person because his crimes meant he should be ostracized and excluded. Full Sutton, a much larger prison, with no official forum for dialogue, and no regular meetings to air grievances and discuss concerns, felt like a more anonymous environment, with prisoners left to navigate the prison social system on their own. I do not mean to imply here that the residents of Grendon did not have concerns around personal safety; rather that such feelings were less prevalent in Grendon than in Full Sutton.

Prisons are often characterized as places of intimidation and extortion. Since 2010, I have spent time in a variety of male prisons where macho-culture presides, swagger and control of the informal economy carry currency, and prisoners adopt a hyper-masculine 'front' as a means of survival (Jewkes, 2005a). In entering prison, prisoners must learn to navigate the complex social relations within it, a place where there is a 'right' way to behave (Liebling, assisted by Arnold, 2004), and getting it wrong can lead to social exclusion, suspicion and extortion.

Tied up with notions of masculinity, solidarity, physical prowess and reputation, prison communities traditionally revolve around hierarchies of power and influence related to status, control (for example, of the informal economy) and gang allegiances. Sex offences and burglary ('don't rob from your own') carry a level of shame, while bank robbery (requiring courage and involving 'sticking it to the man') afforded respect (Crewe, 2009). Regardless of index offence, 'grasses' and 'pad thieves' are also lower down in the prisoner hierarchy, along with men who struggle with their incarceration. This includes the 'physically defenceless', those 'lacking in emotional fortitude', heroin users and self-harmers (Crewe, 2009, p 251).

Within the vulnerable populations, the 'machismo' and 'banter' prevalent in the mainstream population were not present. In their article on the moral community of sex offenders, Ievins and Crewe (2015) state that there was no struggle for power or hyper-masculinity, no 'gangster' culture, fewer drugs, and closer friendships. In Sparks, Bottoms and Hay's (1996) seminal study, prisoners in the VPU at

HMP Albany were seen as 'more compliant' than the mainstream prisoners, resulting in a 'quieter, less pressurized, less dangerous, and less confrontational mode of working' (1996, p 209). Although the prisoners still raised issues around a lack of trust in the officers (they claimed that some staff clearly disliked sex offenders in general), staff could, in some cases, build better interpersonal relationships with them, and in others, bully them. In contrast, at the time of the Sparks et al study, the people convicted of sexual offences in HMP Long Lartin were mixed in with the mainstream population. The researchers stated that the mainstream population 'tolerated' these prisoners in exchange for the more liberal regime the prison ran, but that it remained unacceptable to be friends with them.

When held on 'normal' location, among the mainstream prisoners, people convicted of sexual offences are shunned and suffer verbal abuse and physical intimidation (Sparks et al, 1996). They are usually separated for their own protection, and although there was no discernible hierarchy within the VPU at Full Sutton, their designation as 'vulnerable prisoners' signifies the 'rank' of this population in the wider prisoner community.

The feeling of social rejection is particularly acute for sex offenders. They are rejected and ostracized from society more vehemently by the wider society as well as by the prison community, and often have little to no contact with family and friends on the outside (Ievins and Crewe, 2015). Unlike other offences, being accused and convicted of a sexual offence carries with it a high level of moral condemnation. People convicted of sexual offences, once incarcerated, often find themselves without any contact with those in the outside world, and without friends on the inside.

My experience of teaching the VP population confirms much of what has been said here. The atmosphere surrounding the prisoners in the VP community was starkly different to that which prevailed among the mainstream population; the VPs were quiet, calm, polite and compliant. Issues of trust and stigmatization still permeated our discourse but, in general, it was easier to manage the groups and form a positive working relationship.

Reflecting the prisons literature, interactions within the mainstream half of the prison were characterized by bravado, one-upmanship and competition (see Crewe, 2009, for example). In particular, mainstream participants came from different sociodemographic groups in the prison and some of the more heated interactions, I was later informed by one of the participants, related to specific 'power plays' between prisoners. It was evident from the outset that these men did not respect each other, and that I would have to earn their respect and trust, as I feel I eventually did, if I was going to attempt to maintain order in the classroom.

Liebling et al's trust project (2016) provides a potential explanation for the lack of hierarchy in Grendon and the VPU in Full Sutton. They found that more cooperative environments allowed for respectful negotiation of acceptable behaviours. Grendon's cooperative structure allowed prisoners to have a sense of ownership and responsibility over their community. Hierarchies and power-seeking become unnecessary, as prisoners have a voice in their community and a sense of control over their environment. However, in the VPU at Full Sutton, the cooperative culture related more to the passivity and compliant nature of the vulnerable population than to the cultivation of a sense of community in the prison.

In stark contrast, among the Full Sutton mainstream population, hierarchies and masculine identities were evident. Men marched down the corridor with over-developed muscles, projecting authority, and sometimes proudly displaying their faith identities through their clothing and general appearance. How these hierarchies worked, who was on top and how power was wielded was hidden in the complexities of social encounters. The only real divide of which I was aware – and that became specifically relevant to this research project – was the divide I have referred to between Muslims and non-Muslims.

Muslim prisoners, as we have seen, are subject to particularly acute levels of distrust from the establishment's staff and, as in wider society, are often incorrectly grouped together as though they are one homogenous group. In recent years, the need to include the perspective of Muslim prisoners in research has become apparent due to the changing nature of the prison population. In 2011, only 4 per cent of the prison population identified as Muslim. By 2013, this proportion had risen to 13 per cent (House of Commons Library, 2013), leading to a new interest in Muslim prisoners within public and political discourse. In-prison conversion to Islam is a factor in the rising proportion of Muslim prisoners, the reaction to which has been described as a 'moral panic' (Spalek and El-Hassam, 2007), reflecting a significant amount of 'scaremongering' in the British popular press around the role of Islam in prison 'gang' culture.

Descriptions of the characteristics of the Muslim group in HMP Whitemoor by Liebling et al (2011) resonate closely with my own experience in Full Sutton. The authors argue that, although not ostensibly a 'gang' in the traditional sense, some pressures within the Muslim group did bear some 'gang-like' qualities. In Whitemoor, prisoners displayed their Islamic identity as a symbol of power, and the feeling among prisoners was that the Muslims should be joined in order to enjoy a 'quiet life' in prison.

I had several conversations with staff in Full Sutton around the issue of pressured or forced conversions. There seemed to be an understanding that some prisoners were converting to the faith due to bullying and threats of violence if they did not. I had some dealings with in-prison converts, some of whom discussed how other Muslims had told them they had to be either "with us or with them" – a "proper" Muslim or not – and that, as a result, they had begun to re-establish their faith.

In Whitemoor, according to Liebling et al, there was an emphasis in the regime on 'threats posed by terrorist risk, extremism and radicalisation' (2011, p 124), leading to staff fearing 'conditioning and manipulation' (2011, p 30). Prisoners in Whitemoor did not 'trust the system' (risk assessments and procedures for progression) and became disengaged and frustrated. The authors conclude that 'explanations for the low levels of trust by prisoners included an increasing social and cultural distance between staff and prisoners' (2011, p 124). They go on to say:

> ... ethnicity was a "barrier to trust"; [other factors included] information sharing, report writing and the lack of confidentiality in the prison (prisoners felt "misrepresented" on file); a (growing) prisoner culture of disengagement from staff; with negative peer perceptions of extended contact ("screw-boy"); experiences of inconsistency in the rules/ regime/staff attitudes and friendliness; the job description of an officer, which denotes that in some circumstances a good relationship is irrelevant and is over-ridden by security; and prisoners witnessing staff breaking the rules (for example, taking short cuts) or acts of "unprofessionalism".... (Liebling et al, 2011, pp 124–5)

Liebling et al's research revealed that the rise in the Muslim population in Whitemoor led to a feeling that 'they' (the Muslims) had too much power and influence, and that others (for example, white Catholics) needed to muster support to counter this power relationship. Their research highlights the perception among non-Muslim prisoners that the Muslim group were in some way a unified collective. In reality, Liebling et al (2011) found them to be a fragmented community. However, the authors also point out that some among the Muslim community behaved somewhat like a gang, using violence and coercion to achieve their ends, an observation borne out by the more recent Ministry of Justice study discussed earlier (Powis et al, 2019).

Importantly, however, Liebling et al's study states that the prison authorities were unable to distinguish between the *supportive* Muslim brotherhood and the *suppressive* Muslim gang. Their Whitemoor study found evidence that faith was a proxy for power among Muslim prisoners in this climate; they watched each other, commenting when another individual was not being 'faithful enough'. The authors state that '... faith following was becoming the organizing principle around which violence was "justified" within the prisoner community' (2011, p 101).

Other high security prisons have been found to have less of this deep distrust and conflict and more fluid religious identities (see Liebling et al, 2016). The truth of the issues of forced conversion, radicalization and terrorist ideologies in prison is complex, and confounded by narratives of fear as well as the prevailing political climate. What was relevant to this study was how the low levels of trust and high levels of suspicion around Islam, conversion and TACT prisoners affected the dialogue, atmosphere and character of the prisoner society. The view of Islam by non-Muslim prisoners and staff, and the display of faith identities as a symbol of power by Muslims in Full Sutton, served to create a feeling of 'us and them', and a divisive atmosphere in the prison. Fundamentally, these concerns led to a climate of suspicion and distrust that, arguably, focused most powerfully on the Muslim population.

Despite the fact that only five Muslim prisoners took part in my research, the role of faith in prisons formed a critical part of the understanding of the relevance of philosophy in prisons. The descriptions in the Whitemoor study of the relationships among prisoners, and between staff and prisoners, resonated deeply. A key distinction was that, during my time in Full Sutton, there was an emphasis from the senior leadership team on bringing about a 'change in culture'. Although I personally observed staff–prisoner relationships to be distant and watchful, in speaking to staff they often had a positive attitude towards the prisoners.

There was one incident that was an exception where a staff member pointed out someone I had been talking to and referred to him as a "woman beater", saying something along the lines of "We don't like that type around here", a comment that shocked me considering I was in a high security prison. However, this attitude seemed out of step with the wider prison. Towards the end of my research, staff and prisoners in one wing had begun to set up a 'staff–prisoner relationship committee', which was central to the launch of a 'rehabilitative culture' in Full Sutton. Where staff–prisoner relationships at Whitemoor were arguably at a low trust point at the time of Liebling et al's study, staff–prisoner relationships at Full Sutton seemed to be at a turning point during my research, in part as a result of the findings of the trust project led by Liebling.

Lack of trust was not, however, only relevant to the Muslim prisoners. Sparks et al (1996) noted the lack of trust many prisoners have in prison regimes, and described the suspicion prisoners felt towards the establishment's motivations. This echoed my experience of Full Sutton and, to a lesser extent, at Grendon. The participants in the philosophy class, particularly among the VPs, would discuss the prison staff and management as a collective with specific motivations and untrustworthy actions. They would discuss their files and their disappointment and anger when discovering what staff had written about them. Such occurrences served to undermine relationships and trust between prisoners and staff.

The participants in my philosophy class used such examples to explain why they had to be constantly careful of what they said and how something, seemingly innocuous, could be perceived. One of the more well-known participants in my class had been the subject of several TV documentaries that showed staff discussing him when he was not present. What he heard them say, and the way they interpreted his actions and motivations, was a source of shock to him, and he stated "Well, if that's what they think, then fuck 'em, I'll do my own thing." The culture of distrust could be highly damaging.

Cultivating a safe space

Trust is a key aspect of fostering identity, personal development and friendship. People have to feel safe, and have a level of trust in their environment, if they are to be themselves. Trust is rare in prison, and is difficult to cultivate when the only thing known for certain about a person is that they are convicted of an offence (Ievins and Crewe, 2015). Without trust, sharing of personal information is seen as 'risky', with socializing being suspicious (Sparks et al, 1996; Liebling and Arnold, 2012). In Whitemoor, relationships between prisoners were described as being underpinned by fear, with prisoners acutely aware of certain allegiances hindering progress (Liebling et al, 2011). These themes became most prevalent in Full Sutton due to the lack of trust in that environment, whereas in Grendon, the community ethos meant that establishing trust and relationships was relatively straightforward. However, the culture of a prison often involves complex power structures, negotiations of relationships and high levels of distrust.

Overall, the distrustful and divisive atmosphere in Full Sutton provided an interesting and informative context in which to explore the role of philosophy in developing a community. It became apparent that achieving a community of philosophical inquiry meant developing positive relationships, respect and trust among participants, and also, with me. With the benefit of hindsight, and comprehensive and detailed fieldwork notes, the progression made by the participants became clear. The experience provided me with an opportunity for an in-depth exploration of the way in which philosophy can prevail, even in the face of difficult circumstances.

The issue of trust did not become apparent until I worked in Full Sutton. In hindsight (and a little speculatively), the reason for this may be that Grendon's therapeutic communities had their existing mechanisms for establishing, developing and maintaining trust. As such, because trust already existed in Grendon, I did not have to work to establish it within the philosophy classroom. In Full Sutton, by way of a clear contrast, the divided and distrustful atmosphere, both within the community of prisoners and in the interactions between prisoners and uniformed staff, meant I had to work to build trust.

Establishing trust in the course and its purpose could only be achieved over time. Through open, non–judgemental and fair treatment, the participants came to realize that I had no ulterior motive; I did not wish to change their opinions or persuade them away from their religion, and took no interest in their past deviance or offending activities.

The pedagogy of the philosophy course allowed me to demonstrate that, as a teacher, my aim was to encourage critical and open conversation. I introduced conversational topics through the work of specific philosophers, some of whom I agreed with, while others went profoundly against my own views of the world. I demonstrated that my aim was to introduce a range of ideas and thinkers (not simply those that fitted with my own biased world view), and, by being clear about my standpoint on each philosopher, I modelled my expectations of open, non–judgemental dialogue.

Confirming that I did not wish to persuade them to my way of thinking did not mean I shied away from what I perceived to be challenging, unpalatable or controversial worldviews. Furthermore, by challenging their views I demonstrated to the participants that they could equally challenge mine. On the whole, I received their challenges calmly, responding openly and honestly and admitting when (to their great delight) one of them managed to 'stump' me with an insightful riposte to my contribution. By being open, honest and consistent in my views of the world, as well as having the humility to admit when a participant's contribution had effectively challenged my own, the participants developed trust in me.

9

Personal Self-Exploration

'Seriously, from … Monday night, there was anticipation of the class. Tuesday morning, up until 12 o'clock, you were outside the prison, because you were doing something that was … it's very, very seldom that you get time to be able to think on a higher level, if that makes sense.' (Keith, Full Sutton, VPU)

> ### The Stoics (Week 8, Stage 1)
>
> Today, 'to be philosophical' about something, means learning to accept what you cannot change.
>
> This comes from the philosophy of the Stoics. The founder of Stoicism is Zeno of Citium (ca 334–262 BC) who said that we should only worry about the things we have control over and not get worked up about anything else. Stoics maintained that we are responsible for what we feel and think, and we should control our emotional responses.
>
> For example, Cicero, another well-known Stoic, said that we should not worry about old age but rather accept it as a natural process. Rather than worrying about being able to do less, we should recognize that because older people are more experienced, any work they do is more effective. Therefore, they are able to do less to achieve the same results.
>
> The idea is that we should recognize that it is not growing older that is the problem, but our attitudes towards growing older. If we control our emotions, we can have an optimistic view of old age.

In each of the four groups, at least one member of the group found Stoicism appealing. Those who did would align themselves with Stoic philosophy, claiming that this was how they had managed themselves during their sentence. One participant went as far as saying that "Stoics will be the happiest people you meet" (Peter, Full Sutton, mainstream).

However, many took issue with the perspective, noting, in particular, that the philosophy seemed quite cold. One person said, "Is it not a good thing to cry behind my cell door?" (Paul, Full Sutton, VPU), with another saying that, prior to coming to Grendon, he would never cry "in front of me missus" (Charlie). Having spent time in Grendon, he now would.

The Stoics perspective provided opportunities to discuss some important aspects of expressing emotions while in prison. In several of the discussions, we examined the difference between suppressing emotions and controlling them, and the difference between acceptance and resignation.

Fundamentally, however, Stoicism offers a perspective on 'the good life', a philosophical way of living a meaningful life. Participants reflected on what it meant to live 'the good life', considering what it means to live a simple, quiet existence. They argued that life is complex and multilayered, and different approaches can be appropriate for different situations. Some claimed this would be useful in prisons, while others felt that Stoicism would only be relevant to people who already lived that way (but perhaps it might offer a philosophical framework to express their way of living).

In discussing Stoicism with fellow prison-based philosophy teachers, we often note the relevance of this particular perspective for people in prison. Stoical thinking could be particularly useful for people who are facing long prison stretches. Crewe et al's (2020) research into life in prison suggests that prisoners who are some years into their sentences have resigned themselves to the situation and have found ways to accept the frustrations and limitations of prison life. Stoicism seems to fit with this attitude, suggesting that acceptance might be a good way to cope. There are risks to such acceptance – passivity, acquiescence, political 'quietism' – and not all prisoners approved of Stoic philosophy for these reasons. However, the philosophy did always generate a good debate among the prisoner-participants due to its relevance to their situations.

Stoicism stems from the Ancient Greeks. It sits alongside cynicism, Epicureanism and scepticism as a philosophy that offers a perspective on living 'the good life'. Here, philosophers are not referring to living a morally *correct* life, but instead to finding *eudaimonia*, or 'happiness'. These philosophies offer a way to live that relates to personal welfare and human flourishing. For these philosophers, happiness is the goal for life and they offer a way of 'being' to achieve this. The Stoics articulated a philosophy that encouraged acceptance and emotional control and offered methods of resilience. Unlike many areas of philosophy, Stoicism has never been a purely academic discipline and has always appealed to those seeking guidance in how to live (see Baltzly, 2019, for more on Stoicism).

Here, then, Stoicism provides a basis to start thinking about the questions of wellbeing. In particular, we should recall that much of desistance literature can be articulated as the need to consider the questions of 'Who do I want to be?' and 'How do I want to live?' In this session, for the first time, we offered a perspective that offers an answer to these questions. With its focus on emotional control and acceptance of our situations, we can begin to understand its relevance to people in prison.

Here, in this final 'findings' chapter before we summarize, I begin to draw together findings from both HMP Grendon and HMP Full Sutton. In the first half, I focus on Full Sutton to explore the way in which provision of a philosophy class could promote wellbeing among the participants, even – or perhaps especially – when those participants are confined to a maximum security environment. In particular, wellbeing relates both to the need for mental stimulation (to guard against boredom) and the need for a safe space to articulate an opinion (to drop the mask). In prison, this matters.

The focus, however, is on *conversation*. Through philosophical dialogue the participants gained skills in expressing their points of view, developed their own opinions, and began to learn how to philosophize. Philosophy, with its focus on abstract concepts, ultimately allowed for some personal explorations. Here, we build towards an understanding of how this happened.

Wellbeing and self-expression

Engaging in the philosophy course was purely a matter of choice for the participants. They signed up because they wanted to, for their own interest in the subject matter. The classes would not affect the conditions under which they were held or the likelihood of parole. They would not help them move through the system quicker, and they would not gain a qualification. For many, the classes were simply an enjoyable distraction and a means to pass the time:

> 'Just, like I say, you know, having an intelligent conversation
> with people and learning other people's views and other
> people's points of view on life, and these unanswerable

questions, isn't it, that's interesting me.' (Harry, Full Sutton, VPU)

Interviewer: 'What did you personally get out of being in the class?'
Paul, Full Sutton, VPU: 'Entertainment's the wrong word, just....'
I: 'I think it's a good word.'
P: 'Freedom. Freedom and bit of ... a bit of freshness. Stimulus, a break from the banality, the drudgery of everything.'

In entering the philosophy classroom, the participants found that their status as prisoner or offender was rarely mentioned. Nothing in what we were doing related to the fact that they were in prison – no part of the work related to their sentences or the requirements of the system. This had a particular relevance to the participants in the VPU. For them, the opportunity to be defined as 'learners' and 'philosophers' as opposed to 'sex offenders' was important. The profound gratefulness of the participants towards me for coming to the prison to deliver this course, and treating them with humanity, was surprisingly deep. It seemed that the class meant a great deal to them, and they all expressed sadness at its end:

'[The philosophy classes] normalize people and everything. Maybe it gets people thinking.... A positive outlook, you know. They have a voice, they do matter, they do care, as well, you know. Their thoughts are everything and all that.... It gives me something to say to me wife when I ring up.' (Paul, Full Sutton, VPU)

'I just think it gives people opportunity to do something different. 'Cause to me, it's, like, a little bit of a getaway, a little bit.... And I think that's needed sometimes.' (Martin, Full Sutton, mainstream)

The participants clearly articulated the need for mental stimulation, for something to do. In fact, one of the participants said that the content of some of the materials helped him "sleep a bit better" (Bruce, Full Sutton, VPU). Another went on to say,

'Flipping heck, there's a definite need for it. We'd be all buggered without it, you know, like you say, I'm crying out for it…. I'd rather have me education than me gym sessions, if I have something to do with all that. Oh, it's very much just as important.' (Paul, Full Sutton, VPU)

A key part of this enjoyment for the participants related to the opportunity to express themselves. In an environment where a person's every comment could be subject to analysis, where their behaviour and associations could come under scrutiny, and autonomy was stripped from them, freedom of expression was both rare and important:

> 'You got the opportunity to express what you thought, even if it was wrong and everybody else thought it was wrong, it was a situation where you could do that openly and feel confident that what you were saying wasn't gonna be vilified, it wasn't gonna be repeated everywhere, and that's rare in here.' (Keith, Full Sutton, VPU)

The philosophy classroom provided a safe space for this to occur. The participants enjoyed feeling able to disagree without fear of recriminations. It was a place where they could be open and honest with their fellow participants, and where they trusted that the conversation would not be discussed beyond the classroom:

> 'I wouldn't say we all agreed on everything, but it was just nice to have a chat about things … and disagree with people and know that there's no hard feelings and you could just talk to people and just get ideas, I think.' (Dave, Full Sutton, VPU)

> '… good articulation, and other little skills like that, the socializing, being part of those mechanics in the group. But I thought you got from people, whether it was you or your simple idea, the mechanics of it works, is what I'm saying. There's an efficiency there. Get something from people.' (Jonny, Full Sutton, mainstream)

For Toby, known for his passionate outbursts, the philosophy classroom provided an insight into his own behaviour. Although the participants recognized that his "heart was in right place", they (and I) struggled throughout with his "pantomimic" (as he called them) outpourings of opinion that often disregarded what others said, and failed to take account of previous comments. His passion belied a deep sense of worry regarding the beliefs of the prison community. He cared about the people he was in prison with, and wanted them to have a better understanding of logic, history and politics. In the classroom, however, this would come across as stubborn, unyielding, and, on occasion, disrespectful. During the post-participation interview, I was stunned by the following comment:

> 'For me, learning to present my views in a more moderate fashion, because I realize I lose listeners by how I present my case, or my opinion. So for me it has been an education in seeking to understand … how to put a point across without losing the audience, without being misunderstood. And that has been crucial for me, because I'm extremely poor in that area.' (Toby, Full Sutton, mainstream)

The ability to present oneself openly is an important skill in social interaction. Not only does it allow for better interpretation and understanding of other people, but it also makes it easier to understand how others are interpreting you. For Toby, the sessions encouraged reflection on how to say things in a more acceptable fashion.

Part of the process of learning to articulate oneself better is developing a more sophisticated language for self-expression that can be used in daily life:

> 'What I've learned, I practise in daily life, yeah, definitely. Especially in prison, 'cause there's always problems, in prison, you know. Whether that's people being rude to staff or staff being rude, or just people being inefficient, you know, in what they're doing. So people, like, crying over something that they can't change. You know, I try and teach them the Stoic method, you know, or maybe you need to write your own paper and stop moaning about it, you know. Because you're moaning all the time, maybe it's time to take some action, affirmative action.' (Peter, Full Sutton, mainstream)

The philosophy course meant they could engage in wider conversations that had previously been inaccessible. The participants began to appreciate the role philosophy played in developing their ideas concerning society today, and to understand what philosophers have said. In time, many began to form their own opinions:

'I think, for me, yeah, it's to learn people's diverse thoughts. That was one of the main reasons why I came to the class, to see the diverse amount of thinking. I think generally, the subject, history, kind of, is the subject of my interest as well, yeah. I like to know about civilization and the contribution and this sort of thought, yeah. And philosophy, to me it seems like philosophy's contributed a lot to the betterment of humanity. I think I find modern philosophers more related to my life than classical philosophers, although they can have a lot of wisdom in their statements. Like that one you just mentioned, about Socrates. That's gonna stay with me, and it's always gonna resonate in anything I do, and it's gonna always have that effect on me to ask questions and whys, hows, I can understand something better, you know. And I'm glad you did say that 'cause I didn't know that.' (Jason, Full Sutton, mainstream)

'I think I've learned about philosophy that I'd never heard of. If someone mentions their names now, I can say I've heard of them now. I can take it outside. I want to turn my life around. The positive things are learning how to treat people properly and what is a just society.... The Socrates thing. What makes you happy? I thought it was 75 per cent inside, 25 per cent outside and I thought everyone would just agree with me but others thought different. It comes from within – happiness comes from within yourself. I wondered why others thought differently about it.' (Henry, Full Sutton, mainstream)

For people in prison, this latter point is particularly important. This participant was one of the youngest in the class and, when asked to describe different aspects of his personality, he had responded by saying, "What do you mean, who I am? Because who I am is a criminal. That's all there is."

For those who have engaged in criminal activity most of their life, appreciating that there are different ways of thinking and living is clearly important. For this participant, realizing that there was more to him than this simple label was significant.

Developing our own opinions

Focusing on the ideas of philosophers allowed for self-expression around abstract and impersonal topics. These topics and conversations could have relevance of a deeply personal nature. However, the 'safety' of the conversation revolves around its abstract content. This provided a freedom of self-expression not often achieved in a prison environment.

In Full Sutton, the atmosphere that prevailed in the general prison environment meant the participants had to be on their guard, take care in what they said, be cautious of who they associated with and felt the constant, watchful gaze of the prison regime. Within the prison, talk that occurred in the philosophy classroom could be dangerous on the wings.

As we developed the community atmosphere, however, these issues slowly dropped away. In the philosophy classroom, the participants were equal and were free to offer opinions. They also had to accept that their opinions were open to scrutiny. In the early days, this scrutiny was often taken as a personal affront (recall the incident of one of the participants walking out of a Week 4 session). It took time to cultivate an atmosphere where the participants felt comfortable in changing their minds and accepting a critique of their views. This change was built on the development of trust and positive relationships.

The session on Julian Baggini's 'ego trick' serves to illustrate this point. I wanted to bring in a modern philosopher, somebody contemporary, so the participants understood that the ideas of philosophers continued to be developed today. This appealed to the participants in both Grendon and Full Sutton, and his work was received with enthusiasm.[1]

I introduced Baggini in Week 7. The participants now had some experience in philosophical conversation including several about identity (Theseus' ship, Descartes' dualism, Hume's bundle theory of the self, and so forth). Compared to earlier discussions, the participants responded to this topic with confidence. They now had opinions of their own.

---

[1] In Grendon, one of the participants asked to borrow a copy of Baggini's book, which was then passed to several other participants over the next few weeks.

Baggini's ego trick (Week 7, Grendon; Week 9, Full Sutton, Stage 2)

Julian Baggini (1968–) broadly adheres to Hume's bundle theory of the self. This states that there is no unitary self or soul; instead, we are simply a bundle of perceptions, thoughts and experiences.

However, Baggini goes on to state that we cannot ignore the fact that human beings have a continuous sense of self. This is what Baggini refers to as the 'ego trick'. He claims, because we have no central control system that contains our identity, we are able to construct a sense of self that is unified over time.

Narrative identity (Week 7, Grendon; Week 9, Full Sutton, Stage 3)

Baggini goes on to claim that the 'ego trick' allows us to create an internal narrative. We construct autobiographical accounts of ourselves that allow us to tell our life stories. It is this that unifies us with our past selves.

Baggini is not the first person to discuss the idea of a narrative identity. In sociology, many scholars claim that in order for a person to have a coherent sense of self it is *necessary* for them to have a coherent life story. In other words, a person's identity is dependent on being able to understand one's present in terms of one's past.

Many of the participants immediately took issue with Baggini's idea that we can 'construct' an identity for ourselves. There was a specific difference between the groups in Grendon and the groups in Full Sutton on this particular issue. Perhaps reflecting their engagement with therapy, in Grendon, the participants agreed that understanding the past is key to understanding the self. In Full Sutton, however, the participants argued that this was not necessary. In a possible reflection of their own prison journeys, they felt it was possible to understand your present self without having to engage in deep reflection on the past.

Despite the differences in perspective, all of the groups engaged in conversation around the relevance of experiences, culture, environment, choices and behaviours and, perhaps most relevant to the overarching theme of this book, what makes us who we are.

What was particularly striking in the fieldwork notes, however, is that the participants were becoming more expressive. Now, seven or eight weeks into the course, they had begun to listen to each other. In kind, they became more open to offering opinion and more willing to be constructive in their responses to others. It seems that collaborative exploration of ideas had begun to occur.

Learning how to philosophize

> 'The engagement with everybody, the ideas swimming around, and the fact that everybody's idea is valid. That there was no well, no, "that's wrong" and "you shouldn't be thinking that way." It was ... even the more right-wing, left-wing views aren't shuttered down, but explored and opened up. And it allowed us to open up into different areas, where people were talking about how they felt personally about things, and we were able to challenge their negativity towards that. Loved that.' (Keith, Full Sutton, VPU)

To understand the progress the participants made in these areas, I return to the example of Plato's *Republic* discussed in Chapter 3. This session highlighted the difficulties some of the participants had in early sessions in grasping abstract and theoretical concepts. I started by introducing a story of being shipwrecked on a desert island, and asking participants what they would do to ensure their survival and that of the other shipwrecked people.

In Full Sutton, in the mainstream group, several participants struggled to grasp the metaphor in this stimulus. They initially focused on the specific wording of the text, reminding the group that it was set '2,500 years ago'. They attempted to point out what life would have been like then, drawing on their knowledge of the geography of the Pacific Ocean, and the history of migration and sea travel in the region. For a period, the group got drawn into these debates, and I had to work out a way to return to the question.

To encourage the participants to start thinking about the story in its abstract sense, I asked the participants to consider the author's motivations. Why did he describe the scenario in such a way? Why did he set it 2,500 years ago? What did they think the author was asking the reader to consider? Eventually, after some discussion and questioning, we were able to come round to the idea that the story was a 'scene-setting' exercise to help us consider the question of societal structure:

FIELDWORK NOTES
Full Sutton, mainstream, Session 2, 24 June 2015

They were not so good about talking about the "ought" [how things ought to be and how we ought to behave]; they spent more time thinking about the reality and drawing on historical and current examples rather than thinking about the "right" way of doing things in principle.

Among the VPs, dialogue also focused more on the practical skills required to survive on a desert island. As we progressed through the stages, the participants began to discuss society, the need to 'belong', the role of vocation and the importance of having a voice. However, their opinions were often pre-conceptions that lacked nuance. They made sweeping statements such as "You have it easy over here" (in reference to the UK benefits system); "You're a feminist, Miss? Doesn't that mean you hate men?" (recall Chapter 8).

Although the participants were capable of having an intellectual discussion around different ideas and concepts, they were not used to looking deeply at the reasons *behind* a certain point of view. Particularly among the mainstream groups, but also among the VPs, there was a constant need in those first few weeks to push the participants towards thinking about questions philosophically. The technique of Socratic questioning proved valuable in this context:

FIELDWORK NOTES
Full Sutton, mainstream, Week 2, 24 June 2015

I had to try hard to keep coming back, pushing them to the philosophical point.... The bigger, more abstract picture is much more difficult to get them to focus on, they focus on the minutiae, the detail. So I had to keep pushing them and say, "Well, I think the question that underpins this idea is, what is a just society?" or "How do we judge whether a society is fair?"

The participants made clear progress in their philosophical thinking skills. As set out in Chapter 1, to 'think philosophically' requires the use of accurate and clear language (Thompson, 2003). Further, to examine an issue with a structured *philosophical* approach involves interrogating questions and ideas systematically through reflection and inquiry (see Grayling, 1995, or Law, 2007, for example).

As the week progressed, my role as facilitator also progressed. In some sessions my position was closer to being a 'co-inquirer' who engaged in conversation alongside the men. In others, however, I had to act as more of a referee or coach. In the case of the referee role, I would try to mediate between the participants and pull them back towards the focus of the session (most frequently in the Full Sutton mainstream group but also, on occasion, in other groups). When acting as a sort of 'coach', I would be offering encouragement, gently persuading them to elaborate and put forward an opinion.

These shifts in my position in the group are evident from the fieldwork notes, and offer the means to understand when the participants were being philosophical in their contributions. For example, in Grendon I acted as a 'co-inquirer' from the outset, with the majority of the discussion involving only passive facilitation as the group monitored themselves. This reflected the participants' skills, in respectful group dialogue, but also their careful approach to a topic and their skills in reflecting on the thoughts and opinions of other members the group.

By way of contrast, in Full Sutton I had to engage in active facilitation in both groups. Among the VPs this involved encouraging discussion by asking questions and gently pushing the participants to interrogate the question more deeply and thoroughly. Among the mainstream group, I focused on encouraging the participants to listen to each other, to reflect on their own point of view, and to develop their opinions in more subtle and nuanced ways. By Week 3, the VPs had begun to engage in more active dialogue and by Week 5, we had achieved an excellent philosophical discussion where I felt able to participate as a co-inquirer as opposed to facilitator. Among the mainstream group, it was not until Week 7 that the participants began expanding on philosophical points of view and exploring complex philosophical ideas. However, even at these later stages, I rarely relaxed, always feeling the need to engage in active facilitation. Characterized by a lack of fluidity in the conversations, the mainstream participants struggled to work *together* to build understanding.

The changing dynamics in the classroom also began to reveal how philosophical dialogue works. I drew on my training and experience as a teacher to encourage philosophical thinking. The method of philosophical inquiry I employed provided the opportunity for the participants to explore and understand philosophies at their own pace, and to discuss the ideas in their own words. I used open questioning techniques to help the participants develop their understanding of the topics, and the meanings behind the stimuli. In both groups, over time, the participants began to put forward their own philosophical ideas, became more skilled at reflecting on the material, and started to discuss how the philosophies related to their own way of thinking.

Through the Socratic method, the participants improved their own knowledge of philosophy, became more sophisticated in how they integrated their knowledge into their own ways of thinking and their lifestyles, and developed skills in assessing knowledge for accuracy, relevance, meaning and implications:

> 'I had a different direction of articulating it, so what I thought I knew I didn't quite know. What I knew, I could, sort of, say in a better way.' (Jonny, Full Sutton, mainstream)

A key attribute of the course was the *dialogue* – the learning took place *within* and *through* social interaction. The mainstream participants discussed both their enjoyment of this interaction and their frustration with the difficult dynamics of the class. They also discussed what they gained from this type of interaction – what they learned about themselves, other people and society as a whole:

> 'Well, I think, because of the mechanics of the group.... I met people there who I respect and would have plenty of time for, who I might just have said hello before ... it made us as a group more positive towards each other.' (Jonny, Full Sutton, mainstream)

Among the mainstream group, Session 7 provided the first clear indication that one participant had reflected on the philosophical content, and had developed his own perspective on what he had heard:

> 'When it comes to morality there are three levels – some things are clear-cut, you don't murder, you don't steal. And that's clear-cut. And then, some things are about experience – you learn from experience that certain things are right and wrong. And then, other things come from interpretation – it's the way you interpret things that help you figure out what's right and wrong.' (Martin, Full Sutton, mainstream)

As already indicated, Session 7 constituted a turning point in relations in the mainstream classroom. However, it also constituted a turning point in their philosophical thinking. By Session 7, the participants had discussed various aspects of morality including the ideas of Kant,

Bentham and Mill. As their knowledge of different philosophical ideas increased, their ability to offer a nuanced view improved:

'… we don't have to be that extreme. As always, we can take the middle road and recognize that there is a value in thinking about our past to make sense of who we are today but it doesn't mean we should do it all the time.' (Peter, Full Sutton, mainstream, Session 10)

Through emphasis on philosophical conversation and careful facilitating, the participants began to appreciate the importance of listening to each other. They learned that working together to understand what Kant, Descartes or Plato were saying was more useful than trying to outdo each other (mainstream group) or simply saying what they thought I expected them to say (the VPs).

In the mainstream group, in Session 11, the participants were able to discuss Mill's ideas on liberty, and appreciate the distinction between individual choice and what a government has the right to legislate on. Mill's 'harm principle' took the participants around to the topic of the teachings of Islam:

FIELDWORK NOTES
Full Sutton, mainstream, Session 11, 12 August 2015

We discussed how in Islam you are taught not to engage in behaviour that will harm yourself. They agreed on the point that this is your personal choice to follow that doctrine but also that there is a distinction between moral guidelines and legality – you might agree that this is a good rule to follow but it does not mean the government has the right to legislate on such matters. This is Mill's principal point. It is only harm to others that matters.

The participants understood the philosophy of Mill and also the context in which it was meant. They appreciated the subtleties required in understanding and properly critiquing his philosophical point of view. Despite the complex religious backdrop in Full Sutton, by Week 11, the participants engaged in thoughtful conversation involving religious content, accepting differences of opinion and reflecting on different contributions.

In the mainstream group, breaking down barriers between the prisoners proved a difficult and complex task. Over the course of delivery, I maintained a 'no nonsense' attitude whereby I was willing to engage in conversation and state my point of view, regardless of whether it went against the grain of the conversation. I was also consistent in my insistence on respect for one another's opinions, allowing the participants to speak, and encouraging an open and honest dialogue.

This is not to say that I maintained a perfect attitude throughout – the volatile nature of the mainstream group and the difficult 'larger-than-life' personalities I had to deal with often meant that I felt frustrated, struggled to maintain order and made errors in the way I handled some of the incidents. However, over the course of delivery, the participants came to realize that my ultimate goal was to get them to think philosophically, to enjoy learning and to work together to improve our understanding of the ideas of the philosophers presented:

> 'This is what struck me ... everyone had something to say and we was all on equal terms. It didn't matter if someone was a little bit cleverer than the next.... I might have been a little bit more efficient when I was making my point sometimes than maybe one or two others, but only 'cause I was aware that that's how you should be ... what I was thinking ... with all your knowledge you just argued at our level, and I don't say that our level is below your level. What I'm trying to say to you is you argued at the same level, you argued in the same way, that's what I mean.... I kind of, felt it was, kind of, like that with everyone. Everyone was valid.' (Jonny, Full Sutton, mainstream)

A key part of developing a community atmosphere involved developing an environment where everyone felt they *could* join in and that they were part of the community of inquiry. This had a humanizing affect that involved developing a safe space to discuss controversial topics. In theory, this meant the participants could express their point of view without fear of personal insult or prejudices being formed.

Further to this, the participants articulated the benefits of being in an educated circle. Through the constant dialogue with different people voicing their opinions, ideas and perspectives on the material presented, they developed a sense of being part of the community:

> 'In an educated circle ... you can learn enough.... And that was the first and foremost reason why I started.... Then, seeing the subject matters as well as the diverse amount of thinking, ... people's rationale and that, I thought, yeah, I

think I should stay here, I'll definitely benefit by opening up my horizon, expressing my ideas, taking in new ideas. Because I think everybody takes ideas from everybody.... I think, [the] majority of people, they learn from other people, innit, and then they define themselves. So if I'm in an educated circle I think that's gonna have a good reflection on me. Whereas if I was in a criminal circle, that's gonna have a reflection on me. And to a certain extent, depending how strong the person is, but, yeah, it's something that I'd like to always get engaged in, definite educational circles.' (Jason, Full Sutton, mainstream)

By getting to know each other, the participants began to understand one another's perspectives more fully. In Week 10, I described mainstream discussions as 'vibrant' and 'lively', and in Week 11 I was excited and impressed by the participants' ability to discuss controversial and sensitive issues in a calm and controlled manner. In this late session, we discussed the question of art, and the participants and I enjoyed the discussion immensely. At the end of this session, the atmosphere in the classroom 'buzzed' with excitement as the participants stated that they had appreciated hearing each other's views.

Philosophy as personal self-exploration

Full Sutton provided an environment to 'dig deep' into the role of philosophy in prisons. Where Grendon allowed for comparison of different types of Socratic dialogue and the content of discussion, Full Sutton allowed for closer scrutiny of the *process* of philosophical inquiry. In an environment characterized by division and distrust, Full Sutton provided an opportunity to test the pedagogy of dialogic philosophy in establishing community and cooperation among the participants. The findings demonstrate that providing a space for self-expression based on a shared experience of philosophical conversation can develop trust and relationships, and *how* that can be achieved through philosophy, even in some unlikely places or contexts.

The prison experience is characterized by social isolation, loss of autonomy and fear of violence. These issues contribute to psychological stress, with scholars arguing that imprisonment – and particularly long-term imprisonment – leads to deterioration. Some psychological studies have equated imprisonment to a 'deep freeze', claiming there is no evidence that prison results in deterioration or long-lasting emotional damage (see Zamble and Porporino, 1988).

Furthermore, some evidence suggests that the most damaging and distressing period of imprisonment is at the start, with pains gradually dissipating over time (Zamble and Porporino, 1988).

This is supported somewhat by Liebling's (1992) conclusion that suicide is much more likely in the early stages of imprisonment. However, the impact of imprisonment varies and the ability of long-term prisoners to 'psychologically survive' the experience, and even grow and develop in the face of adversity, may speak more to the strength of the human spirit than the notion that prison is not damaging (see, for example, O'Donnell's *Prisoners, Solitude and Time* [2014] for a full discussion of this possibility).

The work in Full Sutton develops our thinking around what it takes to establish a growth identity. It highlights the way in which providing a space for positive interaction allows prisoners opportunities to practise and develop alternative presentations of the self. Furthermore, the philosophical focus of the dialogue encouraged the participants to engage in reflexive activity, providing insights into themselves and others' ways of thinking.

Arendt (1998 [1958]) argued that we form our identities in a social world and adjust our behaviours according to how others react to them. The philosophy classroom provided a specific social situation for this to occur; behaviours are emphasized and brought to the fore, peers react to one another – negatively and positively – and if conversation is going to be fruitful, the participants develop skills in presenting their case in a manner conducive to positive interaction. For some participants, this meant learning about their own behaviour; for others, engaging in philosophical dialogue shone a light on their weak arguing skills or inappropriate behaviour.

Open conversation provided the participants with the opportunity to rationally discuss each other's points of view and to have others reflect on their own. Such conversation and learning not only encouraged the participants to reflect on appropriate behaviour, but also developed their self-worth. With a platform where others would listen to, and reflect on, their contributions, they realized they had something worthwhile to contribute:

> 'Learning how to listen or how to pick up on people's behaviours. Knowing when to be rude to someone and when not to – knowing when being rude might get you beaten up, or when it will teach someone. And asking the right questions; sometimes.... I might ask a question, not because I have to understand, but because I know someone

else is embarrassed to ask the same question.' (Peter, Full Sutton, mainstream)

'It's helped me understand that the way I've been expressing myself, whatever the idea, however fruitful or non-fruitful it is, my attitude has pushed people away, the loudness, the pantomimic aggression, 'cause I'm not really aggressive … it's just pantomimic. And it's not worked.' (Toby, Full Sutton, mainstream)

'I feel like I've opened up because I feel more confident with myself about what I stand for, and the philosophy sessions, for instance…. Stoicism, where we only worry about … what we can control, I think that has affected me, and now I'm able to sleep a little bit better…. I think maybe it was a confidence thing, and for me, I was listening to other people, you know, especially … 'cause there was a couple of people on the course that are quite outspoken, are quite confident with what they were saying, so I was quite happy sitting there and listening to them…. But now, I think I've gained a little bit of confidence. I think that as the weeks went on, I was giving more, I was adding more to the conversation.' (Bruce, Full Sutton, VPU)

In contrast to these statements, one of the participants voiced some concerns. He discussed the problem with having an open way of thinking and a willingness to engage in questioning when in an unstable and potentially violent situation (such as prison), and the need to develop mental techniques to cope with the pains of imprisonment. This raises the question of the role of philosophy for those who have yet to develop a survival strategy in prison. In order for prisoners to participate, do they need to have a level of resilience to the environment in the first place? The participants in my philosophy class – those who had the confidence to sign up from the outset – included those intertwined with the prisoner hierarchy, those from educated and skilled backgrounds, and those who were trying to make the 'best' of their situation in prison.

The class was also relevant to the participants' personal philosophies. Philosophy involves 'thinking about thinking' (Honderich, 1995), and engaging in philosophical conversation encourages participants to reflect on their own opinions and beliefs. In Full Sutton, the participants discussed how they incorporated other people's (including the philosophers') points of view into their way of thinking. Philosophy seemed to enrich the participants' philosophies of life, adding new dimensions, developing understanding and encouraging reflection on the reasons behind a point of view. Through a constant expression of thoughts, and hearing different views on how we ought to live, the participants reflected on how *they* lived.

Philosophy asks fundamental questions about actions, morality and identity. The social process and interaction within the class highlighted the participants' own behaviours with respect to their interaction and contribution in the dialogic setting. They noticed traits about themselves – that they contributed more than others, or that they contributed less than they thought they would, or that their confidence grew over time – which encouraged them to reflect on their behaviour in the classroom and to consider what it meant for who they were:

'What I'm thinking is, if I'm talking to somebody and I've got my rigid views, and they say something that I think maybe gets me to wake up about them … wake up may be the wrong word, but snap out of my rigid views.' (Dave, Full Sutton VPU)

'Just exercising my brain. You know, like, asking questions, debating about it, and them [other participants] sometimes reanalysing what I thought, and then changing my own original thoughts. You know, like, little things like that, and interacting with other people. That's about it, truthfully.' (Martin, Full Sutton, mainstream)

'I would say I have insights into things that really matter.… It was the mechanics of the group, it was you with your silly little four questions, the simplicity of it.' (Jonny, Full Sutton, mainstream)

'I like the topics about how you should be in life – interesting how others say you should be.' (Henry, Full Sutton, mainstream)

'Because it questions your morals … it questions your integrity. It questions you basically. I mean, by putting these subjects and everything you, sort of, argue the toss and listen to other people's point of view that what you might have thought of as being the wrong thing in the first place

might be in question, basically, if you know what I mean.'
(Harry, Full Sutton, VPU)

'How do people perceive me? How do I ... do I perceive myself in the right way?' (Paul, Full Sutton, VP)

The subject matter and course materials encouraged the participants' personal reflections. Several weeks focused on theories of moral action, asking the participants to consider how we, as people and members of society, *ought* to behave. They were explicit in discussing how this encouraged them to reflect on their own behaviour – past and present – and to think about how certain behaviours might affect others around them:

'I've looked at my behaviour and I've introspected, and it's made me question, what am I doing here?... What is the purpose of my existence here? And I've looked back at my life and I've thought to myself right.... I've just bobbed along with my actions, ... not followed people, as such, I've just tried to lead this life where you get a job and you settle down with someone, you have children, and it, you know, 'cause that's, like, acceptable, that's, like, the norm. And I've just, kind of, like, followed it with actually no plans really.' (Bruce, Full Sutton, VPU)

This participant went on to discuss how this reflection also helped him highlight positive traits in himself as well as negative:

'Here's some things that I have come to realize since doing these sessions ... some of these traits I do have already. I have ambition, and I do have commitment. I'm not one of these that goes round and says "Oh, I can do that".... If I say I'm gonna do something I'll do it.... I find that that's a good trait. But there's other traits in me which I've come to understand in these philosophy groups, that ... maybe sometimes I'll say something and not understand how it can affect others.... I think I'll stand for something, you know, like violence against people, yet I will come down if someone upsets me, or something like that. So these philosophy sessions have ... made me realize and come to understand that living a morally right life and sticking to these things that hopefully will make me ... well, I can become.... I don't know, what's the word, a man of integrity, maybe, or something like that.

What did I personally get? I think my confidence has grown. I think that I've started to look at myself and understand myself a lot more, and following more, and more introspection from each individual session, it's given me a path to go down. Like I've said before, moral, right path, a path to find the truth. You know, goals, and I've looked at my life and I can see now where life's a bit of a journey, it's a bit of a path. There's minefields, and there's things to avoid, and things like that. And maybe on the outside I was quite materialistic and the fact that I thought that maybe accumulating wealth and materialistic things and, you know, like cars and motorbikes and stuff, that would give me ultimate happiness. But now I've started to look, I think "Hang on a minute, no, no that's not what life's about." Life's about helping people and going to work and sharing good times with people. It's about memories and being with your children and ... discovering the world and discovering truths about things, and you know, like ... opening your mind, exploring, like.' (Bruce, Full Sutton, VPU)

Several of the participants were already on a path of self-exploration. Prison constituted a shock to them, having never thought they would find themselves there (see also Liebling, 1992). Therefore, they used the time to understand how they had got there, what it meant for who they were as people, and how they could move forward. The participants discussed how the philosophy classes encouraged and supported this self-exploration. For some, it helped them develop a better understanding of themselves and how others perceived them. As the philosophy class is an educational class focusing on development rather than deficit, the participants identified positive attributes that they had either forgotten or not realized before.

Much of the power of this type of educational opportunity seemed to lie in what it did not focus on as opposed to what it did. In particular, the philosophy classroom focused on learners' philosophical thinking and dialogue skills. By focusing on educational outcomes, the participants' trust that it was safe to openly articulate themselves evolved naturally. Trust cannot be forced. It develops over time. However, *through* philosophical thinking and practised dialogue, the participants were able to gain the skills that *allowed* for trust to be built and self-expression to flourish. This seemed to be relevant to the participants' wellbeing, which, in turn, has a bearing on their experience of the prison.

Overall, the philosophy course constituted a rare opportunity to engage in an intellectual activity for the sake of interest and self-improvement. Providing a space in which prisoners are able to build on their strengths rather than work on their deficits could have a profound impact on a prisoner's frame of mind as they work their way through the system. Some participants stated that programmes available in the prison to address 'criminogenic deficits' had often been useful and meaningful to them. However, consistent with recent literature, building a positive self-image and an optimistic outlook among people in prison went beyond the 'offender' on which the prison tended to focus.

10

Towards a Framework
for Understanding
Philosophy in Prison

On a warm summer's afternoon, I find myself navigating the maze of a high security prison. My footsteps echo down the empty halls and my key chain rattles at my side. My route through involves unlocking barred gates and heavy doors, travelling down a series of identical corridors, passing prison officers watching and waiting at their stations. A lack of windows throughout the prison means no daylight permeates the atmosphere. Instead, cheap strip lighting, low ceilings and once-white walls create a sense of enclosure.

Clutched in my hands is a homemade certificate and a set of teaching materials. The lesson that day had involved a discussion of all the conversations we had had throughout the course: What is society? What is knowledge? How do we choose how to act? What is morality? What makes us who we are? What constitutes change? Over the past three months, along with a group of passionate, opinionated and thoughtful men, I had interrogated some of the big questions in life.

On the final day of teaching, I head towards one of the wings. When I arrive, I am told the men are on 'lockdown'. There had been 'an incident'. I ask the prison officers on duty if I am able to talk to one of the men. The prison officer tells me that they can't unlock anyone but I could go and talk to him through his door. I am hesitant, but it's my last day teaching in the prison, and he had missed the class. I want to give him his certificate and check how he is doing. The prison officer asks if I need escorting to the cell door, but I wave my key chain to him to demonstrate I can make my own way.

I rarely visited the wings. My work meant I spent most of my time in education departments. Usually, on the wings, depending on the time of day, there were men wandering around in dressing gowns and cheap, well-worn slippers, or perhaps flip-flops and tracksuit bottoms. Sometimes they were going to make a cup of tea, sometimes they were trying to get a prison officer's attention, sometimes they were chatting to another prisoner. I was often asked who I was by the men in prison. In earlier years I was usually assumed to be a psychologist; these days, as I am older, an inspector. I have always been asked my nationality – Polish, Spanish, once Albanian. Occasionally, I am asked if I am Jewish. I always answer and explain what I am doing there.

Visiting wings is always interesting and there is usually a conversation to be had. However, with the men on lockdown, the wing is quiet and there is no one to be seen. The men are all behind their doors, on their own in their cells. As the prison officer said, there had been some sort of incident on the wing. I don't know what the incident was, I rarely ask for details. I would rather not know.

That day marked the end of three months teaching philosophy in the prison. In fact, it marked the last day of my teaching philosophy in any prison, for this project at least. I was annoyed that one of my most enthusiastic participants had missed it because of an incident he was not involved in, but I knew this was the reality of prison life. With this in my mind, I walk over to the metal gate that leads to the cells. Heavy and clunking, I pass through and head down to the other end.

There are two floors to the wing, a long wide corridor down the centre, with cells down either side. Walking down the length of the wing, I pass door after door, each with a man inside. It is surprisingly quiet. In prison, just because the doors are locked, does not mean there is no noise. Today is quiet, though, almost peaceful.

I get to his door and knock. "Who's that?" He shouts out. I respond and say he had been missed in the philosophy class that day. He is enthusiastic and tells me to "open the hole, open the hole!" He is referring to the metal flap, about 12 by 4 inches, which covers the window. The prison officers open them and look in, without asking. I am not a prison officer, though, and I would feel I was intruding on his privacy, so I wait for an invitation.

The cell door is cold metal and grey. He is on one side, and I the other. We chat about the course and I tell him I have brought this week's materials and a certificate (homemade) for him. He says to "slide it under the door, slide it under!" I do, and he is pleased.

Half an hour ago, he should have been in my classroom, sitting, as an equal, discussing deep questions of philosophy with his fellow learners and me. In the classroom, we were philosophers – inquirers questioning and considering different points of view. Now, at this moment, the stark reality of his situation became apparent. This man was a prisoner and could not open his door.

Philosophy

> 'Philosophy's changed worlds innit, it's changed ways of thinking in whole continents. So, if we can learn to kind of like ... make that a microcosm, we could do that in out our lives personally....' (Charlie, Grendon)

At the outset of this book, I defined philosophy as an 'activity of thought' (Law, 2007) or 'thinking about thinking' (Honderich, 1995). To engage in active philosophizing is less about discussing opinions and conclusions, and more about exploring how and why these opinions have been formed. This subtle but key distinction lies at the heart of the idea of *collaborative* dialogue; we are not there to make people think the way we think, and nor ought we to engage in philosophical dialogue with such an agenda. Instead, we go into dialogue with the intention of taking an interest in our fellow participants' worldviews, seeking to understand the reasoning and principles that lie behind them.

Philosophy can be understood as a conversation that human beings have been engaged in for millennia. The participants understood that their discussions in the prison classroom formed part of a long line of philosophers who have argued over these ideas, discussing the same issues and contemplating the same paradoxes. They enjoyed being able to place themselves on a spectrum of philosophical ideas.

The act of taking part in this conversation, even in a small way, had meaning. For these men, to be given the space to engage in a conversation that people have been having with each other for thousands of years meant feeling part of something. They, too, were people with valuable opinions. They, too, had something to offer.

This understanding – of being part of a greater whole, of recognizing your place within the history of humans – seemed to provide the foundation for more nuanced thinking about the world. While their views may not change the course of history, these small contributions to the wider conversation of life, morality and how to live, all matter.

Over the course of this book I have endeavoured to authentically describe what happened in the philosophy classroom, and to provide a clear overview of the findings of the research. Taking an ethnographic approach, the research developed into an exploration of the possibility of growth in an environment characterized by survival. I am not the first prison sociologist to articulate the importance of meaning-making in the prison environment, and nor am I the first to notice the deep, personal reflections entering prison seems to induce (see, in particular, work from Liebling or O'Donnell). However, this research has demonstrated that, over time, it is possible to cultivate a space within a prison for self-expression, self-reflection and meaningful interactions.

In this chapter, I draw these ideas together into a 'framework' for understanding the relevance of philosophy to the lives of people in prison. In summarizing the findings, I build towards a final reflection on growth. I articulate some key moments of reflection from the participants, moments I witnessed by spending a period of time working with them to cultivate a community of philosophical inquiry.

Through these detailed observations of a small group of participants in two prisons, I gained an insight into the lives of the participants and the realities of living in prison. As Liebling (2019) describes, prisons, in their restrictions, can become a place where we gain an understanding of what is fundamental; they have the capacity to '… concentrate the mind on what it means to be human' (2019, p 85). In this research project, I learned that context matters.

Prisons shaping the 'front'

Where a person is, the type of environment that they spend their time in and the people with whom they associate all contribute to the way in which they see themselves. Throughout the fieldwork, I learned that prisons can incubate suspicion and fear. Confirming much of the wider prison sociology literature (which I have discussed at length), the prison community rarely allows the individual to relax. Instead, the prison can become a place where the prisoner is preoccupied with survival and a need to protect who they are from the wider effects of living in the prison.

The two prisons offered very different environments in which to explore the role of philosophy education. HMP Grendon, in many ways, represented a safe space for me as a researcher. The prisoners were unchallenging, forgiving, sympathetic, and willing to engage. I could test out my materials and engage in conversation without being concerned with aggressive, confrontational contributions or tangential discussions. This is not to say that the course was easy. The men I worked with had lived complicated lives and were engaged in deep therapeutic work. As a result, they were open, trusting, willing to reflect and entrenched in conversations of their past, present and future. They brought these reflections to the philosophy classroom, steeping the content with passion and personal interest.

The broader political climate in HMP Full Sutton meant the participants were closed, suspicious, often filled with either shame or anger. They were searching for ways to find meaning in the context of long prison sentences. All were engaged in some kind of 'self work', using the scant resources available to find ways to fill their time. Entering Full Sutton was difficult.

Although at the time I did not fully appreciate it (as it was necessary to experience Full Sutton before I could assess this), the community ethos of Grendon meant that the participants were open to my presence and willing to engage in the process. They were, to varying degrees, skilled in Socratic dialogue and group conversation, and had a clear understanding of how to go about disagreeing with a point of view without causing offence. They were able to show humility, happily changed their minds, and enthused about how philosophy had developed their thinking through the introduction to new ideas. For these participants, the content of the conversation, and the actual *act* of philosophizing in a group, provided the context for their reflections on the impact of the course when it concluded.

In Full Sutton in particular, but also in Grendon, issues of trust permeated the social environment, with relationships being negotiated in an environment where there was a 'right way to behave' (Liebling, assisted by Arnold, 2004). Among the Full Sutton mainstream population, this manifested itself most overtly around the Muslim population. With talk of forced conversions and radical ideologies, staff (and prisoners) were suspicious of the motives of all Muslims, regardless of the truth of their involvement in such issues.

The VPU was no less tense, albeit in a different way. Among the VPs, prisoners were suspicious of the motives of the regime, ever cautious to speak openly for fear of statements being recorded and taken out of context. This meant I observed (and discussed directly with the participants) prisoners in Full Sutton presenting carefully orchestrated fronts in response to their environment and as a means of self-protection.

The notion of prisoners developing 'fronts' is well established in the prison sociological literature, and I have discussed this in detail over the course of the book. I continue to use this language of 'frontstage' and 'backstage' selves because Goffman's perspective of the dramaturgical self helps us describe the conscious effort many prisoners make to project a particular front in order to successfully navigate prisoner society (see, for example, Jones and Schmid, 2000). However, the dichotomy of 'frontstage' and 'backstage' selves is, perhaps, an oversimplification (see Crewe et al, 2013, for example). In reality, an individual has a range of 'selves' that they present in different circumstances. These selves are not necessarily dissonant, and nor are they unavoidably a departure from the true self. Rather, they reflect different aspects of a person's identity, with different versions of the self being allowed to come to the fore according to what is appropriate in different social settings. As such, conceptualizing different presentations of the self as modes of 'survival' is, as I point out in the Chapter 3, something of a leap. However, it is an appropriate leap in the context of a prison environment given prisoners' preoccupation with personal safety and the need to negotiate the complex and unwelcoming environment of the prison.

Presenting a 'front' is not unique to prisons. In everyday life, we present versions of the self suitable to a given situation. However, in prison (and other environments), the survival 'mask' all too often involves developing a hyper-masculine sense of self that shows no fear, emotion or distress in the face of the prison community; that takes violence, bullying and deprivation in its stride, relying on no one else to get through the prison day. The fear, expressed by some of the participants, was that this cultivated 'macho' self gradually becomes who they are – no longer a front, but an expression of the fundamental self because, after 10, 15, 20 years in prison without spaces in which they can present different, more pro-social, versions of the self, this macho front becomes all they know.

The implication here is that spending long periods of time in the prison community can fundamentally affect a person's identity. As Sykes, one of the earliest prison sociology scholars, said, in prison the '... individual's picture of himself as a person of value ... begins to waiver and grow dim' (1958, pp 78–9). Further, in general, prison environments damage a person's sense of self. Words such as survival, coping, adaptation, deprivation and stagnation are all common in the prison sociological literature.

In such an environment, is growth possible? In the following, I explore this question drawing in particular on desistance literature. However, as we draw to the closing arguments of this book, the findings of this research have shaped my understanding of growth in the prison environment. In the subsequent sections I build towards an understanding of the needs of people living in a prison environment.

Growth

Underpinning the discussion thus far is the question of what a 'growth' identity looks like in a prison environment. To answer this, I began with criminological literature, starting my considerations of identity with the concept of desistance. Researchers in this area concern themselves with questions of identity and place self-understanding at the centre of their analysis. While desistance is not the focus of this study (as I have emphasized, the research focused on life in prison), the desistance literature provided me with a route into considerations of identity. The narrative self, the relevance of self-reflection and the opportunity for self-development were all relevant to the findings of this research.

Two studies from the early 2000s shaped my understanding of identity and helped articulate the idea of growth: from Maruna (2001) and Giordano et al (2002). Both Maruna's articulation of 'redemption' scripts and Giordano's 'hooks for change' theory emphasize the need for the individual to self-reflect. Both consider it important for the individual to frame their past behaviour in such a way as to be able to move forward. They also agree on the need for a person to envision a 'future self' that they can work towards. However, they place emphasis on different areas. In Maruna's theory, we must look to the past in order to understand our present; in re-biographing ourselves in a more positive light, we are able to move forward towards a constructed, desired self. For Giordano et al, crafting of the future self happens earlier, with the view of past behaviours coming as the final stage in the process. Either way, by looking at desistance we can move towards a perspective on identity and consider how individuals (with experience of the criminal justice system) might start moving towards a positive future.

Desistance theory often draws on the tradition of the narrative self, most notably, the work of McAdams (1993) Within this tradition, life is articulated as a 'narrative quest' that helps us understand ourselves and our place in the world (MacIntye, 1984; Schechtman, 2011). At the centre of this process is the way the person understands him or herself. In the tradition of Giddens, our ability to develop self-understanding relates the language we use to describe ourselves. Desistance theorists, in discussing the need to 'craft a satisfying *replacement self*' (Giordano et al, 2002, p 1027; original emphasis), and to have a future 'desired self' (Bottoms and Shapland, 2016) to work towards (see also Chapter 4), offer us a way of thinking about identity. While self-reflection, understanding the past and developing a sense of the future are all important processes, the key is how we articulate who we are to ourselves.

The narrative perspective of identity recognizes the relevance of the community that surrounds us; as I have said before, we are co-authors in our stories (see Schechtman, 2011; see also Chapter 4, this book). As a result, underlying much of the discussion throughout this book has been recognition of the essentially interactive process of internal self-reflection and social presentations of the self. Identity formation is both a private endeavour and a public demonstration. It is a lifelong process of personal development, conceptualized as an internal narrative of the self (in the tradition of Giddens and McAdams) that is constructed in public, and presented and renegotiated through reflection and feedback from others.

This perspective is taken from Hannah Arendt's ideas presented in *The Human Condition* (1998 [1958]). While she recognizes the presence of an internal, subjective understanding of the self, she also emphasizes its interactions with presentations of the self in a public sphere. According to Arendt, it is through our actions and our speech that we reveal ourselves to others. In this way, the internal self and the projected external self interact with the environment and the community, with the reactions of others (to our presented selves) serving to shape our internal understandings (see also Kreider, 2014, for reflections on Arendt's perspective). What happens, then, if the feedback and public demonstration of the self takes places in a prison?

In recent years, some scholars have begun to discuss the idea of 'meaning-making' in the prison environment. Crewe et al (2020), interviewing people in prison who had received a life sentence at a young age (under 25), argue that there are some important differences between those who are 'early' in their sentences, those who are 'mid' and those who are 'late'. Their participants described the need for some 'self-modification' entering prison. However,

> ... as the emotional fog of the early years [of incarceration] are lifted, prisoners found that they had the psychological strength and space to consider the existential questions that in the past they had been unable to contemplate or had judiciously ignored. (Crewe et al, 2020, p 265)

Liebling also argues that entering prison often leads to a form of existential crisis (Liebling et al, 2011), and surviving the environment involves processes of meaning-making. Personal development involves helping others and exercising the positive attributes of their personhood (Liebling et al, 2016). Crewe et al, who dedicate a chapter to identity and personhood, refer to McAdams' narrative theory (the same theory Maruna draws on), saying '... prisoners' change narratives were often imbued with a sense of meaning and value' (2020, p 270). They go on to say that 'most' were able to achieve Maruna's redemption narrative and understand their 'shameful' past in terms that would allow them to see themselves as being able to lead a meaningful life (Maruna, 2001).

This research into the prison experience in England implies that some people in prison do achieve a sense of purpose in the prison environment. This indicates that we are right to ask how this might be at all possible, given the circumstances and limited opportunities. However, it is important to note that while Crewe et al's research provides interesting insights into identity, they rely on a series of interviews with people at different stages in their prison journey. Their work does not articulate *how* prisoners achieve a 'change narrative'. Furthermore, it does not discuss the different contexts in which their participants are living or have lived.

My research indicates a more complex journey of meaning-making by prisoners. I worked closely with 24 men over the course of several months. By engaging them in philosophical conversation for hours at a time, I got to know the participants, and they got to know me. I tracked the content, progress and nature of these conversations through detailed fieldwork notes, and both during and after, gathered the reflections of the participants through interviews, feedback forms and, on occasion, letters.

The interaction of the individual with their environment is complex. The dichotomy of 'survival' versus 'growth' among prisoners relates directly to the prison environment (see Liebling, 2012). Prison sociologists discuss stagnation, marking time and social isolation as elements of the reality of prison life (see O'Donnell, 2014). Hierarchies, power relations and fear all serve to encourage a 'survival' identity (see, for example, Sparks et al, 1996). An enabling environment, on the other hand, provides the opportunity for personal development with a focus on relationships and a humanistic approach to the individual (Haigh et al, 2012).

Therefore, it is not simply that Grendon provided a more positive environment (or 'enabling' environment) and Full Sutton a more stifling environment. The expectations of the therapeutic community had its own challenges. Four out of the 12 participants in my philosophy group left Grendon without completing their therapeutic journey. In particular, one participant chose to leave the therapeutic community in Grendon as he felt the environment would *not* help him progress. Therapeutic dialogue 'entails the exploration and expression of painful material and disturbing emotions' (Greenwood, 2001, p 48). Although the prisoners were more open and personable in their interactions, the environment did not necessarily lend itself to encouraging them to 'be themselves'. Instead, a different 'front' is played out in the therapeutic environment, albeit one that is arguably more oriented towards growth.

On the other hand, in Full Sutton, some of the participants preferred to stay in the maximum security environment despite being potentially eligible to move to a lower category (that is, lower security) prison. Among the participants, for some of those on fixed-term sentences, the need to progress within the prison system was not relevant,[1] and the atmosphere of Full Sutton suited them. In Full Sutton, they had their own cell, could cook their own food, and, as the prison was primarily made up of long-term prisoners, could 'do their own time' as they could find their 'place' in a reasonably stable prison population. However, for others their desire to stay may have reflected a 'fear of the unknown' that moving to another prison would involve rather than indicating an acceptance of the prison social climate.

My understanding of identity and growth has been developed by, and through, philosophical conversations with the participants. While desistance researchers often refer to processes of 'change', I prefer to consider growth. In doing so, we alter our focus. Instead of thinking about how a person goes from being an 'offender' to being an 'ex-offender', we consider how a person develops over time. Instead of seeking to categorize, we seek to understand. By focusing on growth, we stop focusing on ideas of redemption and judgement, and instead take account of the whole person with a past, a present and a future, a future that they can work towards, a past they need to understand, and a present that they have to come to terms with. In this way, we focus on the whole person, the human being at the centre of their story.

A framework for growth

In delivering philosophy in two contrasting prisons, I developed an initial framework for emerging themes. The focus here, as articulated earlier, is on the role of philosophy for the person-in-context, that is, the person in prison. To organize my findings, I employed four key 'orienting concepts'. These are 'forming relationships', 'developing

---

[1] For those on a fixed-term sentence, the majority will be automatically released from prison after serving a specific number of years. However, those on life sentences can only be released from open conditions, that is, when they have reached category 'D' status. For those on a life sentence in this study it was therefore necessary to 'progress' through the system and move on from Full Sutton.

trust', 'becoming more open-minded' and 'wellbeing'. These, in turn, provided a basis for understanding how philosophy relates to 'a space for self-expression' and 'opportunity for self-reflection'. I now consider each in turn.

Forming relationships

In the pilot work in HMP Low Moss, in Grendon, and in Full Sutton, nearly every participant discussed how the philosophy class provided opportunities to get to know and interact with people with whom they would not normally associate. With its focus on collaborative dialogue, philosophy provided a space for the participants to get to know each other and to begin to form relationships.

Importantly, these relationships were based on positive, pro-social interaction in a learning environment. In the philosophy classroom, the participants' crimes became irrelevant as they got to know each other – not because they resided in the same block, or had attended the same behavioural therapy programme, but because they had discussed Socrates' ideas of 'the good life' and Plato's arguments around the dangers of free-thinking artists and playwrights. Philosophy provided an environment that allowed positive relationships between these often very different participants to develop and grow. They began to understand, and therefore tolerate, each other as they heard and reflected on each other's reasoning and thinking.

Developing trust

Through a shared experience, philosophy 'grew' trust both among the participants and between the participants and myself. Trust was key to understanding how relationships developed within the philosophy classroom. The deep-rooted suspicion many prisoners have for the motivations of the prison regime has been well documented (see, for example, Sparks et al, 1996), and my entry into the field constituted a suspicious move in the eyes of many in the prison, with several of the prisoners unsure of my motives or status. In Full Sutton, the lack of trust related to the complex, 'charged' atmosphere in the prison, and I had to work hard to develop trust within the philosophy classroom. In Grendon, with its community ethos and space in the prison for dialogue and conversation, trust came more easily. In both prisons, with a focus on exploratory enquiry, abstract topics and collaborative dialogue, the philosophy classroom provided a structure to the conversations that allowed for trust to flourish.

However, the success of the philosophy course also depended on establishing trust. In order for the participants to engage openly and honestly in conversation, they had to trust that their fellow participants would not judge them for their comments, and that any contributions made would be treated with respect. For philosophical conversation to flourish, I needed to earn the trust of the participants (and vice versa). Perhaps the most accurate description would be to say trust and philosophical dialogue grew together, each encouraging the other. This took time.

Becoming more open-minded

Throughout the interviews, feedback forms and informal conversations, the participants discussed how the subject matter of, and dialogue in, the philosophy classroom had 'opened their minds'. They articulated the enjoyment they got from being allowed the time to listen to others and to consider different points of view on the topics presented. The participants were exposed to a range of views and opinions that allowed for a broad discussion of ways of thinking, and engaged in discussion that analysed, considered and developed a range of ideas.

The focus on *how* people think, as opposed to *what* people think, meant the conversation did not challenge the particulars of the participants' beliefs, but instead encouraged more developed or complex ways of thinking. The abstract nature of the course content – on philosophers' ideas as opposed to individual opinions – meant discussions could focus on the 'ought'. How 'ought' we to behave? How 'ought' society be structured? What principles 'ought' to underpin our theories of moral action? The participants were encouraged to *understand* a philosopher's point of view and offer an opinion where they could.

As a consequence, a key theme emerging from the research findings centred round 'open-mindedness'. This theme emerged primarily in Grendon, but built on the work from Low Moss, and became relevant to the work in Full Sutton. As a somewhat abstract concept I turned to the participants' own words in an attempt to capture their thoughts. For them, being more 'open-minded' meant being willing to critically reflect on their own opinions, able to listen to others and appreciate different ways of thinking. Over time, they became more willing to change their minds and able to take account of the wider society and community of which they were a part.

Wellbeing

The participants enjoyed the course – it was fun and engaging. Although this might seem a trivial observation, the value of this in the context of a prison should not be overlooked. With prison being characterized by boredom and stagnation, the opportunity to exercise intellectual capacity proved particularly relevant in the prison environment. The philosophy classroom presented a space in which they could be "normal … and be meself, not have to watch me tongue or anything" (Paul, Full Sutton, VPU). They discussed finding "people who are actually that deep.... I've opened more possibilities of spending my time well…" (Steven, Full Sutton, VPU). As with the mainstream population, the participants in this group were intelligent and, for the most part, engaged in some form of self-exploration, personal improvement or education outside of the philosophy classroom.

For many, however, it was simply about activity and stimulation. It gave them something to do, something to think about, a topic to occupy the mind. For some, the subject matter itself seemed to have an impact. Many discussed taking the ideas back to their cells and thinking over the discussions, taking time to reflect on the moral lessons and ideas presented. Finally, for others, it went deeper, with the space in the philosophy classroom providing a humanizing environment, where prisoners could be themselves and be treated as an equal and as a person. This was particularly relevant to the VP population in Full Sutton who, as has been discussed previously, can be subject to acute stigmatization and social rejection within the prison community. For these participants, the opportunity to engage in dialogue around something not related to their offence or life in prison presented an opportunity to engage in an activity as people as opposed to 'sex offenders' or 'prisoners'.

A space for self-expression

In conversational philosophy, participants are given the opportunity to talk. In a prison, with a constant need to be careful about what you say, having a space where they could freely air their views was meaningful.

In Grendon, the participants articulated the importance of these conversations in relation to the other activities. Unlike in therapy, no philosophy participant was expected to reveal an aspect of their past or personal circumstances if they did not wish to, and their engagement in the dialogue was voluntary. The participants welcomed this 'break' from the 'heavy' therapeutic work and enjoyed the opportunity.

In Full Sutton, the space for self-expression was more fundamental. The philosophy classroom served to provide an area of 'common ground' where they could interact with each other away from the complex social relations in the wider prison. For the mainstream prisoners, the philosophy classroom provided a context to overcome difference; the participants moved from laughing *at* each other to laughing *with* each other. The course became a rare safe haven in which they felt comfortable 'dropping the mask' and speaking their minds.

Here, we begin to see the relevance of these themes to the perspective of identity articulated in this book. Identity development involves a constant renegotiation of the self, both in private and in public. To do this, people need a space for self-articulation, where they can test out ideas, reflect on who they are in the company of others, and feel able to ask questions and get things wrong. For this to occur, vocabulary for self-definition is relevant, and the opportunity to 'try out' fledgling identities and potential future selves is particularly important. The ability to express oneself accurately and articulately is key.

Opportunity for self-reflection

There were clear moments of self-reflection, both in the classroom and outside. The participants, in entering the classroom, would relate how they had been thinking about the content of the previous week, and that it had given them a different way of understanding themselves. One participant said that Hume's 'bundle theory of the self' had "really struck a chord" and helped him understand that to give "different parts of myself to people ... [is] not abnormal" (Alex, Grendon). He went further and said that it helped him understand "... how little parts of me had changed gradually – I can see the gentle gradual change to become who I am today."

The philosophy course, the content and opportunity to explore different ideas allowed the participants the opportunity to reflect on how these ideas applied to them. Importantly, the course materials allowed them to control the direction of the course. While I maintained a focus on *philosophical thinking*, the content of the conversation would vary significantly between groups. Where one group would use Hume's perspective on knowledge to discuss the relevance of observation, another took the opportunity to question the motivations of philosophers themselves; some discussed the relevance of feelings and experiences, and others sought concrete examples to make their point. In having this flexibility, the participants could approach the stimulus from their own perspective. This, in turn, allowed them to reflect on how the discussion related to their own lives.

Bringing the themes together

Through the Socratic method and the development of a community of philosophical inquiry, this research has shown that philosophy can encourage people to ask questions and consider principles that lie behind an opinion. Prisoners followed in the Socratic tradition exploring complex ideas in the company of others. With language being the medium of philosophy, the participants articulated their arguments, expressed their thoughts and feelings, and engaged in critical reflection on the thoughts and feelings of others. Through these interactions, they got to know, and learned to tolerate, each other. They became more willing to listen to different points of view and to express their own views in the company of others. They learned to trust the environment of the philosophy classroom as a safe space for open, honest dialogue.

The different, but interrelated aspects of philosophy articulated in this framework all contributed towards an understanding of growth and development in prison. In reality, associations between these themes are not linear. Relationships, trust, open-mindedness and philosophical dialogue emerged alongside each other. Over time, a sense of community developed and, alongside it, the opportunity for self-expression and personal reflections. The dialogic aspect of philosophy indicated the importance of providing a space where prisoners can learn to articulate who they are in ways that are meaningful to them. In cultivating a community based on a principle of growth and development, philosophy encouraged self-reflection and provided a safe space for participants to 'be' and become.

So, we have established that moments of self-reflection occurred as part of this research process, and that the individual can find room for personal realizations in the context of a prison. However, we now need to understand *how* philosophy achieved this. What was it about philosophical dialogue that provided the means for the participants to self-reflect?

How philosophy helped develop a space to grow

Throughout this book, I have provided illustrative examples of the philosophy classes that have served to develop the reader's understanding of the techniques I employed in delivering the course. The stages of each of the sessions were organized in such a way as to demonstrate how philosophers build their arguments from first principles. Each session introduced counter-arguments and different schools of thought on the same idea. This contributed to encouraging more complex ways of thinking, as new stages would challenge the opinions offered during the previous stage's discussions.

This was no accident. I took time and care to plan the structure of the sessions to coax, or almost 'trick' the participants into agreeing with a certain point of view. I would do this by providing a robust foundation, argument and conclusion from a particular perspective that, at first glance, would seem logical and obvious. I would follow this by introducing a classic and well-known counter-example that would force the group to reconsider and reflect on previously stated points of view. In general, the participants enjoyed these 'tricks' and, over time, their skills of critically reflecting on philosophical ideas improved as they learned how to question a position before accepting a conclusion. They learned to be critical thinkers.

In delivering the course, I used careful methods of posing questions that served to draw the participants through the philosophical content and encourage philosophical thinking. The course focused on encouraging the participants in active philosophizing, which involved recognizing, articulating and interrogating underlying principles. Therefore, in response to a participant's comment, I would endeavour to ask a question that would encourage them to clarify what *their* principles were, or on what principles participants based the opinion that they had just offered. As an established method of teaching I drew on the principles of Socratic dialogue, widely recognized for encouraging learners to engage in thinking problems through. It proved a particularly useful technique in the context of philosophy in prison as it allowed the participants the time and space to put forward their own thoughts, interrogate them and respond to each other through collaborative exploration.

In addition to the pedagogy of philosophical inquiry, my professional perspective played a part in establishing trust. I take a humanistic view of education. I aim to facilitate a learning space that allows learners the time and space to pursue their interests, in their own time and at their own pace. Maintaining this perspective proved key in developing a philosophical space as the participants, particularly among the mainstream Full Sutton group, challenged my skills as a teacher. To overcome these challenges, I returned to the fundamental principles of philosophical dialogue and its pedagogy (see Chapter 1), which served to re-establish the aims of my educational course in my own mind and emphasize the teaching techniques in which I had trained. Importantly, I re-established what 'good' philosophical inquiry ought to look like, and then used principles of Socratic questioning. I found that maintaining a clear perspective on what philosophy is, as a subject and discipline, and responding to the participants' contributions with a question that aimed to encourage philosophical thinking, served as important techniques in the prison classroom.

On reflection, part of the process involved demonstrating humility. Coming in as a Cambridge graduate, the participants received me with previously conceived (and often incorrect) notions of my background, my privilege and my attitude. Over time, by treating all participants as equals and demonstrating a willingness to recognize when they had 'outfoxed' me, they began to realize that, despite my education, my opinions were no more valid than their own. This was confirmed when two colleagues from Cambridge sat in on one of my classes and one of the participants observed that their contributions were on a par with everyone else's. The pedagogy of the philosophy classroom proved an *equalizer*, where sex offenders, convicted murderers and repeat prisoners could go toe-to-toe with a Cambridge graduate, a Cambridge research associate and a Cambridge professor. I also demonstrated a human side to myself by my consistent failure to spell check or read through my teaching materials. The participants would good-naturedly laugh at my mistakes, which I would take with humour, admitting my weakness and demonstrating that this did not diminish my confidence or reflect on my ability to deliver the programme.

This all contributed towards a sense of community. In general, this aspect of the philosophy course proved to be complementary to the ethos of Grendon, but counter to the prevailing culture of Full Sutton. In both environments, the course successfully established a sense of community that was based on the positive, shared experience of philosophical inquiry. Importantly, this shared experience was *not* based on their status as prisoner, but instead allowed them to engage in an activity as a person, as a learner and as an amateur philosopher. Such an environment served to break down stereotypes, promote tolerance and understanding, and develop different social networks. For some, this meant they could grow as individuals away from the influences of their normal social circles.

So we now come to the final question: is growth possible in the prison environment? Can people in long-term confinement find ways to understand themselves better? Are personal realizations possible?

Or perhaps we should be more specific – is there evidence of growth within *this* research project?

Moments of growth

Thinking about the men I worked with over the course of this research, there were clear moments where they demonstrated poignant personal realizations. For some, these moments occurred during the philosophical conversations or while the course was running (recall, for example, Toby's realization that his "pantimomic" outrage was counterproductive to getting people on side).

For others, these moments came in post-participation interviews when we were reflecting together on the relevance of the course. Michael, for example, used the 'Theseus' ship' paradox to discuss his own process of change in his group therapy session. He said it helped him articulate his journey and explain to others his process of change.

Another, Charlie, learned the value of his own contributions. He was funny and quick-witted and I recall one particular conversation when we were discussing issues of class versus income. I related a conversation I had had with an archaeologist friend who had learned the digger driver was earning twice what he earned. Charlie cut across and said, "Yeah, well, you have to understand, an archaeologist often needs a digger driver, but a digger driver never needs an archaeologist."

Charlie was good-natured, but often 'played the fool'. He would make out that he did not have as much to say as others in the class, he had not engaged in much formal education prior to, or in, prison. His contributions could be blunt, so much so that after he would make his point, the rest of the class would fall silent. I spoke to him about this in his post-participation interviews. He voiced his concerns that he did not think he was really saying anything that useful. What he had not realized was that, while others chattered on, mused out loud about different ways of thinking about the stimulus, he would sit and listen. Eventually, he would cut across the conversation with a short, succinct and on-point comment. His sharp wit meant his contribution would often get to the heart of the issue that others were skirting around. When I explained this to him and said "the way you describe philosophy shows you totally understand what it is, you completely get the purpose of it", he responded by simply saying, "Thank you. That means a lot" (Charlie, post-participation interview, Grendon).

For some participants, their demonstrations of growth related to the process of engaging in philosophical conversation. One of the Muslim TACT prisoners had an open disposition and clear desire to understand how his circumstances had led him to interpret his faith in such a way that he had engaged in activities that contravened the Terrorism Act. He and I had a range of conversations (after class, in the breaks and in interviews) about the role of faith in people's lives and what he had learned from the philosophy class. For him, he saw the role of philosophy as a potential guide to life: on how to live and how to behave. He saw its importance for many people, but he reflected, for him, he could turn to the Qu'ran for guidance. He respected and understood the need for philosophy for those without such a strong guiding faith. Through philosophy, he had opportunity to articulate tolerance and understanding for others.

Finally, there were two participants who seemed to reflect directly on their offences as a result of the philosophy class. I will keep these accounts somewhat vague so as to protect their identity. Both had been convicted of particularly serious crimes against women involving violence and sexual assault. However, they had very different dispositions. One was nervous and reflective, understood the severity of his crimes and seemed to want to find a way to understand his behaviour. The other was more bold – he would discuss what he had done in detail, demonstrated little shame and, while he clearly knew he had done something wrong, he seemed to want to find excuses.

In the case of the former, in the post-participation interview we discussed the question of feminism again (he was the one who had recommended an author and seemed to understand the ideas of feminism well). I carefully asked him about how he had come to understand feminism and, on realizing that he had grown up with these perspectives, gently asked how he squared his views with the crimes he had committed. He looked at me thoughtfully and simply responded, "I missed something there, didn't I?"

In the other's case, the post-participation interview involved a candid conversation about trust in relationships. We discussed the importance of openness and honesty, and eventually he said, "But Kirstine, I was honest. I told her. I told her that I had a temper." I paused at this comment, and carefully said, "Can you see that that is a little threatening?" His eyes widened in surprise and said, in clear astonishment that he had not seen that before, "It is, isn't it! That is a little threatening."

The purpose of relating these stories is not to argue that philosophy had long-term or lasting effects on the participants. I did not seek to achieve this, and nor did I measure it. It is, instead, to articulate how philosophy provided small moments of growth, incidences where the participants made clear breakthroughs in self-reflection and self-understanding. By developing a working relationship with the participants, we were able to engage in a level of candour that provided moments of insight.

One further example illustrates this point. Over the course of 12 weeks, and after some resistance, I developed a good rapport with one of the Muslim participants who had been convicted of terrorism offences. Unlike the other Muslims who had either converted while in prison, came from liberal Muslim families or were willing to reflect openly on their faith, this participant maintained a careful interaction with me throughout. It was evident he followed strict scriptures, but he also seemed to be carefully considering his personal faith narrative. On several occasions, he pushed me on my own beliefs. In these situations, he was not challenging me, but instead asking me questions so as to understand my perspective, and, perhaps, his own.

On one of these occasions he told me that a few years prior he would have refused to shake my hand because I was a woman, and he asked how I would feel about that. I told him, frankly, that regardless of your religion I expect to be treated the same as a man, particularly in a professional context. In my view, to refuse to shake my hand could be reasonably seen as an insult. This was towards the end of the philosophy classes and we had established an understanding that views can be expressed and must be considered. I felt confident in being able to express my true feelings about this without insulting his faith because we had cultivated a level of trust. His response was to nod thoughtfully, and we did not discuss it again.

Over the months that followed the course, I exchanged a few letters with this participant. We discussed logic, faith and reason. The point of recounting this is to demonstrate that, perhaps, by engaging with individual participants as equals, and being genuinely interested in their wellbeing, development and worldviews (as opposed to only engaging with them in terms of their offending), we can provide openings to challenge some of their existing ways of thinking. By showing that they are part of our community, as opposed to them being 'others', outside and expelled, we find space to engage on the topics that really matter.

To grow, we need space to be. This involves space for self-expression, space to get things wrong, space to ask questions and space to forge new ways of being. I wonder whether this is ever truly possible in a prison, but there seems to be some strength of the human spirit that can forge through, given the right opportunity. The themes raised through philosophical conversation relate both to what communities of philosophical conversation can offer and to that which is lacking in the prison environment. The participants articulated attributes of the philosophy class they enjoyed precisely because they are lacking in the wider environment. Trust, positive relationships, space to be open and improved wellbeing through the opportunity for self-expression were all highlighted – because they were not available elsewhere, and because they were important to the people in prison.

In taking philosophy into the prison classroom, I learned that opportunities for exploring and expressing ideas were rare. Philosophy provided a space that went beyond the prison walls and allowed the opportunity for self-expression. The participants were given the time to develop new ideas, were introduced to new concepts and were able to articulate, in the company of others, what their views were on a range of issues. I also learned that in the restrictive environment of a prison, any opportunity to articulate the self and to present yourself to others in an authentic way is meaningful. Perhaps, most importantly, I learned that in a deeply dehumanizing environment, philosophy had the power to change the way people thought about themselves.

11

Final Reflections

Over the course of this research, I have found that the prisoner-participants were deep thinkers, fully capable of intellectually challenging conversation, and with perspectives that often proved insightful. Many were earnest in their attempts to find meaning in the prison environment, and engaged in philosophical conversation with a passionate interest in self-improvement. The importance of trust, the relevance of relationships and the provision of a safe space for self-articulation in a prison environment are all present in literature on the prison experience.

Many of the participants will not be released from prison for a significant period of time. The relevance of this course is therefore about survival – survival of one's identity in the face of a complex and volatile prison culture. It is in this context that the 'survival' versus 'growth' dichotomy takes on relevance. In a prison, survival *requires* the opportunity to grow. Without it, in the harsh and austere prison environment, prisoners stagnate, suspended in time and space with little stimulation. Education therefore takes on a particular meaning in the prison and is, arguably, not simply desirable, but necessary.

At the outset of this project, nearly 10 years ago now, there was no literature around philosophy in prisons. I seem to have 'caught a wave', however, and there is now a range of philosophy courses being run and some literature has begun to emerge on the subject. However, my research remains significant and novel. As an in-depth, ethnographically led study of philosophy in prisons, I immersed myself in the context, worked closely with the participants, and considered the relevance of education through the lens of philosophical conversation. It constitutes a unique study that provides a new and important perspective on the role of prison education by drawing on the experience of researcher-as-teacher, and articulating the experience of prisoners in engaging in philosophical conversation.

This research has delineated between a 'survival' identity and a 'growth' identity. At the outset of this book I related the 'survival' identity to Goffman's dramaturgical self. Goffman's discussions around presentations of the self postulates that a 'frontstage' self is performed according to the social expectations of a particular situation. The 'backstage' self is reserved for when the individual feels comfortable and they allow themselves to drop the 'mask'. In this book, and in wider prison research, this idea is used to articulate prisoners' methods of 'survival' within the context of a complex prison social system, with presentations of the self being steeped in the complexity of human emotions that arise in the face of the prison environment. 'Growth' has been related to development, and the book began with desistance literature to develop an understanding of the narrative self.

The research has been shaped by my own subjective experience of delivering philosophy in prisons. By drawing on ethnographic techniques of data collection and analysis, I was able to work with my biases to produce rich and detailed findings. Throughout, I engaged in reflexive practice, refining research questions through a system of 'progressive focusing' and 'sense checking' emerging themes by returning to the field and asking for the participants' feedback. With an iterative research process involving stages of data collection, analysis, theory-building and literature searching, validation and triangulation were built into the research process. Furthermore, throughout, I articulated and justified the perspective from which I was working. In doing this, my biases and interests were actively used to shape the book and direct the investigation.

The research in HMP Full Sutton revealed that philosophy provided a space to cultivate relationships and trust, and to promote the wellbeing of the participants. This research also demonstrated that it was only when trust and relationships were established that philosophical conversation could flourish, but also that it was through philosophical conversation that trust and relationships emerged – like some kind of perfect circle, trust and relationships 'grew' together. In HMP Grendon, I was able to focus more closely on the relevance of the content of the conversations and the construct of 'open-mindedness' emerged from the work there. In developing more open-minded dispositions, growth identities are given the space to emerge.

In the philosophy classroom, the individual is met as a 'whole person'. In the prison context this was both rare and important. As desistance research has shown us, the change narrative is complex and requires opportunity for self-reflection. Identity work involves being able to 'try out' ways of being in different contexts. If a person spends all their time in an environment that encourages or creates the need for a macho front, how can we expect them to develop in any other way?

The dialogic nature of the class provided a space for the participants to communicate with each other and to articulate the self in a safe environment. In Grendon, the 'safe' environment refers to the distinction between the dialogue engaged in therapy and dialogue in philosophy. Whereas therapy can be personal, specific and often involves the exploration of disturbing emotions, philosophy can be abstract and involve the exploration of a philosophical idea. The outcome of interest in therapy is psychological change, while the outcome of interest for a teacher in a philosophy setting is that their students have simply *learned* something. Both these attributes of philosophy contributed to developing a safe space for open dialogue.

In Full Sutton, the philosophy classroom provided a space to overcome complex interpersonal relationships that are formed by the underlying prisoner 'society'. The participants were able to drop their 'mask' and engage in the dialogues as educational and stimulating activities. However, this took time to establish. I had to develop trust and respect among the participants before relationships could emerge and the participants could 'relax' and be themselves. With trust in place, there was an indication from this research that philosophical dialogue could serve to ameliorate the impact that imprisonment can have in contributing to survival identities. There is some suggestion from this research that education, and in particular, philosophical dialogue, can contribute to a growth identity, and to the personal development of individual participants. In particular, philosophical dialogue seemed to provide the space in which explorations of the self can occur.

This research has highlighted the importance of offering programmes that go beyond the offender, to the person. I have offered here an exploration of *how* this might be achieved in the context of a prison. The findings support the importance of education for education's sake – the power of an individual prisoner engaging in a programme for personal self-improvement alone cannot be overstated. Scholars in the desistance field discuss the need for 'strength-based' programmes (see, for example, McNeill and Weaver, 2010) to enhance our understanding of the process of change. In general, desistance research has yet to be fully 'operationalized', and this study highlights a need to ensure these efforts do not lead to the instrumentalization of programmes for the express purposes of achieving desistance. Instead, we should be focusing on process of growth. By taking a 'whole person' approach to this research, and considering personal development as it is experienced by prisoners undergoing study-for-its-own-sake, I offer an insight into how this type of growth might be cultivated in the context of a prison educational classroom. Perhaps giving people in prison an opportunity to be seen as more than just an offender means that they will start seeing themselves as something different.

Since I completed my fieldwork, I have had some contact with my participants. Some have written letters to update me on their work, and others have written brief notes to thank me for the time I spent with them. One wrote to me to relate an argument over an overcrowded fish tank in his wing. He related how too many eggs had hatched in the tank, meaning the whole community of fish would be at risk if nothing was done. He was disappointed that his fellow prisoners could not understand his perspective that it would be better for the whole community if some of the eggs were removed so that a smaller number were allowed to survive. He used utilitarian arguments to make his case, and lamented the lack of philosophical understanding among his fellow prisoners, as they could not appreciate the argument he was making.

A second prisoner wrote to thank me for the 'head start' philosophy had given him in his Critical Thinking A-Level, and discussed how he could apply some of the lessons he had learned with me in further studies. In both cases, I was delighted to hear that the course had taken on relevance beyond the classroom.

I wish to end this book by acknowledging what the participants themselves taught me about philosophy, life and how to live. During the philosophy sessions, I engaged in philosophical exploration with the prisoner-participants. I reflected on the materials alongside them, listened to their points of view, and, through this dialogue, developed my own views and understanding of the topics. In Grendon in particular, the participants articulated what it meant to actively philosophize in clear and eloquent terms. Through their descriptions of the experience of philosophy, I improved my own understanding of what philosophy is for, and what it means to philosophize. In Full Sutton, they helped me understand why these philosophical conversations are important in the human context of a prison.

For these men, this was about freedom – freedom of self-expression, freedom to disagree and freedom to engage. I hope that for the short time I worked with these men, I was able to provide a space outside and beyond the prison walls where they could be philosophers for a time.

A final word

The final word of my book I leave to one of the participants. A thoughtful and engaging man, always concerned with others, and earnest in his passionate attempts to reform and rebuild his life, he sadly passed away in prison less than a year after engaging in this research. I was fortunate enough to see him again before his passing, and it seems fitting to close this discussion in the way that I opened it, with his words:

> 'I saw a different side to the people I already knew. And it gave me more, it made me see other people in a different way. Because, before, I'd never heard other people's opinions. Being able to work together, being able to argue together, develop ideas together; it's always been "you're right, I'm wrong, this is the way it is, no it ain't" and so forth. To see people work on the thing together, to build and come to some sort of conclusion together, in some cases, it was enlightening. And, I suppose, that's sort of rubbed off.... I listen more to people because I realize people have got their own ideas and they can think about things logically. So I've given other people more time as well and I'm more interested in what other people have got to say as well rather than, well, you've got nothing to say.'

Appendix: Technical Methods

Methodological framework

Layder's *Sociological Practice* (1998), the primary source for the methodological framework of this research, provides a critique of both purist qualitative and 'verificationist' quantitative methodologies. However, Layder does not wholly reject either perspective, instead offering a third way that allows the researcher to draw on emergent, data-driven analysis as well as extant literature known as 'adaptive theory'. In this Appendix I provide a more technical account of data collection and analysis, and the underlying methodological framework used to produce these findings.

Layder argues that to maximize theory generation there should be a dialogue between all resources available (general theory, substantive theory, theory-testing, sensitizing concepts and empirically emergent theory). Thus, he offered a framework that allows for use of extant theory, combining what is known about philosophy in general, prison sociology and desistance to guide data collection and analysis, and adapt and refine the emergent theory. Extant theories are used in conversation with the data through developing 'orienting concepts', engaging in 'memo writing' and organizing data through a system of 'pre-coding'. However, Layder's account of research methods lacks detail, and I therefore draw on a variety of appropriate methodologies to enhance my data collection and analysis.

Research design

My research design took a staged approach – pilot, HMP Grendon, HMP Full Sutton. At each stage, fledgling theories emerged. These provided direction and orientation for the subsequent data collection while also ensuring data collection tools allowed for new themes and issues to emerge. I engaged with the literature alongside data collection, with desistance literature and prison sociology offering particular guidance. The research involved reflexive practice and triangulation to increase validity and reliability (Golafshani, 2003). Throughout each stage of the research, I undertook initial analysis on the qualitative data, developing orienting concepts and refining and testing theories in the field (Layder, 1998).

The lens of this research has been focused on the lives of prisoners. Taking a 'humanistic' approach allowed the participants the opportunity to articulate the prison experience, their status as prisoner and the role of education from the dual perspectives of the prisoner-participants and the teacher-researcher (Liebling, 2015). Liebling's descriptions of such work as 'emotional edgework' resonate with my own experience in the field; this research has been intimate, intrusive and emotionally demanding (Liebling, 2015), yet, at the same time, it has been informative and worthwhile. The opportunity to engage men in prison in philosophical conversation is not granted to everyone, and the research design produced accurate and careful descriptions of the prisons, prisoners and philosophical inquiries.

The research design took an iterative process of data collection, analysis and reflection to produce an overall theory. Data collection included interviewing participants before and after course delivery using semi-structured interview schedules refined and developed during the piloting phase and throughout the research process. I drew on qualitative arguments that the individual at the centre of the research ought to be heard most clearly in the emerging theory (Rubin and Rubin, 2012). As a subjective participant, my own experience and insight held relevance, with systematic and extensive fieldwork notes providing key insights. Analysis, however, always began with the participants' own words, starting with post-participation interviews before drawing on fieldwork notes and other data collection strands.

Figure A1: The research process

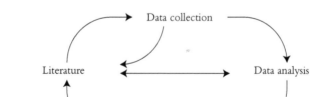

Research questions

Drawing on ethnographic methods of 'progressive focusing', each stage of the research included systematic focusing and refinement of the research questions (Wilson and Sapsford, 2006). The following two research questions underpin the inquiry:

- How is engaging in philosophy education relevant to a prisoner's personal development?
- How does the environment of a prison impact the role of philosophy in the lives of the participants?

Each data collection period resulted in new research questions. In Grendon, the following research questions emerged:

- How does the dialogue in philosophy differ from the dialogue employed in the therapeutic community?
- Does philosophy complement or contradict the work of a therapeutic community?

Emergent themes from Grendon encouraged a greater focus on wellbeing and personal development:

- Does philosophical inquiry encourage personal development among participants, and if so, in what way(s)?
- Does philosophy improve participants' wellbeing, and in what way does it impact prisoners' psychological survival?

The environment of Full Sutton produced its own research questions:

- How does philosophy establish trust among its participants?
- What role does philosophy play in establishing positive, pro-social relationships among prisoners?

Finally, working with the vulnerable prisoner (VP) population in Full Sutton produced:

- Why is the humanizing effect of philosophy particularly relevant to prisoners held in the vulnerable prisoner units (VPUs) of maximum security environments?

Data collection

Observations and fieldwork notes

Throughout, extensive and detailed notes recorded a range of observations (Bernard, 1994). I delivered the course in the education department alongside other educational programmes. For the duration of delivery, I spent two days in each prison per week using my time outside of the classroom to learn about the prison context and engage prisoners and staff in conversation around 'life inside'. I adapted the length and structure of the course according to the regime schedule, so each session lasted between 2½ and 4 hours (12.30 pm until 4 pm in Grendon and 8.15 am until 12.30 pm in Full Sutton VPU and 8.15 am until 11 am in the mainstream half).

Fieldwork notes included observations of the prison in general, recording everything from the particulars of a casual conversation with a member of staff to my own feelings of walking down the prison corridors. Staff on wings, in the education department and in the chaplaincy provided useful insights into the prison environment. I also sought out specific members of staff to discuss particular themes that had emerged in my data. For example, I spent time with members of the psychology department in order to understand the psychological courses available, and I spoke with the chaplaincy in Full Sutton to improve my understanding of faith in prison.

Each philosophy session produced specific and separate fieldwork notes. During delivery of the course, I took the role of full participant when engaged in facilitating philosophical conversation (Schensul et al, 1999), refraining from taking fieldwork notes during delivery of the course to ensure that I gave the dialogue my full attention. I therefore took fieldwork notes directly after each philosophy session, recording them via a dictaphone during my journey home.

Observations are passed through the 'interpretive filter' of the observer (Foster, 2006). As such, fieldwork notes reflect my interpretation of what was interesting and what was important. However, by employing Layder's methods of analysis, I consciously recognized and worked with my own subjectivities and interests, and employed several techniques to guard against bias and poor note-taking. This included ensuring my notes were as detailed as possible, thereby capturing a wide range of data, and having my supervisor review some fieldwork notes and offer advice throughout that served to encourage clarification of thought (Murchison, 2010).

Finally, all my fieldwork notes were subject to triangulation (Foster, 2006). In addition to my own observations, I 'tested' my thoughts through respondent validation (Murchison, 2010). Throughout delivery, feedback forms and informal conversations with the participants provided the opportunity to check my analysis of the environment and philosophy sessions. I discussed my conclusions regarding the atmosphere of the prison and the classroom with staff members, within the education department and beyond, and with the prisoners. The following section discusses these methods in more detail, where I dedicate a section to triangulation, validation and reflexivity.

Interviewing participants

I conducted three types of interview over the course of the research (Wilson, 1996):

- Pre-course interviews
- Informal, conversational interviews throughout delivery
- Post-course formal interviews.

Each of these interview stages adopted different interview styles and had distinct purposes Pre-course interviews had three purposes: to inform the participants of the research; to meet and gain rapport with the participants (Bailey, 2007); and to gain insight into the participants' educational backgrounds and attitudes (Roberts, 2002). I recorded these interviews through note-taking and conducted them in a conversational style.

During delivery, I engaged the participants in purposeful conversation to validate my observations of the class dynamics (Foster, 2006). Most of these conversations happened casually, in corridors, as I walked with the participants towards our separate tea break areas, or as we waited for other participants to arrive before the class began. On some occasions, I sought out specific participants to discuss something that had happened in the class, and engaged them in discussion in their wings or their workshops.

Finally, each of the participants engaged in a formal post-participation interview. Most (23/24) of these interviews were recorded using a digital voice recorder, with one participant asking not to be recorded; I recorded his interview through note-taking. The interview schedule took a semi-structured approach (Wilson and Sapsford, 2006), starting with open-ended, exploratory questions. The second half of the interview asked participants more direct questions that related to my own theories about the use of philosophy in prisons (these questions were also adapted and altered at each stage of the process as theories emerged).

All interview schedules were piloted. The wording of the questions ensured they were open-ended, neutral, singular and clear, while the order of questions allowed for exploration of the participants' experiences, opinions, feelings and knowledge (Patton, 2002). I amended and adapted the interview schedule as the research progressed to allow for exploration of new and emerging themes in the data, and the semi-structured approach allowed the participants time to explore their own thoughts and ideas about the role of philosophy.

Participant feedback

Throughout delivery, the participants completed feedback forms after each session, giving them the opportunity to reflect on sessions and provide feedback. This allowed me to keep abreast of how the participants felt about the course, their engagement, and their view on the topics.

I also captured participant responses through focus groups and correspondence. In order to develop and refine emerging theories, some participants reviewed draft chapters and were asked to respond in writing if they had time. I returned to each of the prisons several months after course delivery to hold focus groups with the participants. In each of these sessions, I outlined my preliminary findings, asking the participants to provide feedback in writing and verbally. These sessions proved particularly useful in sense checking interpretations of themes (Foster, 2006). In some cases, the participants corrected my findings, allowing for a more refined and developed theme. In others, they agreed with and confirmed my analysis, serving to validate my findings (Atkinson and Hammersley, 2007).

Ethics

Negotiating entry and recruiting participants in Grendon and Full Sutton involved different processes. In both prisons, I established contact with the governor of the prison through my supervisor, Alison Liebling. Each of the governors gave initial approval for the research. I then sought, and gained, official approval for the research from the National Offender Management Service (NOMS) and the University of Cambridge Ethics Committee. Each institution required a different level of security clearance, and provided safeguarding training prior to the research commencing.

All participants were fully informed of the research, assured of anonymity, the voluntary nature of participation, and of the right to withdraw. All were given a participant information sheet and I reiterated the distinction between the course and the research. All participants consented to taking part in both the research and the course. One participant withdrew his consent, leaving the course part way through. He is not included in this research. Several other participants left the course without completing due to being transferred to other prisons. These participants are also not included in the research.

I recorded post-participation interviews using a digital voice recorder. At the end of each day, I transferred all recordings on to a laptop and encrypted the files. I deleted the original recordings from the digital voice recorder and transcribed the interviews with the original transcriptions also being encrypted. Some interviews were transcribed by an outside source that was recommended by my department. The transcribers were made aware of the sensitive nature of the research, and agreed to confidentiality. Files were transferred in a secure manner. I provided a code and a pseudonym for all participants, and altered transcripts so that they referred to the participants only by these pseudonyms, and any identifying comments were redacted. This allowed the transcripts to be imported to NVivo (version 10.1.1) for analysis. These protocols were in accordance with the guidelines of the University of Cambridge's Institute of Criminology at the time of the research, and I am only person with access to the encrypted files.

Data analysis and developing theory

After each period of fieldwork (including the pilot stage), I began my analysis by reviewing and coding post-participation interview transcripts. From there, I developed themes, orienting concepts and theoretical memos, allowing the participants' words to shape my thinking. I used techniques of open-coding in the early stages to generate themes (Glaser and Strauss, 2012 [1967]). As themes and theories began to emerge, I switched to Layder's method of 'pre-coding' whereby I read through the transcripts and fieldwork notes, pinpointing 'theoretically relevant' (Layder, 1998, p 57) sections. Throughout, I kept theoretical memos that tracked and explored emerging theories.

Analysis of data occurred in stages, with each period of data collection being independently analysed while building on the one that came before. In Grendon, the interview transcripts from the 12 participants were analysed together, triangulating emerging theories with fieldwork notes and feedback forms. In Full Sutton, however, the distinction between delivering philosophy in the VPU and in the mainstream wings led me to analyse these two groups distinctly. The assumption was that, because my experience was so distinct in the two prisons, so, too, would be the participants' experience, which would, in turn, lead to distinct outcomes.

As Layder points out, theorizing and data analysis are distinct processes, but should work in conjunction. As such, periods of fieldwork, data analysis, theorizing and engaging with the literature occurred several times at different stages in the research. Having developed the key orienting concepts from the data – open mind, trust and community/wellbeing – as well as drawing orienting concepts from the literature – identity, self-understanding – the next stage was to draw these concepts together to develop an overarching theory (Bendasolli, 2013).

Triangulation, validation and reflexivity

From the design stage of this research, reflexivity has been seen as a key tool in the data collection process, and one of particular importance when engaging in subjective, person-centred research. Interview schedules were adapted and developed between each stage of data collection, and observational notes became more specific and refined by engaging in evaluation and critique of content (Shaw, 1999; Murchison, 2010). Methods of 'respondent validation' ensured findings were regularly sense checked with research participants to check that I had an accurate understanding of a particular situation (Bloor, 1978; Atkinson and Hammersley, 2007).

I triangulated my findings by cross-referencing fieldwork notes with interview transcripts and feedback forms. This allowed for a rich, data-driven thematic analysis of the research (Wilson and Hutchinson, 1991). I also drew on the experiences of other researchers in maximum security environments and literary accounts, which provided the opportunity to compare and contrast my own experience and findings with those of researchers who have come before me.

As the research progressed, and I delivered the course in different environments, my understanding of the role of philosophy changed and developed. The straightforward delivery of the course in Grendon contrasted with the complex social relations of Full Sutton. I entered the field somewhat naively and left it with a much deeper understanding of the difficulties of the lives of prisoners. Utilizing methods of progressive focusing allowed the research to unfold and develop according to the natural evolution of the project, including the development of trust and respect between the participants and the researcher, and among the participants themselves. It provided the scope for incorporating emerging theories, testing and refining them as the research progressed, resulting in an in-depth account of philosophy education in two prisons in England.

Researcher-teacher

Finally, the research was strengthened by the in-depth insight the dual role of researcher-teacher perspective provided. However, this also meant that the analysis passed through the 'interpretive filter' of the researcher (Foster, 2006), and my findings constitute a subjective, systematically recorded account. It has been driven by my belief in and passion for education, shaped by my training and background in the teaching profession and my perspective of what education ought to look like.

This perspective relates to the approach to the prisoner as an 'experiencing subject' as opposed to an 'experienced object' whereby I recognize that I, too, am an 'experiencing subject' in this research process (see also, Duguid, 2000). My experience as a teacher in the prison classroom provided a specific and unique perspective in the data, with findings shaped by my approach to philosophy, the topics I chose to cover, the way in which I conducted myself in the classroom and the relationships I developed with the participants. These, in turn, were driven by my understanding of what a 'good' learning environment looks like – one that builds learners' confidence, that encourages a thirst for knowledge, that looks to work with learners' strengths and interests, and, most importantly, one that encourages them to think critically about that which is presented to them, allowing space and time for them to challenge both what is being taught and the way in which the teaching is being delivered. For me, a positive learning environment is one that is 'buzzing' with energy and enthusiasm, where learners have not only learned something, but also enjoyed themselves in the process. To achieve this, in my experience, it is imperative for learners to understand that I, as their teacher, care about their progress in my classroom, about their educational journey and consequently, about them as people who live in the world.

In prison, motivations for entering education, the ability to progress within the classroom and the capacity to apply the learning beyond the classroom are all constrained by the prison environment. It is therefore important that a teacher, in such an environment, recognizes and works with this distinct context, with concepts such as pastoral care, wellbeing and safety taking on specific meanings relevant to the lives of these particular learners. My role as philosophy teacher was to develop participants' skills in active philosophizing and encourage their acquisition of knowledge in the subject of philosophy. It was important to create a positive learning environment for all participants where learners, participants, pupils or students must feel safe and able to engage in the learning process. The wellbeing of the learners underpins practice, which, in the prison environment, meant striving for an environment where the participants felt able to participate in conversation without fear of being undermined, with an understanding that their contribution had equal value, and where they were, first and foremost, learners in a classroom.

A note on information sources

Teaching materials were developed and adapted during the course of delivery. Some were used in both prisons, others just in one prison.

The following books were consulted regularly:

- Dave Robinson and Chris Garratt (1999) *Introducing Ethics*.
- Christopher Hamilton (2003) *Understanding Philosophy for AS Level*.
- Nigel Warburton (2004) *A Little History of Philosophy*.
- Stephen Law (2007) *The Great Philosophers: The Lives and Ideas of History's Greatest Thinkers*.
- Philip Stokes (2010) *Philosophy: The Great Thinkers*.
- Peter Worley (2011) *The 'If' Machine: Philosophical Enquiry in the Classroom*.
- Stephen Trombley (2012) *Fifty Thinkers Who Shaped the Modern World*.
- Tom Butler-Bowdon (2013) *50 Philosophy Classics: Thinking, Being, Acting, Seeing*.
- Gary Hayden (2013) *You Kant Make It Up! Strange Ideas from History's Great Philosophers*.

I also consulted the following websites:

- The Stanford Encyclopaedia of Philosophy: http://plato.stanford.edu/
- Aeon: https://aeon.co

Bibliography

Arendt, H. (1998 [1958]) *The Human Condition* (2nd edn), Chicago, IL: The University of Chicago Press.

Atkinson, P. and Hammersley, M. (2007) *Ethnography: Principles in Practice* (3rd edn), New York: Taylor & Francis.

Auty, K. and Liebling, A. (2020) 'Exploring the relationship between prison social climate and reoffending', *Justice Quarterly*, 37(2), 358–81. doi:10.1080/07418825.2018.1538421

Bachman, R. (2007) *The Practice of Research in Criminology and Criminal Justice*, Los Angeles, CA: SAGE Publications Ltd.

Bailey, C.A. (2007) *A Guide to Qualitative Field Research* (2nd edn), Thousand Oaks, CA: Pine Forge Press.

Baltzly, D. (2019) 'Stoicism', *The Stanford Encyclopedia of Philosophy* (Spring edition) (edited by Edward N. Zalta). Available at: https://plato.stanford.edu/archives/spr2019/entries/stoicism

Barrow, W. (2010) 'Dialogic, participation and the potential for Philosophy for Children', *Thinking Skills and Creativity*, 5, 61–9.

Batuik, M.E. (1997) 'The state of post-secondary correctional education in Ohio', *Journal of Correctional Education*, 48(2), 70–2.

Batuik, M.E., Lahm, K.F., McKeever, M., Wilcox, N. and Wilcox, P. (2005) 'Disentangling the effects of correctional education: Are current policies misguided? An event history analysis', *Criminal Justice*, 5(1), 55–74.

Beckford, J.A. (2005) 'Muslims in the prisons of Britain and France', *Journal of Contemporary European Studies*, 13(3), 287–97.

Beckford, M. (2015) 'Revealed: First UK jail where half the inmates are Muslim and others are pressured to convert to Islamic "protection racket"', *Mail Online*, 17 October. Available at: www.dailymail.co.uk/news/article-3277502/First-UK-jail-half-inmates-Muslim-pressured-convert-Islamic-protection-racket.html

Behan, C. (2007) 'Context, creativity and critical reflection: Education in correctional institutions', *Journal of Correctional Education*, 58(2), 157–69.

Behan, C. (2008) 'From Outside to Inside: Pedagogy within Prison Walls', in R. Wright (ed) *In the Borderlands: Learning to Teach in Prisons and Alternative Settings*, San Bernadino, CA: San Bernadino State University, pp 119–35.

Behan, C. (2014) 'Learning to escape: Prison education, rehabilitation and the potential for transformation', *Journal of Prison Education and Reentry*, 1(1), 20–31.

Bendasolli, P.F. (2013) 'Theory building in qualitative research: Reconsidering the problem of induction', *Forum: Qualitative Social Research*, 14(1).

Bennallick, M. (2019) 'Exploring Learning Cultures in Prison', PhD thesis, London: Royal Holloway.

Bernard, H.R. (1994) *Research Methods in Anthropology*, Thousand Oaks, CA: SAGE Publications Ltd.

Biesta, G. (2011) 'Philosophy, exposure, and children: How to resist the instrumentalisation of philosophy in education', *Journal of Philosophy of Education*, 45(2), 305–19.

Blackburn, S. (1999) *Think*, Oxford: Oxford University Press.

Bloor, M. (1978) 'On the analysis of observational data: A discussion of the worth and uses of inductive techniques and respondent validation', *Sociology*, 12(3), 545–52.

Bonta, J. and Andrews, D.A. (2007) *Risk-Need-Responsivity Model for Offender Assessment and Rehabilitation*, User Report 2007–06, Ottawa, ON: Public Safety Canada.

Bottoms, A. (2002) 'Morality, Crime, Compliance and Public Policy', in A. Bottoms and M. Tonry (eds) *Ideology, Crime and Criminal Justice: A Symposium in Honour of Sir Leon Radzinowicz*, Cullompton: Willan Publishing, pp 39–42.

Bottoms, A. and Shapland, J. (2016) 'Learning to Desist in Early Adulthood: The Sheffield Desistance Study', in J. Shapland, S. Farrall and A. Bottoms (eds) *Global Perspectives on Desistance: Reviewing What We Know and Looking to the Future*, Oxford: Routledge, pp 99–125.

Bouffard, J., Mackenzie, D.L. and Hickman, L.J. (2000) 'Effectiveness of vocational education and employment programs for adult offenders', *Journal of Offender Rehabilitation*, 1–41.

Bovill, M. and Anderson, C. (2020) 'Changing the subject: A community of philosophical inquiry', *European Journal for Research on the Education and Learning of Adults*, 11(2), 183–98.

Brandon, J. (2009) *Unlocking Al-Qaeda: Islamist Extremism in British Prisons*, London: Quilliam.

Brewster, D.R. and Sharp, S.F. (2002) 'Educational programs and recidivism in Oklahoma: Another look', *The Prison Journal*, 82(3), 314–34.

Brubaker, R. and Cooper, F. (2000) 'Beyond "identity"', *Theory & Society*, 29, 1–47.

Bruner, J. (1987) 'Life as narrative', *Social Research*, 54(1), 11–32.

Buber, M. (2000 [1923]) *I and Thou* (translated by R.G. Smith), New York: Scribner Classics.

Burman, J. (2015) 'Why are Muslim terror gangs allowed to run Sharia extortion rackets in UK jails?', *Express*, 4 November. Available at: www.express.co.uk/news/uk/616260/Britain-Prisons-Category-A-Michael-Gove-Steve-Gillian-Jizya-Tax-ISIS-Belmarsh-Inmates

Bushway, S.D., Thornberry, T.P. and Krohn, M. (2003) 'Desistance as a developmental process: A comparison of static and dynamic approaches', *Journal of Qualitative Criminology*, 19(2), 129–53.

Butler-Bowdon, T. (2013) *50 Philosophy Classics: Thinking, Being, Acting, Seeing*, London: Nicholas Brealey Publishing.

Butrus, N. and Witenberg, R.T. (2013) 'Some personality predictors of tolerance to human diversity: The roles of openness, agreeableness, and empathy', *Australian Psychologist*, 48, 290–8.

Callan, V. and Gardner, J. (2005) *Vocational Education and Training Provision and Recidivism in Queensland Correctional Institutions*, Adelaide, SA: National Centre for Vocational Education Research.

Carr, D. (2002) 'Moral education and the perils of developmentalism', *Journal of Moral Education*, 31(1), 5–19.

Casey, S., Day, A., Vess, J. and Ward, T. (2013) *Foundations of Offender Rehabilitation*, Abingdon: Routledge.

Clare, E. and Bottomley, K., assisted by A. Grounds, C.J. Hammond and A. Liebling (2001) *Evaluation of Closed Supervision Centres*, Home Office Research Study 219, London: Home Office.

Clemmer, D. (1958) *The Prison Community*, New York: Holt, Rinehart & Winston.

Clinks (2016) *The Rehabilitative Prison: What Does a 'Good' Prison Look Like?*, Discussion Paper. Available at: www.clinks.org/clinks-discussion-paper-what-might-good-look-prison-estate

Coates, S. (2016) *Unlocking Potential: A Review of Education in Prison*, London: Ministry of Justice. Available at: www.gov.uk/government/uploads/system/uploads/attachment_data/file/524013/education-review-report.pdf

Cohen, S. and Taylor, L. (1972) *Psychological Survival: The Experience of Long-Term Imprisonment*, Harmondsworth: Penguin.

Costa, P.T. and McCrae, R.R. (1992) 'Four ways five factors are basic', *Personality and Individual Differences*, 13(6), 653–65.

Costelloe, A. and Warner, K. (2008) 'Beyond Offending Behaviour: The Wider Perspective of Adult Education and the European Prison Rules', in R. Wright (ed) *In the Borderlands: Learning to Teach in Prisons and Alternative Settings*, San Bernardino, CA: San Bernardino State University, pp 136–46.

Crawley, E. and Sparks, R. (2005) 'Older Men in Prison: Survival, Coping and Identity', in A. Liebling and S. Maruna (eds) *The Effects of Imprisonment*, Cullompton: Willan Publishing, pp 343–65.

Creese, B. (2015) *An Assessment of the English and Maths Skills Levels of Prisoners in England*, Centre for Education in the Criminal Justice System, London: UCL Institute of Education.

Crewe, B. (2009) *The Prisoner Society: Power, Adaptation and Social Life in an English Prison*, Oxford: Oxford University Press.

Crewe, B., Hulley, S. and Wright, S. (2020) *Life Imprisonment from Young Adulthood: Adaptation, Identity and Time*, London: Palgrave Macmillan.

Crewe, B., Warr, J., Bennett, P. and Smith, A. (2013) 'The emotional geography of prison life', *Theoretical Criminology*, 18(1), 1–19.

Cronin, J. (2011) *The Path to Successful Reentry: The Relationship Between Correctional Education, Employment and Recidivism*, Report 15-2011, Columbia, MO: University of Missouri, Institute of Public Policy.

Daniel, M.-F. (2008) 'Learning to philosophize: Positive impacts and conditions for implementation, A synthesis of 10 years of research (1995–2005)', *Thinking: The Journal of Philosophy for Children*, 18(4), 36–48.

Davis, L.M., Bozick, R., Steele, J.L., Saunders, J. and Miles, J.N. (2013) *Evaluating the Effectiveness of Correctional Education: A Meta-Analysis of Programs that Provide Education to Incarcerated Adults*, RAND Corporation. Available at: www.rand.org/pubs/research_reports/RR266.html

de Viggiani, N. (2012) 'Trying to be something you are not: Masculine performances within a prison setting', *Men and Masculinities*, 1–21.

Deci, E. and Ryan, R.M. (2009) 'The "what" and "why" of goal pusuits: Human needs and the self-determination of behavior', *Psychological Inquiry: An International Journal for the Advancement of Psychological Theory*, 1 (4), 227–68.

DeMarzio, D. (2009) 'Dialogue, the care of the self, and the beginning of philosophy', *Thinking: The Journal of Philosophy for Children*, 19(4), 10–16.

Deutsch, H. (2008) 'Relative Identity', in E.N. Zalta (ed) *The Stanford Encyclopedia of Philosophy*, Winter. Available at: http://plato.stanford.edu/archives/win2008/entries/identity-relative/

Dewey, J. (1990 [1902]) *The School and Society, the Child and the Curriculum*, London: The University of Chicago Press.

Duguid, S. (1997) 'Confronting worst case scenarios: Education and high risk offenders', *Journal of Correctional Education*, 48(4), 153–9.

Duguid, S. (2000) *Can Prisons Work? The Prisoner as Object and Subject in Modern Corrections*, Toronto, ON: University of Toronto Press.

Duguid, S. (2008) 'The Professor in Prison: Reflections', in R. Wright (ed) *In the Borderlands: Learning to Teach in Prisons and Alternative Settings*, San Bernardino, CA: California State University, pp 113–18.

Duguid, S. and Pawson, R. (1998) 'Education, change, and transformation: The prison experience', *Evaluation Review*, 22(4), 470–95.

Duguid, S., Hawkey, C. and Knights, W. (1998) 'Measuring the impact of post-secondary education in prison', *Journal of Offender Rehabilitation*, 27, 87–106.

Durkheim, E. (1973) *On Morality and Society: Selected Writings, Volume 1* (edited by R.N. Bellah), Chicago, IL: The University of Chicago Press.

Ellison, M., Szifris, K., Horan, R. and Fox, C. (2017) 'A rapid evidence assessment of the effectiveness of prison education in reducing recidivism and increasing employment', *The Probation Journal*, 64(2), 108–28.

Evans, J. (2013) *Philosophy for Life and Other Dangerous Situations*, London: Ebury Publishing.

Eysenck, H. J. (1998 [1947]). *Dimensions of Personality*, Piscataway, NJ: Transaction Publishers.

Farrall, S. (2016) 'Understanding Desistance in an Assisted Context: Key Findings from Tracking Progress on Probation', in J. Shapland, S. Farrall and A. Bottoms (eds) *Global Perspectives on Desistance: Reviewing What We Know and Looking to the Future*, Oxford: Routledge, pp 187–204.

Farrall, S. and Bowling, B. (1999) 'Structuration, human development and desistance from crime', *British Journal of Criminology*, 39(2), 253–68.

Farrall, S., Bottoms, A. and Shapland, J. (2010) 'Social structures and desistance from crime', *European Journal of Criminology*, 7(6), 546–70.

Feely, M.M. and Simon, J. (1992) 'The new penology: Notes on the emerging strategy of corrections and its implications', *Criminology*, 30, 449–74.

Foster, P. (2006) 'Observational Research', in R. Sapsford and V. Jupp (eds) *Data Collection and Analysis* (2nd edn), London: SAGE Publications Ltd, pp 57–92.

Frede, D. (2016) 'Plato Ethics: An Overview', in E.N. Zalta (ed) *The Stanford Encyclopedia of Philosophy*. Available at: http://plato.stanford.edu/archives/win2016/entries/plato-ethics

Fredrickson, B.L. (2001) 'The role of positive emotions in positive psychology: The broaden-and-build theory of positive emotions', *The American Psychologist*, 56(3), 218–26.

Freire, P. (1996 [1970]) *Pedagogy of the Oppressed* (translated by M.B. Ramos), London: Penguin.

Gadd, D. (2000) 'Masculinities, violence and defended psychosocial subjects', *Theoretical Criminology*, 4(4), 429–49.

Gadd, D. (2003) 'Review essay: Making criminology good: A response to Shadd Maruna', *The Howard Journal*, 42(3), 316–22.

Gagné, R.M. (1977) *Conditions of Learning* (3rd revised edn), Thompson Learning.

Gehring, T. (1997) 'Post-secondary education for inmates: An historical inquiry', *Journal of Correctional Education*, 48(2), 46–55. Available at: www.jstor.org/stable/23294132

Genders, E. and Player, E. (1995) *Grendon: A Study of a Therapeutic Prison*, Oxford: Oxford University Press.

Gergen, K.J. (2011) 'The Social Construction of the Self', in S. Gallagher (ed) *The Oxford Handbook of the Self*, Oxford: Oxford University Press, pp 633–53.

Giddens, A. (1989) *Sociology*, Cambridge: Polity Press.

Giddens, A. (1991) *Modernity and Self-Identity*, Stanford, CA: Stanford University Press.

Giordano, P.C. (2016) 'Mechanisms Underlying the Desistance Process: Reflections on "A Theory of Coginitive Transformation"', in J. Shapland, S. Farrall and A. Bottoms (eds) *Global Perspectives on Desistance: Reviewing What We Know and Looking to the Future*, Oxford: Routledge, pp 11–27.

Giordano, P.C., Cernkovitch, S.A. and Rudolph, J.L. (2002) 'Gender, crime, and desistance: Toward a theory of cognitive transformation', *American Journal of Sociology*, 107(4), 990–1064.

Glaser, B. and Strauss, A.L. (2012 [1967]) *Discovery of Grounded Theory: Strategies for Qualitative Research*, New Brunswick, NJ and London: Aldine Transaction.

Glueck, S. and Glueck, E. (1940) *Juvenile Delinquents Grow Up*, Oxford: Commonwealth Fund.

Goffman, E. (1961) *Asylums: Essays on the Social Situation of Mental Patients and Other Inmates*, New York: Anchor Books.

Goffman, E. (1969) *Presentations of the Self*, Plymouth, NH: Latimer Trend & Co.

Golafshani, N. (2003) 'Understanding reliability and validity in qualitative research', *The Qualitative Report*, 8(4), 597–606.

Golding, C. (2011) 'Educating philosophically: The educational theory of Philosophy for Children', *Educational Philosophy and Theory*, 43(5), 413–14.

Gorard, S., Siddiqui, N. and See, B.H. (2016) *Philosophy for Children: Evaluation Report and Executive Summary*, Durham: Durham University, Education Endowment Foundation.

Gordon, H.R. and Weldon, B. (2003) 'The impact of career and technical education programmes on adult offenders: Learning behind bars', *Journal of Correctional Education*, 54(4), 200–9.

Gottfredson, M.R. and Hirschi, T. (1990) *A General Theory of Crime*, Stanford, CA: Stanford University Press.

Graham, H. and McNeill, F.F. (2017) 'Desistance: Envisioning Futures', in P. Carlen and L. Ayres França (eds) *Alternative Criminologies*, London: Routledge, pp 433–51.

Grayling, A.C. (1995) 'Editor's Introduction', in A.C. Grayling (ed) *Philosophy: A Guide Through the Subject*, Oxford: Oxford University Press, pp 1–6.

Green, L. (2009) 'Education for democracy: Using the classroom community of inquiry to develop habits of reflective judgement in South African schools', *Thinking Skill and Creativity*, 4, 178–84.

Greenwood, L. (2001) 'Psychotherapy in Prison: The Ultimate Container?', in J.W. Saunders (ed) *Life within Hidden Walls: Psychotherapy in Prisons*, London: Karnac Books, pp 37–54.

Habermas, T. and Bluck, S. (2000) 'Getting a life: The emergence of the life story in adolescence', *Psychological Bulletin*, 126(5), 748–69.

Haigh, R., Harrison, T., Johnson, R., Paget, S. and Williams, S. (2012) 'Psychologically informed environments and the "enabling environments"', *Housing, Care and Support*, 15(1), 34–42.

Hamm, M.S. (2013) *The Spectacular Few: Prisoner Radicalization and the Evolving Terrorist Threat*, New York and London: NYU Press.

Hamilton, C. (2003) *Understanding Philosophy for AS Level*, Cheltenham: Nelson Thornes Ltd.

Hannam, P. and Echeverria, E. (2009) *Philosophy with Teenagers: Nurturing a Moral Imagination for the 21st Century*, London: Network Continuum.

Harper, G. and Chitty, C. (2005) *The Impact of Corrections on Re-offending: A Review of 'What Works'*, London: Home Office.

Harvey, J. (2007) *Young Men in Prison: Surviving and Adapting to Life Inside*, Cullompton: Willan Publishing.

Harvey, J. and Smedley, K. (2010) 'Introduction', in J. Harvey and K. Smedley (eds) *Psychological Therapy in Prisons and Other Settings*, Abingdon: Willan Publishing, pp 1–25.

Hatfield, G. (2016) 'René Descartes', in E.N. Zalta (ed) *The Stanford Encyclopedia of Philosophy*. Available at: http://plato.stanford.edu/archives/sum2016/entries/descartes/

Hayden, G. (2013) *You Kant Make It Up! Strange Ideas from History's Great Philosophers*, London: Oneworld Publications.

Healy, D. (2014) 'Becoming a desister: Exploring the role of agency, coping and imagination in the construction of a new self', *British Journal of Criminology*, 54, 873–91.

HM Chief Inspector of Prisons (2013) *Report on an Announced Inspection of HMP Full Sutton: 3–7 December 2012*, London: Her Majesty's Inspectorate of Prisons.

HM Inspectorate of Prisons (2015) 'Close Supervision Centres – a well run system which contains dangerous men safely and decently', News Release. Available at: www.justiceinspectorates.gov.uk/hmiprisons/media/press-releases/2015/08/close-supervision-centres-a-well-run-system-which-contains-dangerous-men-safely-and-decently/

Hochschild, A.R. (1979) 'Emotion work, feeling rules and social structure', *The American Journal of Sociology*, 85(3), 551–75.

Hogg, M.A., Abrams, D., Otten, S. and Hinkle, S. (2004) 'The social identity perspective: Intergroup relations, self-conception, and small groups', *Small Group Research*, 35(3), 246–76.

Hollin, C.R. (2007) 'Criminological Psychology', in M. Maguire, R. Morgan and R. Reiner (eds) *The Oxford Handbook of Criminology*, Oxford: Oxford Handbook of Criminology, pp 43–77.

Home Office (1966) *Report of the Inquiry into Prison Escapes and Security* (The Mountbatten Report), London: HMSO.

Honderich, T. (1995) *The Oxford Companion to Philosophy*, Oxford: Oxford University Press.

Hopkins, K. (2012) *The Pre-Custody Employment, Training and Education Status of Newly Sentenced Prisoners: Results from the Surveying Prisoner Crime Reduction (SPCR) Longitudinal Cohort Study of Prisoners*, London: Ministry of Justice.

Horn, A.S. (2012) 'The cultivation of a prosocial value orientation through community service: An examination of organizational context, social facilitation, and duration', *Journal of Youth Adolesence*, 41, 948–68.

Hospers, J. (1997) *Analysis: An Introduction to Philosophical Analysis* (3rd edn), London: Routledge & Regan Paul.

House of Commons Library (2013) *Prison Population Statistics*, Social and General Statistics, London: House of Commons.

Hughes, E. (2009) 'Thinking Inside the Box: Prisoner Education, Learning Identities, and the Possibilities of Change', in B.M. Veysey, J. Christian and D.J. Martinez (eds) *How Offenders Transform Their Lives*, Cullompton: Willan Publishing, pp 87–103.

Hughes, E. (2012) *Education in Prison: Studying through Distance Learning*, Farnham: Ashgate Publishing Ltd.

Hulley, S., Crewe, B. and Wright, S. (2015) 'Re-examining the problems of long-term imprisonment', *British Journal of Criminology*, 1–24.

Hunsberger, B., Pratt, M. and Pancer, S. (1994) 'Religious fundamentalism and integrative complexity of thought: A relationship for existential content only?', *Journal for the Scientific Study of Religion*, 33(4), 335–46.

Hurry, J., Brazier, L., Parker, M. and Wilson, A. (2006) *Rapid Evidence Assessment of Interventions that Promote Employment for Offenders*, Research Report No 747, London: Department for Education and Skills.

Ievins, A. and Crewe, B. (2015) '"Nobody's better than you, nobody's worse than you": Moral community among prisoners convicted of sexual offences', *Punishment and Society*, 62, 315–19.

Inside Time (2014) 'HMP Grendon', 13 December. Available at: www.insidetime.org/hmp-grendon-visiting-information/

Irwin, J. and Owen, B. (2005) 'Harm and the Contemporary Prison', in A. Liebling and S. Maruna (eds) *The Effects of Imprisonment*, Cullompton: Willan Publishing, pp 94–117.

Janaway, C. (1995) 'The Pre-Socratics and Plato', in A.C. Grayling (ed) *Philosophy: A Guide Through the Subject*, Oxford: Oxford University Press, pp 336–97.

Jarman, B. (2020) 'Only one way to swim? The offence and the life course in accounts of adaptation to life imprisonment', *The British Journal of Criminology*, 60(6), 1460–79. Available at: https://doi.org/10.1093/bjc/azaa036

Jarvis, P. (1995) *Adult and Continuing Education: Theory and Practice* (2nd edn), London: Routledge.

Jeffrey, C.R. (1959) 'The historical development of criminology', *Journal of Criminal Law and Criminology*, 50(1), 3–19.

Jenkins, H.D., Steurer, S.J. and Pendry, J. (1995) 'A post release follow-up of correctional education program completers released in 1990–1991', *Journal of Correctional Education*, 46(1), 20–4.

Jenkins, P. and Lyle, S. (2010) 'Enacting dialogue: The impact of promoting Philosophy for Children on the literate of identified poor readers, aged 10', *Language and Education*, 24(6), 459–72.

Jenkins, R. (1996) *Social Identity*, London: Routledge.

Jenson, E.L. and Reed, G.E. (2008) 'Adult correctional education programs: An update on current status based on recent studies', *Journal of Offender Rehabilitation*, 44(1), 81–98.

Jewkes, Y. (2005a) '"Doing" masculinities as an adaptation to imprisonment', *Men and Masculinities*, 8(44), 44–63.

Jewkes, Y. (2005b) 'Loss, Liminality and the Life Sentence: Managing Identity through a Disrupted Lifecourse', in A. Liebling and S. Maruna (eds) *The Effects of Imprisonment*, Cullompton: Willan Publishing, pp 366–90.

Jewkes, Y. and Bennett, J. (2008) *Dictionary of Prisons and Punishment*, Portland, OR: Willan.

Johnson, J.A. (2009) 'Lifetech Institute: Leading change through transitional centers', *Community College Journal of Research and Practice*, 33(11), 942–4.

Jones, M. (1980) 'Desirable Features in a Therapeutic Community in Prison', in H. Toch (ed) *Therapeutic Communities in Corrections*, New York: Praeger.

Jones, R.S. and Schmid, T.J. (2000) *Doing Time: Prison Experience and Identity among First-Time Inmates*, Stamford, CT: JAI Press Inc.

Jordan, M. (2011) 'The prison setting as a place of enforced residence, its mental health effects, and the mental healthcare implications', *Health Place*, 17(5), 1061–6.

Kazantzis, N., Fairburn, C.G., Padesky, C.A., Reinecke, M. and Teesson, M. (2014) 'Unresolved issues regarding the research and practice of cognitive behavior therapy: The case of guided discovery using Socratic questioning', *Behaviour Change*, 31(1), 1–17.

Kelso, J.C. (2000) 'Recidivism rates for two education programs' graduates compared to overall Washington State rates', *Journal of Correctional Education*, 51(2), 233–6.

Kennedy, D. (1999) 'Philosophy for Children and the reconstruction of philosophy', *Metaphilosophy*, 30(4), 338–59.

Kennedy, D. (2004) 'The role of a facilitator in a community of philosophical inquiry', *Metaphilosophy*, 35(5), 744–65.

Kennedy, D. and Kennedy, N. (2011) 'Community of philosophical inquiry as a discursive structure, and its role in school curriculum design', *Journal of Philosophy of Education*, 45(2), 265–83.

King, R. (1985) 'Control in Prisons', in M. Maguire, J. Vagg and R. Morgan (eds) *Accountability and Prisons*, London: Tavistock.

King, R. and McDermott, K. (1990) '"My geranium is subversive": Some notes on the management of trouble in prisons', *The British Journal of Sociology*, 41(4), 445–71.

Knowles, M. (1975) *Self-Directed Learning*, Chicago, IL: Follet.

Kohan, W. and Wozniak, J. (2009) 'Philosophy as a spiritual exercise', *Thinking: The Journal for Philosophy for Children*, 19(4), 17–23.

Kreider, K. (2014) *Poetics and Place: The Architecture of Sign, Subjects and Site*, London: T.B. Tauris Ltd & Co.

Lacey, A.R. (1971) 'Our Knowledge of Socrates', in G. Vlastos (ed) *The Philosophy of Socrates: A Collection of Critical Essays*, London: Palgrave Macmillan, pp 22–49.

Laub, J.H. and Sampson, R. (2001) 'Understanding desistance from crime', *Crime and Justice*, 28, 1–69.

Laub, J.H., Nagin, D.S. and Sampson, R.J. (1998) 'Trajectories of change in criminal offending: Good marriages and the desistance process', *American Sociological Review*, 63(2), 225–38.

Law, S. (2007) *The Great Philosophers: The Lives and Ideas of History's Greatest Thinkers*, London: Quercus Publishing PLC.

Layder, D. (1998) *Sociological Practice: Linking Theory and Social Research*, London: SAGE Publications Ltd.

LeBel, T.B., Burnett, R., Maruna, S. and Bushway, S. (2008) '"The chicken and the egg" of subjective and social factors in desistance from crime', *European Journal of Criminology*, 5(2), 131–59.

Lebow, R.N. (2012) *The Politics and Ethics of Identity: In Search of Ourselves*, Cambridge: Cambridge University Press.

LeCompte, M.D. (1987) 'Bias in the biography: Bias and subjectivity in ethnographic research', *Anthropology and Education Quarterly*, 18(1), 43–52.

Liebling, A. (1992) *Suicides in Prisons*, London: Routledge.

Liebling, A. (2004) 'The late modern prison and the question of values', *Current Issues in Criminal Justice*, 16(2), 202–19. doi:10.1080/10345329.2004.12036316

Liebling, A. (2012) 'Can Human Beings Flourish?', Prison Phoenix Trust Lecture, London.

Liebling, A. (2012) 'Vulnerability, Struggling and Coping in Prison', in B. Crewe and J. Bennett (eds) *The Prisoner*, Oxford: Routledge, pp 53–66.

Liebling, A. (2015) 'Description at the edge? I–it/I–thou relations and action in prisons research', *International Journal for Crime, Justice and Social Democracy*, 18–32.

Liebling, A. (2019) 'Finding George Eliot in prison: Reflections on its moral life', in *George Eliot Review Online*.

Liebling, A., assisted by Arnold, H. (2004) *Prisons and their Moral Performance: A Study of Values, Quality, and Prison Life*, Oxford: Oxford University Press.

Liebling, A. and Arnold, H. (2012) 'Social relationships between prisoners in a maximum security prison: Violence, faith, and the declining nature of trust', *Journal of Criminal Justice*, 40, 413–24. doi:10.1016/j.jcrimjus.2012.06.003

Liebling, A. and Crewe, B. (2013) 'Prisons beyond the New Penology: The Shifting Moral Foundations of Prison Management', in J. Simon and R. Sparks (eds) *The SAGE Handbook of Punishment and Society*, Thousand Oaks, CA: SAGE Publications Ltd, pp 283–307.

Liebling, A. and Williams, R.J. (2017) 'The new subversive geranium: Some notes on the management of additional troubles in maximum security prisons', *BJS: The British Journal of Sociology*, 69(4), 1194–219.

Liebling, A., Arnold, H. and Straub, C. (2011) *An Exploration of Staff–Prisoner Relationships at HMP Whitemoor: 12 Years On*, Cambridge University, Prisons Research Centre, London: National Offender Management Service and Ministry of Justice.

Liebling, A., Price, D. and Elliot, C. (1999) 'Appreciative inquiry and relationships in prison', *Punishment and Society*, 1(1), 71–98.

Liebling, A., Williams, R. and Lieber, E. (2020) 'More mind games: How "the action" and "the odds" have changed in prison', *British Journal of Criminology*, 60(6), 1648–66. Available at: https://doi.org/10.1093/bjc/azaa046

Liebling, A., Armstrong, R., Bramwell, R. and Williams, R. (2016) 'Locating Trust in a Climate of Fear: Religion, Moral Status, Prisoner Leadership, and Risk in Maximum Security Prisons – Key Findings from an Innovative Study', Unpublished, Prison Research Centre, Institute of Criminology.

Liebling, A., Bramwell, R., Armstrong, R., Williams, R., Auty, K.K. and Schmidt, B. (2014) *Full Sutton SQL & MQPL+ Reports, March 2014* , Cambridge: Prisons Research Centre, Institute of Criminology, University of Cambridge.

Lien, C. (2007) 'Making sense of evaluation of P4C', *Thinking: The Journal of Philosophy for Children*, 17(1&2), 36–48.

Liht, J. and Savage, S. (2013) 'Preventing violent extremism through value complexity: Being Muslim being British', *Journal of Strategic Security*, 6(4), 44–66.

Lipman, M., Sharp, A.M. and Oscanyan, F.S. (1980) *Philosophy in the Classroom*, Philadelphia, PA: Temple University Press.

Lockwood, S., Nally, J.M., Ho, T. and Knutson, K. (2012) 'The effect of correctional education on postrelease employment and recidivism: A 5-year follow-up study in the state of Indiana', *Crime & Delinquency*, 58(3), 380–96.

Long, F. (2005) 'Thomas Reid and Philosophy with Children', *Journal of Philosophy of Education*, 39(4), 599–614.

MacIntyre, A. (1984) *After Virtue* (2nd edn), Notre Dame, IN: Notre Dame University Press.

MacKenzie, D.L. (2006) *What Works in Corrections: Reducing the Criminal Activities of Offenders and Delinquents*, New York: Cambridge University Press.

Martinson, R. (1974) 'What works? Questions and answers about prison reform', *The Public Interest*, 35, 22–54.

Maruna, S. (2001) *Making Good: How Ex-Convicts Reform and Rebuild Their Lives*, Washington, DC: American Sociological Society.

Maruna, S. (2010) 'The great escape: Exploring the rehabilitative dynamics involved in "Changing Tunes"', Changing Tunes. Available at: www.artsevidence.org.uk/evaluations/great-escape-explring-rehabilitative-dynamics-invo/

Maruna, S., LeBel, T.P. and Lanier, C.S. (2004) 'Generativity Behind Bars: Some "Redemptive Truth" about Prison Society', in E. de St Aubin, D.P. McAdams and T.C. Kim (eds) *The Generative Society: Caring for Future Generations*, Washington, DC: American Psychological Association, pp 131–51.

McAdams, D.P. (1993) *The Stories We Live By: Personal Myths and the Making of the Self*, New York: Guilford Press.

McAdams, D.P. (2009) 'Personality, modernity and the storied self: A contemporary framework for studying persons', *Psychological Inquiry: An International Journal for the Advancement of Psychological Theory*, 7(4), 295–321.

McCall, C. (2009) *Transforming Thinking: Philosophical Inquiry in the Primary and Secondary Classroom*, London and New York: Routledge.

McCloskey, H. (1972) 'A Non-Utilitarian Approach to Punishment', in G. Ezorsky (ed) *Philosophical Perspectives on Punishment*, Albany, NY: State University of New York Press, pp 119–34.

McCord, J. (1994) 'A review of "Crime in the Making: Pathways and Turning Points Through Life" by Sampson, R.J. & Laub, J.H.', *Contemporary Sociology*, 23(3), 414–15.

McIntosh, J. and McKeganey, N. (2000) 'Addicts' narratives of recovery from drug use: Constructing a non-addict identity', *Social Science & Medicine*, 50, 1501–10.

McNeill, F. (2012) 'Four forms of "offender" rehabilitation: Towards an interdisciplinary perspective', *Legal and Criminological Psychology*, 17(1), 18–36.

McNeill, F. (2016) 'The Fuel in the Tank or the Hole in the Boat? Can Sanctions Support Desistance?', in J. Shapland, S. Farrall and A. Bottoms (eds) *Global Perspectives on Desistance: Reviewing What We Know and Looking to the Future*, Oxford: Routledge, pp 265–81.

McNeill, F. and Schinkel, M. (2016) 'Prisons and Desistance', in Y. Jewkes, J. Bennett and B. Crewe (eds) *Handbook on Prisons*, Abingdon: Routledge, pp 607–21.

McNeill, F. and Weaver, B. (2010) *Changing Lives: Desistance Research and Offender Management*, Glasgow: Glasgow School of Social Work and Scottish Centre for Crime and Justice Research, Universities of Glasgow and Strathclyde.

Merçon, J. and Armstrong, A. (2011) 'Transindividuality and philosophical enquiry in schools: A Spinozist perspective', *Journal of Philosophy of Education*, 45(2), 251–64.

Mezirow, J. (1990) 'How Critical Reflection Triggers Transformative Learning', in J. Mezirow (ed) *Fostering Critical Reflection in Adulthood: A Guide to Transformative and Emancipatory Learning*, San Francisco, CA: Jossey-Bass Publishers, pp 1–20.

Michaud, O. (2009) 'Monastic meditations on philosophy and education', *Thinking: The Journal of Philosophy for Children*, 19(4), 39–42.

Miell, D. (1990) 'The Self and the Social World', in I. Roth (ed) *Introduction to Psychology*, Milton Keynes: The Open University, pp 30–78.

Millett, S. and Tapper, A. (2011) 'Benefits of collaborative philosophical inquiry in schools', *Educational Philosophy and Theory*, 44(5), 546–67.

Ministry of Justice (2010) *Compendium of Reoffending Statistics and Analysis: Executive Summary*, Ministry of Justice Statistics Bulletin, London: Ministry of Justice.

Ministry of Justice (2013) *Transforming Rehabilitation: A Revolution in the Way We Manage Offenders*, London: Ministry of Justice. Available at: https://consult.justice.gov.uk/digital-communications/transforming-rehabilitation/supporting_documents/transformingrehabilitation.pdf

Minstry of Justice (2014) *Surveying Prisoner Crime Reduction (SPCR)*. Available at: www.gov.uk/government/collections/surveying-prisoner-crime-reduction-spcr

Ministry of Justice (2015) *Safety in Custody Statistics England and Wales: Deaths in Prison Custody to June 2015, Assaults and Self-Harm to March 2015*, London: Ministry of Justice. Available at: www.gov.uk/government/uploads/system/uploads/attachment_data/file/449648/safety-in-custody-2015.pdf

Ministry of Justice (2016) *Prison Safety and Reform*, London: Open Government Licence.

Morgan, D.L. (1997) *Focus Groups: As Qualitative Research*, Qualitative Research Methods Series 16, A SAGE University Paper, London: SAGE Publications Ltd.

Morgan, G. and Smircich, L. (1980) 'The case for qualitative research', *The Academy of Management Review*, 5(4), 491–500.

Morris, M. (2001) 'Grendon Underwood. A Therapeutic Prison', in J.W. Saunders (ed) *Life Within Hidden Worlds: Psychotherapy in Prison*, London: Karnac Books, pp 89–112.

Morse, J.M. (1991) 'Approaches to qualitative-quantitative methodological triangulation', *Nursing Research*, 40, 120–3.

Murchison, J.M. (2010) *Ethnography Essentials: Designing, Conducting, and Presenting Your Research*, Research Methods for the Social Sciences, San Francisco, CA: Jossey-Bass.

Murdoch, I. (1977) *The Fire and the Sun: Why Plato Banished the Artists*, Oxford: Clarendon Press.

Murris, K.S. (2000) 'Can children do philosophy?', *Journal of Philosophy of Education*, 34(2), 261–79.

Murris, K.S. (2008) 'Philosophy with Children, the Stingray and the educative value of disequilibrium', *Journal of Philosophy of Education*, 43(3–4), 667–85.

Nally, J.M., Lockwood, S.R., Ho, T. and Knutson, K. (2011) *The Effect of Correctional Education on Postrelease Employment and Recidivism: A 5-Year Follow-Up Study in the State of Indiana*, Working Paper.

Nichols, H. (2021) *Understanding the Educational Experiences of Imprisoned Men: (Re)education*, Abingdon: Routledge.

Niles, W.J. (1986) 'Effects of moral development discussion group on delinquent and predelinquent boys', *Journal of Counseling Psychology*, 33(1), 45–51.

Noonan, H. (2011) 'Identity', *The Stanford Encyclopaedia of Philosophy*. Available at: http://plato.stanford.edu/archives/win2011/entries/identity/

Nugent, B. and Schinkel, M. (2016) 'The pains of desistance', *Criminology & Criminal Justice*, 16(5), 568–84.

Nussbaum, M.C. (1998) *Cultivating Humanity: Classical Defense of Reform in Liberal Education*, Cambridge, MA: Harvard University Press.

Nuttall, J., Hollmen, L. and Staley, E.M. (2003) 'The effects of earning a GED on recidivism rates', *Journal of Correctional Education*, 54(3), 90–4.

O'Donnell, A. (2013) 'Unpredictability, transformation, and the pedagogical encounter: Reflections on "What is effective" in education', *Educational Theory*, 63(3), 265–82.

O'Donnell, I. (2014) *Prisoners, Solitude, and Time*, Oxford: Oxford University Press.

O'Hear, A. (1981) *Education, Society and Human Nature: An Introduction to the Philosophy of Education*, London: Routledge.

Oliver, P. (2004) *Writing your Thesis*, London: SAGE Publications Ltd.

ONS (Office for National Statistics) (2012) *Ethnicity and National Identity in England and Wales: 2011*. Available at: www.ons.gov.uk/peoplepopulationandcommunity/culturalidentity/ethnicity/articles/ethnicityandnationalidentityinenglandandwales/2012-12-11

ONS (Office for National Statistics) (2012) *Religion in England and Wales 2011*. Available at: www.ons.gov.uk/peoplepopulationandcommunity/culturalidentity/religion/articles/religioninenglandandwales2011/2012-12-11

Overholser, J.C. (1993) 'Elements of the Socratic method: I Systematic questioning', *Psychotherapy*, 30(1), 67–74.

Oxford English Dictionary (2013) 'Identity', 13 March. Available at: www.oed.com/view/Entry/91004?redirectedFrom=identity#eid

Pals, J.L. (2006) 'Constructing the "Springboard Effect": Causal Connections, Self-Making, and Growth within the Life-Story', in D.P. McAdams, R. Josselson and A. Lieblich (eds) *Identity and Story*, Washington, DC: American Psychological Association, pp 175–200.

Paternoster, R.P. (1989) 'Decision to participate in and desist from four types of delinquency: Deterrence and the rational choice perspective', *Law & Society Review*, 23(1), 8–40.

Paternoster, R.P. and Bushway, S. (2009) 'Desistance and the "feared self": Toward an identity theory of criminal desistance', *The Journal of Criminal Law and Criminology*, 99(4), 1103–56.

Patton, M.Q. (2002) *Research & Evaluation Methods* (3rd edn), Thousand Oaks: CA: SAGE Publications Ltd.

Pawson, R. (2002) 'Evidence-based policy: In search of method', *Evaluation*, 8(2), 157–81.

Pawson, R. and Tilley, N. (1997) *Realistic Evaluation*, London: SAGE Publications Ltd.

Pearson, F.S. and Lipton, D.S. (1999) 'The Effectiveness of Educational and Vocational Programs: CDATE Meta-Analyses', Presented at the Annual Meeting of the American Society of Criminology, Toronto.

Pecorino, P.A. (2016) *An Introduction to Philosophy: An Online Textbook*, New York: Queens Community College, City University of New York. Available at: www.qcc.cuny.edu/SocialSciences/ppecorino/ INTRO_TEXT/CONTENTS.htm

Phillips, C. (2008) 'Negotiating identities: Ethnicity and social relations in a young offenders institution', *Theoretical Criminology*, 12(3), 313–31.

Phipps, P., Korinek, K., Aos, S. and Lieb, R. (1999) *Research Findings on Adult Corrections Programmes: A Review*, Washington, DC: Washington State for Public Policy.

Pike, A. and Hopkins, S. (2019) 'Transformative learning: Positive identity through prison-based higher education in England and Wales', *International Journal of Bias, Identity and Diversity in Education*, 4(1), 48–65.

Piquero, A.R., Farrington, D.P. and Blumstein, A. (2003) 'The criminal career paradigm', *Crime and Justice*, 30, 359–506.

Plato (1992 [380 BC]) *Republic* (translated by G. Grube), Hackett Publishing Company Ltd.

Plutarch (1960) 'Theseus', in Plutarch, *The Rise and Fall of Athens: Nine Greek Lives: A New Translation* (translated by I. Scott-Kilvert), Harmondsworth: Penguin Books Ltd, pp 13–42.

Pollizi, D. and Maruna, S. (2010) 'In search of the human in the shadows of correctional practice: Atheoretical reflection with Shadd Maruna', *Journal of Theoretical and Philosophical Criminology*, 2(2), 158–97.

Powis, B., Dixon, L. and Woodhams, J. (2019) *Exploring the Nature of Muslim Groups and Related Gang Activity in Three High Security Prisons: Findings from Qualitative Research*, Ministry of Justice Analytical Series 2019, London: Ministry of Justice. Available at: www. investigativeproject.org/documents/testimony/410.pdf

Pratt, M., Hunsberger, B., Pancer, S.M. and Roth, D. (1992) 'Reflections on religion: Aging, belief orthodoxy, and interpersonal conflict in the complexity of adult thinking about religious issues', *Journal for the Scientific Study of Religion*, 31(4), 514–22.

Presser, L. (2009) 'The narratives of offenders', *Theoretical Criminology*, 13(2), 177–200.

Price, D. (2000) 'The origins and durability of security categorisation: A study in penological pragmatism or spies, Dickie and prison security', *British Society of Criminology: Selected Proceedings*, 3, Liverpool: British Society of Criminology, pp 1–15.

Quraishi, M. (2008) 'Researching Muslim prisoners', *International Journal of Social Research Methodology*, 11(5), 453–67.

Ratner, C. (2002) 'Subjectivity and objectivity in qualitative methodology', *Forum: Qualitative Social Research*, 3(3), Article 16.

Rawls, A.W. (1987) 'The Interaction Order Sui Generis: Goffman's contribution to social theory', *Sociological Theory*, 5(2), 136–49.

Reiner, R. (2007) 'Political Economy, Crime and Criminal Justices', in M. Maguire, R. Morgan and R. Reiner (eds) *The Oxford Handbook of Criminology* (4th edn), Oxford: Oxford University Press, pp 341–80.

Reznitskaya, A. (2007) 'Empirical research in Philosophy for Children', *Thinking: The Journal for Philosophy got Children*, 17(4), 4–13.

Roberts, B. (2002) *Biographical Research*, Buckingham: Open University Press.

Robinson, D. and Garratt, C. (1999) *Introducing Ethics*, Cambridge: Icon Books Ltd.

Robinson, H. (2014) 'Substance', in E.N. Zalta (ed) *The Stanford Encyclopedia of Philosophy*, Spring. Available at: http://plato.stanford.edu/archives/spr2014/entries/substance/

Rock, P. (2007) 'Sociological Theories of Crime', in M. Maguire, R. Morgan and R. Reiner (eds) *The Oxford Handbook of Criminology* (4th edn), Oxford: Oxford University Press, pp 3–42.

Rogers, C.R. (1969) *Freedom to Learn*, Columbus, OH: Merrill.

Romero, E., Gomez-Fraguela, A., Luengo, A. and Sobral, J. (2003) 'The self-control construct in the general theory of crime: An investigation in terms of personality psychology', *Psychology, Psychology, Crime & Law*, 9(1), 61–86.

Rubin, H.J. and Rubin, I. S. (2012) *Qualitative Interviewing: The Art of Hearing Data*, Thousand Oaks, CA: SAGE Publications Ltd.

Rudisill, J. (2011) 'Transition from studying to doing philosophy', *Teaching Philosophy*, 34(3), 241–71.

Ruess, A. (1997) 'Higher Education and Personal Change in Prisoners', Unpublished Thesis, University of Leeds .

Russell, B. (2005 [1946]) *History of Western Philosophy*, London: Routledge.

Sampson, R.J. and Laub, J.H. (1993) *Crime in the Making: Pathways and Turning Points through Life*, Cambridge MA: Harvard University Press.

Saunders, J.W. (2001) 'An Introduction to Psychotherapy in Prisons: Issues Themes and Dynamics', in J.W. Saunders (ed) *Life Within Hidden Worlds: Psychotherapy in Prison*, London: Karnac Books, pp 1–36.

Sauter, F.M., Hernes, A.W., Blöte, A.W., van Widenfelt, B.M. and Westenberg, P.M. (2010) 'Assessing therapy-relevant cognitive capacities in young people: Development and psychometric evaluation of the self-reflection and insight scale for youth', *Behavioural and Cognitive Psychotherapy*, 38, 303–17.

Savage, S. (2011) 'Four lessons from the study of fundamentalism and psychology of religion', *Journal of Strategic Security*, 4(4), 131–50.

Schechtman, M. (2011) 'The Narrative Self', in S. Gallagher (ed) *The Oxford Handbook of the Self*, Oxford: Oxford University Press, pp 394–416.

Schensul, S.L., Schensul, J. and le Compte, M.D. (1999) *Ethnographer's Toolkit: Essential Ethnographic Methods*, 2, Walnut Creek, CA: AltMira Press.

Schinkel, M. (2014) 'Punishment as moral communication: The experiences of long-term prisoners', *Punishment & Society*, 16(6), 578–97.

Schinkel, M. (2015) 'Fair enough: Long-term prisoners talk about their sentence', *Scottish Justice Matters*, 3(1), 3–24.

Schinkel, M. (2015) 'Adaptation, the meaning of imprisonment and outcomes after release – The impact of the prison regime', *Prison Service Journal*, 219, 24–9.

Shapland, J. and Bottoms, A. (2011) 'Reflections on social values, offending and desistance among young adult recidivists', *Punishment and Society*, 256–82.

Shapland, J., Farrall, S. and Bottoms, A. (2016) 'Introduction', in J. Shapland, S. Farrall and A. Bottoms (eds) *Global Perspectives on Desistance: Reviewing What We Know and Looking to the Future*, Oxford: Routledge, pp 1–9.

Shaw, I.F. (1999) *Qualitative Evaluation*, London: SAGE Publications Ltd.

Shuker, R. and Shine, J. (2010) 'The Role of Therapuetic Communities in Forensic Settings: Developments, Research, and Adaptations', in J. Harvey and K. Smedley (eds) *Psychological Therapy in Prisons and Other Settings*, Abingdon: Willan Publishing, pp 215–30.

Smith, A. (2013) *Her Majesty's Philosophers*, Hook: Waterside Press.

Social Exclusion Unit (2002) *Reducing Re-Offending by Ex-Prisoners: Summary of the Social Exclusion Unit Report*. Available at: www.justice reparatrice.org/www.restorativejustice.org/articlesdb/articles/4219

Soyer, M. (2014) 'The imagination of desistance: A juxtaposition of incarceration as a turning point and the reality of recidivism', *British Journal of Criminology*, 54, 91–8.

Spalek, B. (2007) *Communities, Identities and Crimes*, Bristol: Policy Press.

Spalek, B. and El-Hassam, S. (2007) 'Muslim converts in prison', *The Howard Journal*, 46(2), 99–114.

Sparks, R. (2001) 'Degrees of estrangement: The cultural theory of risk and comparative penology', *Theoretical Criminology*, 5(2), 159–76.

Sparks, R., Bottoms, A. and Hay, W. (1996) *Prisons and the Problem of Order*, Oxford: Oxford University Press.

Splitter, L.J. (2009) 'Caring for the "self as one among others"', *Thinking: The Journal of Philosophy for Children*, 19(4), 33–9.

Splitter, L.J. (2011) 'Identity, citizenship and moral education', *Educational Philosophy and Theory*, 43(5), 484–505.

Splitter, L.J. (2011) 'Agency, thought, and language: Analytic philosophy goes to school', *Studying Philosophical Education*, 30, 343–62.

Sprod, T. (2001) *Philosophical Discussion of Moral Education: The Community of Ethical Inquiry*, London: Routledge.

Sterk, C.E. (1999) *Fast Lives: Women Who Use Crack Cocaine*, Philadelphia, PA: Temple University Press.

Steurer, S.J., Smith, L.G. and Tracy, A. (2001) *Education Reduces Crime: Three-State Recidivism Study*, Lanham, MD: Correctional Education Association.

Stevens, A. (2011) 'A "very decent nick": Ethical treatment in prison-based therapeutic communities', *Journal of Forensic Psychology Practice*, 11(2–3), 124–50.

Stevens, A. (2012) '"I am the person now I was always meant to be": Identity reconstruction and narrative reframing in therapeutic community prisons', *Criminology and Criminal Justice*, 12(5), 527–47.

Stokes, P. (2010) *Philosophy: The Great Thinkers*, London: Acturus Publishing Ltd.

Strawson, G. (2004) 'Against narrativity', *Ratio*, 17(4), 428–52.

Sykes, G. (1958) *The Society of Captives: A Study of a Maximum Security Prison*, Oxford: Princeton University Press.

Szifris, K. (2010) 'Philosophy in Prisons: Exploring the Benefits of Providing a Forum for Philosophical Discussion to Prisoners', Unpublished Dissertation.

Szifris, K. (2016) 'Philosophy in prisons: Opening minds and broadening perspectives through philosophical dialogue', *Prison Service Journal*, 225, 33–8.

Szifris, K. (2017) 'Socrates and Aristotle: The role of ancient philosophers in the self-understanding of desisting prisoners', *The Howard Journal of Crime and Justice*, 56(4), 419–36.

Szifris, K., Fox, C. and Bradbury, A. (2018) 'A realist model of prison education, growth, and desistance: A new theory', *Journal of Prison Education and Reentry*, 5(1).

Tangney, J.P. and Dearing, R. (2002) *Shame and Guilt*, New York: Guilford Press.

Tangney, J.P., Stueqig, J. and Mashek, D.J. (2007) 'Moral emotions and moral behaviour', *Annual Reviews Psychology*, 58, 345–72.

Tavernier, R. and Willoughby, T. (2012) 'Adolescent turning points: The association between meaning-making and psychological well-being', *Developmental Psychology*, 48(4), 1058–68.

Taylor, I., Walton, P. and Young, J. (1973) *The New Criminology: For a Social Theory of Deviance*, Abingdon: Routledge.

Terry, L., with Cardwell, V. (2015) *Understanding the Whole Person: Part One in a Series of Literature Reviews on Severe and Multiple Disadvantage*, Revolving Doors Agency.

Thomas, K. (1990) 'Dimensions of Personality', in I. Roth (ed) *Introduction to Psychology, Volume I*, Milton Keynes: The Open University, pp 131–84.

Thompson, M. (2003) *Teach Yourself Philosophy*, London: Hodder Education.

Toch, H. (1977) *Living in Prison: The Ecology of Survival*, Washington, DC: American Psychological Association.

Toch, H. (1980) 'The Therapeutic Community as Community', in H. Toch (ed) *Therapeutic Communities in Corrections*, New York: Praeger Publishers, pp 3–20.

Topping, K.J. and Trickey, S. (2007) 'Collaborative philosophical enquiry for school children: Cognitive effects at 10–12 years', *British Journal of Educational Psychology*, 77(2), 271–88.

Torre, M.E. and Fine, M. (2005) 'Bar none: Extending affirmative action to higher education in prison', *Journal of Social Issues*, 61(3), 569–94.

Trombley, S. (2012) *Fifty Thinkers Who Shaped the Modern World*, London: Atlantic Books.

Turley, C., Payne, C. and Webster, S. (2013) *Enabling Features of Psychologically Informed Planned Environments*, Ministry of Justice Analytical Series, London: National Offender Management Service and Ministry of Justice.

Vanhooren, S., Leijssen, M. and Dezutter, J. (2015) 'Loss of meaning as a predictor of distress in prison', *International Journal of Offender Therapy and Comparative Criminology*, 61(13), 1411–32.

Vaughan, B. (2007) 'The internal narrative of desistance', *British Journal of Criminology*, 47, 390–404.

Viechtbauer, W. (2010) 'Conducting meta-analyses in R with the metafor package', *Journal of Statistical Software*, 36(3).

Visher, C., Winterfield, L. and Coggeshall, M. (2005) 'Ex-offender employment programs and recidivism: A meta-analysis', *Journal of Experimental Criminology*, 1, 295–315.

Waller, E. (2000) 'Disjunction and Integration in Prison Education', in D. Wilson and A. Ruess (eds) *Prisoner(er) Education: Stories of Change and Transformation*, Winchester: Waterside Press, pp 106–37.

Walmsley, R. (1989) *Special Security Units: A Home Office Research and Planning Unit Report*, London: Her Majesty's Stationery Office.

Warburton, N. (2004) *Philosophy: The Basics* (4th edn), Abingdon: Routledge.

Ward, T. (2012) 'Moral strangers or fellow travellers? Contemporary perspectives on offender rehabilitation', *Legal and Criminal Psychology*, 17(37), 40.

Ward, T. and Marshall, B. (2007) 'Narrative identity and offender rehabilitation', *International Journal for Offender Therapy and Comparative Criminology*, 51(3), 279–97.

Ward, T. and Maruna, S. (2007) *Rehabilitation*, Abingdon: Routledge.

Warr, J. (2020) '"Always gotta be two mans": Lifers, risk, rehabilitation, and narrative labour', *Punishment & Society*, 22(1), 28–47. doi:10.1177/1462474518822487

Webb, E. (ed) (2020) *'The New Syria?' Critical Perspectives on the Deradicalisation and Reintegration of Islamist Offenders*, London: Civitas.

Wheeler, S. (1961) 'Socialization in correctional communities', *American Sociological Review*, 26(5), 397–712.

Whitely, S. (2004) 'The evolution of the therapeutic community', *Psychiatric Quarterly*, 75(3).

Williams, R. (2013) 'Network hubs and opportunity for complex thinking among young British Muslims', *Journal for the Scientific Study of Religion*, 52(3), 573–95.

Williams, R. and Liebling, A. (2018) 'Faith Provision, Institutional Power and Meaning among Muslim Prisoners in Two English High Security Prisons', in K.R. Kerley (ed) *Finding Freedom in Confinement – The Role of Religion in Prison Life*, New York: Praeger, pp 269–91. Available at: https://doi.org/10.17863/CAM.18069

Wilson, D.B., Gallagher, C.A. and MacKenzie, D.L. (2000) 'A meta-analysis of corrections-based education, vocation, and work programs for adult offenders', *Journal of Research in Crime and Delinquency*, 347–68.

Wilson, H.S. and Hutchinson, S.A. (1991) 'Triangulation of qualitative methods: Heideggerian hermeneutics and grounded theory', *Qualitative Health Research*, 1(2), 263–76.

Wilson, M. (1996) 'Asking Questions', in V. Jupp and R. Sapsford (eds) *Data Collection and Analysis*, London: SAGE Publications Ltd, pp 94–120.

Wilson, M. and Sapsford, R. (2006) 'Asking Questions', in R. Sapsford and V. Jupp (eds) *Data Colleciton and Analysis* (2nd edn), London: Sage Publications Ltd, pp 93–122.

Winterfield, L., Coggeshall, M., Burke-Storer, V.C. and Tidd, S. (2009) *The Effects of Postsecondary Correctional Education: Final Report*, Washington, DC: Urban Institute.

Wolcott, H.F. (1990) *Writing up Qualitative Research*, Qualitative Research Methods Series 20, A SAGE University Paper, London: Sage Publications Ltd.

Wong, P. (2012) 'Toward a Dual-Systems Model of What Makes Life Worth', in *The Human Quest for Meaning Theories, Research and Applications*, London: Routledge, pp 3–22.

Worley, P. (2011) *The 'If' Machine: Philosophical Enquiry in the Classroom*, London: Continuum.

Wright, R. (2014) 'Identities, education and reentry (Part One of Two): Identities and performative spaces', *Journal of Prison Education and Reentry*, 1(1), 32–41.

Yorshanky, M. (2009) 'The community of inquiry: A struggle between self and communal transformation for female students and the other', *Thinking: The Journal of Philosophy for Children*, 19(2&3), 42–9.

Yos, T.B. (2007) 'Philosophy for Children and the cultivation of good judgement', *Thinking: The Journal of Philosophy for Children*, 17(1&2), 9–16.

Zamble, E. and Porporino, F.J. (1988) *Coping, Behavior, and Adaptation in Prison Inmates*, New York: Springer Verlag Inc.

Zgoba, K., Haugebrook, S. and Jenkins, K. (2008) 'The influence of GED obtainment on prisoner release outcomes', *Criminal Justice and Behaviour*, 35(3), 375–87.

Index